Advanced Praise for *Out of Silence*

Martin Beck Matuštík's narrative of his discovery of his Mother's two secrets is breathtaking. The first—that he is Jewish—altered his life irrevocably. The second—concerning the reasons for which his Mother concealed their Jewish origins—complicated that origin and that discovery irreparably. Recounting his personal history from the disclosure of the first in the summer of 1997 to his unveiling of the second in the spring of 2012, his book remains a testimony to all of us who live in the wake of disaster, which is to say, who struggle with its posthumous or Lazarean dimensions, which is to say, to all of us.

——Sandor Goodhart, Professor of English and Jewish Studies, Purdue University

Who will stop the resentments of the era of the two twentieth-century beastly regimes? The stories of our fathers and grandfathers? Lord Karel Schwarzenberg, a Czech politician and wise man, recently placed in doubt my fragile optimism, saying, "One can inherit and pass prejudices to another generation, but not life experience." Yes, but the life stories, such as Dr. Matuštík's multigenerational drama, *Out of Silence,* leave visible traces. We should not store them in institutional file cabinets.

——Fedor Gál, Ph.D., author, journalist, and film documentarist (see www.kratkadlouhacesta.cz) was a cofounder and chair of the Public against Violence, the movement that in 1989 brought down Communism in Slovakia. He was born at the end of World War II in the Czech concentration camp Terezin

To re-pair is to bring back together that which has been torn asunder. This poignant memoire, through bringing together the visual and the audible, the olfactory and the gastronomic, the past and the present, reaches forth for the ethical meaning of life as uncovering the spiritual depths of ethical responsibility. As a major critical theorist of philosophy and religion, Matuštík raises the question of becoming a Jew, and this question, as told through the complicated relationship to his mother and, through her, to his extended family and the wider Jewish people, becomes a question of communal self-critique. From Shoa to Communist Czechoslovakia to post-Communist Eastern Europe to the very human and often overlooked dimensions of how individuals and communities part and reconcile, *Out of Silence* is a powerfully naked, movingly poignant, and courageously liberating portrait.

——Lewis R. Gordon, Professor of Philosophy, Africana Studies, and Judaic Studies, UCONN-Storrs; Nelson Mandela Visiting Professor, Rhodes University, South Africa; and EuroPhilosophy Chair, Université Toulouse Jean Jaurès, France

After more than twenty-five years of bringing works on the history of the Holocaust and Jewish culture to the light of print, I can honestly assert we have not read a book which so edifies the theological issues bound up in the history of a family rent apart by war and politics, anti-Semitism and the subsequent clashes of Communist and capitalist cultures. The author's expertise in philosophical and religious studies and his truly advanced perspective in the philosophical and public aspects of his family's journey provide an unusual opportunity for readers follow a memoiristic literary non-fiction narrative while engaging the theoretical and historical issues as well.

——Alan Adelson, Executive Director of Jewish Heritage Project, the International Initiative in the Literature of the Holocaust, New York

MARTIN BECK MATUŠTÍK

OUT OF SILENCE

REPAIR ACROSS GENERATIONS

Library of Congress Cataloging-in-Publication Data
Matuštík, Martin Joseph Beck, 1957–
     Out of Silence: Repair across Generations
     / Martin Beck Matuštík. p. cm.
     Includes bibliographical references and illustrations.
ISBN: 0988373211 (paperback)
ISBN: 13: 978-0-9883732-1-1 (paperback)
ISBN: 978-0-9883732-6-6 (electronic)

Library of Congress Control Number: 2014909735 (paperback)
New Critical Theory, Phoenix, AZ

OUT OF SILENCE

MARTIN BECK MATUŠTÍK

OUT OF SILENCE

REPAIR ACROSS GENERATIONS

NEW CRITICAL THEORY

In 1938 some 89,000 Jews lived in Slovakia. Between March 25 and October 20, 1942, the Slovak State was among the first Nazi satellites to round up and deport some 57,628 Jews, paid Germany five hundred reichsmarks for each Jew, and supplied fifty-seven train transports with cattle wagons free of charge.[1] With the defeat of the Slovak partisans, between September 1944 and March 1945, Germans took over the Slovak operation of the "Final Solution" and deported 12,306 Slovak Jews in eleven transports. More than 71,000 Slovak Jews were slaughtered in the Shoah: of those deported in 1942, 57,553 were murdered; of those deported from 1944 to 1945, approximately eight thousand perished; approximately eight thousand Jews fled from Slovakia to Hungary in 1942, and of those who fled back in 1944 and were deported, two thousand did not return. Three thousand five hundred Jews were killed in Slovakia. Out of 1,566 Jews who fought in the Slovak National Uprising in 1944, 269 were killed. Having survived deportations, killings, and partisan defeat in the Tatra Mountains, my mother, uncle, and their parents were the only Jews who returned to their Slovak village of Myjava in 1945. I was born in Slovakia during the Cold War and grew up in ignorance of my extended Jewish kin and my precarious origins amid annihilation and survival. This is the story I imagine my mother would have told me one day.

Naš dom, naš hrad.
Celé prízemie je otcova velká
ordinácia a čakáreň.

1. "Our house, our castle": Beckov before 1939

Nathan Beck in his Myjava home before 1939

2. Nathan Beck in his home office before 1939

3. Magda Beck in a Purim play in Nové Mesto nad Váhom; March 3, 1942

CONTENTS

AUTHOR TO READER

I was born with an impossible urgency to repair the irreparable and became the child of a Holocaust survivor when I was forty years old and learned that some of my family members had perished in Auschwitz-Birkenau, and surviving relatives had managed to leave Czechoslovakia in 1946. The socialist and capitalist responses to the Shoah characterized the two wings of my surviving Jewish family—those who stayed in Czechoslovakia and those who sought refuge in Israel or Australia in 1946. Both groups are a microcosm of twentieth-century tensions between the secular and spiritual visions of what constitutes a "better world." My mother proudly acknowledged her ties with the Slovak and Soviet Communists, but unlike her surviving Australian and Israeli kin, she cut off any connection to our Jewish origins. While she dreamed of the coming of socialism, her family in Sydney embraced free enterprise. Mother's silence about the Holocaust still speaks of her hidden desire to shield me from harm.

I lived for twenty years in Czechoslovakia and twenty more in America before I drank from Mother's first secret: her hiding our Jewish origins. It took another fifteen years for me to discover Mother's second secret—the hiding of her personal reasons for hiding our Jewish origins. In 2012, when I at last found the key to my mother's story stored in shoeboxes full of public and family secrets, it was locked within moral and spiritual gray zones of her own survival. As in Helen Epstein's iron box for the unspeakables,[2] Mother's archives and afterlives of memory veil multiple silences. Unlocking the nature of traumatic secrets is the first task, but the keys to life are not necessarily left as benefits of one's personal inheritance or group heritage. I invite readers and listeners of my story to accompany me on this voyage of discovery in order to duplicate a new set of keys that we can pass on after we have unlocked the worst and best in us. The ability to mend broken worlds and wake up from our ignorance rests with all of us who listen to silences, pauses, and minor keys of suffering as articulations of hope. Every generation lives on by transforming hope into reasons for living.

I have stolen my memoir from a story about a rabbi who was said to carry with him two pieces of paper. One scrap delivers a message from the future; the other scrap warns that progress emerges from the ashes of history. Perhaps someone put the rabbi's two messages into my pocket as transgenerational fragments of memory. My karmic urgency to repair the irreparable reveals the Janus face of resurrection and ashes. I hope some memoirist, editor, literary agent, or a buddha will steal, create, and retell my midrash when unforgivable disrepair, long shrouded in silence, disturbs the mnemonic traces. One must be joyful because enlightened and liberated sentient beings compassionately imagine and retell our open future.

In Kathmandu, Nepal, December 7, 2014

I

EZEKIEL WRITES FROM SYDNEY

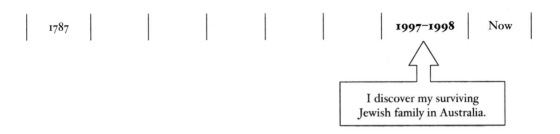

The story opens in Chicago during the summer of 1997. I receive two letters from my lost Sydney relatives, whom I never knew I had. My Australian relatives descend from my mother's surviving Jewish kin in Slovakia. This dramatic scene provides the setting to which I return as I uncover the past before my birth and create my future after this discovery. Resurrection and ashes are two faces of Ezekiel writing from Sydney.

Breaches and Repairs: The Initiating Scenes (1997–1998)

I receive an unusual letter. My curly forehead is giving in to the eastern breeze wafting in through the bay window from Lake Michigan. As I open the first airmail envelope, I fix my eyes on a big oak in front of our Chicago redbrick six-unit flat. Patricia, my life companion, can't hear me when I call out loudly from the living room. So I walk through a long hallway, under skylights shining heavens, into our bedroom, past my wall-to-wall bookcases and a guest sofa near the long French dining table, to Patricia's cozy office in the back of the apartment. She's preparing her seminar on Kierkegaard's *Diary of the Seducer* for Loyola juniors. Huddled over a pile of books, she fiddles with her jacket. I tell her about the mail then walk back to the living room. Dry oak leaves momentarily draw my attention by shivering crisply in anticipation of Indian summer. The faintly warm sun kindles with a purplish dusk glow. I get lost in thought, away from my Habermas lectures for Purdue.

At forty I drink from Mother's first secret: our Jewish origins. Fifteen years will pass before I will unlock Mother's second secret: her singular reasons for hiding our Jewish origins.

Several months ago, having heard in my mother's native village of Myjava that some of my relatives had learned to make shoes and left for Australia long before my birth, I started writing letters to Jewish organizations; searching Sydney, Melbourne, and Perth phone books for shoe factories; and requesting marriage and funeral records for names I know. I've been posting cyber notes on Australian websites, contacting LISTSERVs of genealogical groups, and combing through Red Cross records for Slovak Jewish survivors who might have known my native village table. I pull out the first folded letter hungrily. Late summer of 1997 tastes of an uncanny feast of ancestral foods. Next year I will be at a Shabbos table in Sydney surrounded by my kin.

Silences and Returns: My Life (1957–Now)

Born in Slovakia in 1957, I grew up in Prague behind the Iron Curtain, suffused by the aroma of Mother's pregnant silence. She never spoke to me about the Shoah, and she didn't follow Jewish cookbooks.

Potato pancakes were called by many names throughout Eastern and Central Europe, Scandinavia, the Baltic region, and Russia: *deruny, draniki, placki kartoflan, oladyi, bulviniai blynai, reiberdatschi, kartoffelpuffer, raggmunk;* in Czech they were known as *bramborák* and in Slovak *zemiaková placka.* My *bramborák* did not taste like Jewish food and was a coveted beer-pub delicacy of the poor. As I was born with an urgency for words and foods whose origin I didn't learn with my native grammar, my *bramborák* dripped of a greasy nostalgia for Prague. Mother said nothing about the relatives consumed by the fires of Auschwitz or the survivors who had left their Slovak tables. I became a survivor's child only after I turned forty.

With pungent marjoram, sharp cumin, a secret dash of *Plzeň,* and crispy golden, my *bramborák* held the smell of fall turning into wintery breezes longing for a spiritual home. Mother died when I was fourteen, and I had to flee Czechoslovakia at nineteen. Separated from the cradle by multiple veils, I didn't recognize until my forties that our home cooking *was* Jewish; biblically I didn't know this food's lovemaking. I drank Mother's ancient love at my first US Hanukah when my childhood potato pancakes acquired the texture of latkes' native Yiddish and Hebrew.[3] Olive oil saturates the *levivahs* with hope—the miracle of eight days during which the light of Solomon's Temple was renewed. In a genealogy of intimacy, food speaks by its taste. Nourishment's deep memory sounds birth milks out of silence.

Sydney

August 28, 1997

Dear sir,

Replying to your letter dated 28th July 1997, the following information has been extracted from our archives: MARRIAGES—BECK: David to Rose 1939...Julius to Lilly 1941...Kurt to Hilde 1938...Walter to Elvira 1950...Freda to Leon 1926...Hannah to Louis 1924...Ruth to Jacob 1964.

None of these Beck marriages reflect family connections that are known to me. I want to summon Patricia away from her study, but I examine the archive lists alone. Deaths punctuate marriages.

DEATHS—BECK: Béla 1973...Elisabeth 1960...Gertrude 1966...Helen 1988...John 1982...Phillip 1950...Rudi 1986...DEATHS—VESELY: Erwin 9th June 1980...Kornelia 1984.

Sounds and tastes of something familiar escape from these cursory lines. Béla and Erwin (in Slovakia they called him "Ervín") are my grandpa's younger brothers. I call out the two names of my great-uncles as they step out from this Sydney report on their deaths; I greet them with that double expression of being moved and angry at once. I ask myself, *Why did Mother refuse to tell me anything about her dad and his two brothers? She died; they are buried!* In vein I try to conjure up the cadences of their laughter.

This first of the two letters from Sydney falls ahead of autumn leaves on our Persian rug; my left eyebrow twitches; my cheeks flinch with tension. I comb through my receding hairline with my right hand.

If words were food, I could have cooked them with great-uncles while they lived, even if you didn't wish that I speak with them. I am addressing Mother. I imagine her sitting in the dark corner in front of me. A black ribbon is holding her blond hair up in that curious fashion of the 1960s. She wears a dark-black turtleneck and a white jacket with black stripes rushing down from the collar. Serious and focused on a blank sheet of paper, she leans over her writing desk. This photo records a slightly different memory:

Magda Matustikova, Prague home office, before 1972

4. Magda Beck at her Prague home office before 1972

What will she cook up? I ask myself.

A typical intellectual of her day, she smokes Spartas, a cheap Czech brand. Ashes fall off the lit-up tip into a crooked clay ashtray I made for her in fifth grade.

I decide, *I must interrupt her writing if I want to drink from the future that may speak to me out of her silence.*

I am six years younger than my brother, Pavel, who remembers our mother's dad. Our grandpa Nathan died a year before I arrived into this world. One of Nathan's brothers, Ervín, was still alive when I fled Prague in 1977, and he would have been my closest relative then in the whole "free" world. I thirst for these faces that vanished before my birth. I pick up the letter again but don't recognize other names. The sun has almost set, and faceless lives do not taste with the familiarity of daily bread.

How can I share an uncooked meal if Mother hid the recipe? The letter in my hand hurries to circumnavigate the full life cycle: dust from dust—words flow as mother's milk. The last paragraph announces the cast for my *Hamlet*. Tomb inscriptions read like theater curtains unveiling characters in search of a mystery author: the first in the order of appearance is my grandpa's brother, Ervín, my Slovak great-uncle inscribed into a Sydney burial stone!

TOMBSTONE INSCRIPTIONS—VESELY: Erwin, born 17th October 1913...father-in-law of Michael...grandfather of Karen and Allan.

Did Mother know my great-uncles? Hearing myself utter their names, I taste the spring waters by which refugees in the American Southwest long to quench desert thirsts. I return to inanimate matter drawn in Australian dollars:

Our fee for this research and service is A$ 20.00.

Sincerely,

Irene Rothenberg

The sun sets to paint the dawn when I hear a jolly male voice hollering from the answering machine. I spring up from our oblong Chicago couch, almost trip over its *L*, and run toward the phone. Panting for breath, I arrest my advance. I screen the call but strain to understand its diction.

"Hallo, Martin. Got your letter. My surname is Veselý, but I do not think we are related. Your story is interesting. I wish I could be of help, so should you visit Sydney. Give me a call."

Unable or unwilling to pick up, I spy on the hearty echo from Sydney. My name sounds foreign in down-under diction. The caller pronounces "Veselý" as both Slovaks and Czechs would say it and write it, with a long accent on the ý. Someone has called only to tell me he has nothing to do with my journey.

Czechs would enjoy *bramborák* with an occasional mixture of pork roast or ham. I do not interpret my life as that of a child of a silent Shoah survivor. My Slavic latkes share a bath with the first peoples' Indian fried bread—a mikveh drenched in unkosher lard. Before becoming every goy's potato pancake, the ancient Hanukah dish was made of cheese. During this Indian Chicago summer, my North American applesauce rushes over the Old World latkes, restoring my future taste buds for a richer diet. Choked words conjugate memory with syllables made of forgotten aromas. I eat incense rising from broken burned breads as a Phoenix yearning for waters that would flow from ashes.

Ashes and the Gray Zones: The Costs of Resurrection

A second letter from Sydney arrives a day later. This Chicago summer exhausts all nourishments that have been fed by my two religiously militant atheistic periods. The first atheism mixed for me a native-milk formula from dried-up Communist breasts; I indulged in a second atheism during my struggle for tenure as a philosophy professor in North America. Securing that right to sit at the academic head table is a significant feast for anyone, but it's a feat for an immigrant who arrived without kin and resources. At forty I've succeeded to live as a thinker without wonder, losing myself in an even greater diaspora.

I open a small envelope with a return address from Double Bay a suburb of Sydney. The sender's name, Gary Binetter, on the envelope doesn't sound like a name I've heard of before. *Who is Binetter?* I look at his signature. *Do I hold a letter from another jolly Aussie who has nothing to offer in my search?*

This single-page letter from my Australian second cousin, Gary, takes my breath away. He's my age, and this is the first time I've heard from him. I sink into my office chair; then I jump and run through the long carriage hallway and finally gallop toward Patricia and pull her to my side. We move to the living room. I sit her down on the dark-brown couch and stare at the old wooden frame of the ornate window; the trees are getting ready for their last dance. I open my eyes, touch them, and don't believe their report. I rub them and read again; then I stare at the letter as if it were an apparition.

Born-again atheists may not believe in such resurrections.

"You must read the letter aloud to me!" I whisper to Patricia.

She reads slowly, rewinds, reads fast. Her early gymnastic meets kept her young in midlife once she turned, like me, to sedentary philosophical gymnastics of the soul. Her eyes mime a question. With hair painted almost strawberry blond by the last sun, she gathers my story. Patricia senses something momentous happening in my life—in *our* life. She presses intimately against my thighs to share in my discovery. If words were served at a banquet, Gary's letter would be its entrée. The biblical prophet Ezekiel promised that dry bones will gather their living flesh. Words emerge from Mother's silence—*Am I entering the future of my diaspora?*

Sydney

August 29, 1997

Dear Martin,

My name is Gary Binetter. I faxed you about a month ago, but since I haven't heard from you, I assume you didn't receive it. I have before me a copy of an e-mail you sent to a lady recently. The lady has moved on from the position she occupied; it is now occupied by Tony B. Tony received your e-mail and was about to trash it when he decided to pass it on to his mother, who was born in Žilina, Czechoslovakia. It did not mean anything to her, so she gave it to her mother, Terry. Terry is my grandmother's best friend. Terry came back from Europe recently and whilst there visited Žilina. I was curious to hear from her how she found Žilina and wanted to compare notes. She mentioned your e-mail in passing.

My paternal grandmother was Etelka Becková, your grandfather's sister. I spoke to my father, Emil. He remembers his uncle Nathan very well and with great fondness. He showed me photos of him with his children, Ernest and Magda. It is not clear from your letter, but I assume Magda was your mother.

It is amazing to hear from you. A few years ago, we received a letter from Belgium from Georges Binetter, asking if we were related. Since then I have been busy tracing my paternal grandfather's side and wanted to complete that before I confused myself with my paternal grandmother's side of the family!

I am sending you copy of what I have on record. You also mention family in Israel. Who (and where) are they? Also if your brother in L.A. is interested in meeting any members of the family, please let me know the contact details. We all travel to L.A. from time to time.

All the family in Australia is closely connected with the Jewish community, though we are not religious. My cousin, Michael's son Steven, celebrated his bar mitzvah recently.

I hope to hear from you soon.

Best wishes,

Gary

I repeat Gary's words aloud; I respond to Gary. *It is amazing to hear from you.* Words of responsorial psalmody taste of heavens, but heavens cannot wait for an afterlife. The costs of resurrection ripen with ashes and bear fruit in the here-and-now life. Gary began his family search around the same time I started mine, and we are generational contemporaries. Mysterious aromas of desired dishes have urged us to connect the fragments from the never-before-shared table. We share the same great-grandparents. Our birth showers were shattered over fifty years and three continents. Gary's grandmother and my grandfather were siblings; his dad and my mother were first cousins. We gulped irreversible time and destroyed space. The ashes of the dead, dormant in their survivors, woke up from sleep and rushed the baby milk through the veins of the survivors' children. Gary is beset by my inborn urgency to mend our broken worlds. We share a transgenerational transmission. We recognize each other in convex mirrors signaling across our distance in time, birth, and geography. Our cosmic mirrors draw a calligraphy image that reminds me of Plato's metaphor that the psyche (soul) is a polis (city) written in large letters. These are the letters from the future that wishes to remember the past and then, in mending it, repeat it forward. Wanderers in strange lands, we are the second-generation children of silence who reek of old ovens built in diaspora. Gary is my second cousin.

"In every post-Holocaust generation, in every family, there is a person who awakes with sudden urgency to reconnect the genealogical fragments. That person is called a menorah candle," Sandor Goodhart told me after hearing my story.

Was I brought into the world as a lost child to become a candle of awakening, a bread to be eaten, and wine to be drunk in renewed intimacy? I asked myself as I listened to Sandor, a Jewish scholar and my former Purdue colleague. *Is Gary such a candle in his family? Which philosophical or sacred books tell of such exile, exodus, and twin Shabbat candles? Who prepared the survivors' children for this second coming? Why was my mother silent? Which secret dish or ingredient of care did her silence hide? What good obligated her? Or was she obligated by ashes that couldn't be drawn in the full-color scale, even in their resurrection?* Ezekiel prophesied from Sydney that roots, spices, and aromas would serve the living foods. *What are the costs of this prophesy for my journey?* I live in Phoenix, Arizona, as I now write these words, when desert stones wake up ancient Abrahams.

Resurrection arrives in cheap or costly brands. A well-known Christian philosopher of religion, Alvin Plantinga came to my Purdue department early in the twenty-first century to present a paper with an updated argument for immortality. His was among the best arguments for human immortality, and he presented his case for dualism of an immortal soul or mind and a mortal body with the clarity and conviction of an analytic Christian philosopher pursuing a worthy intellectual mission. I asked him how he would square his own Christian faith with this version of philosophical dualism and why he should bother with any notion of the resurrection of the body if his reason granted him so securely the natural immortality of the soul.

The body doesn't figure much into Platonic immortality. Does not so-called "platonic love" get its name from the preferential love for the soul at the expense of denying love to the body? Plato's teacher Socrates sought to convert the erotic affections of his male followers into an idealized, philosophical loving of the concept of love. Analytically rigorous philosophical proofs of the immortality of Platonized Christianity offer at best a cheap brand of resurrection. Since the time of the Church fathers and Saint Augustine, only mainstream Christianity baptized Plato's case for the immortality of the soul, thereby also running dangerously close to settling for cheaper versions of resurrection.

The Hebrew prophet Ezekiel admitted without embellishment that in death we are dry bones. Should there be resurrection, it cannot be underwritten by Platonized immortality of the soul. Ezekiel proclaimed the act of new creation. Neither Saint Thomas Aquinas's theory of the human person as a psychophysical synthesis of body and soul, nor Søren Kierkegaard's existential drama of spiritual self-transformation, nor Lutheran Pastor Dietrich Bonhoeffer's struggle against the Nazis and his death in Auschwitz could rely on "cheap grace." Along with the best thinkers in Orthodox and modern Judaism, these three mature Christian thinkers held views echoing Ezekiel's biblical prophecy that dry bones shall rise. This faith claim cannot be ensured by philosophical proofs for the immortality of the soul.

In the early-summer months of 1997, anticipating the mail birds from Sydney, I stood next to the pool of ashes that held millions of Auschwitz bones. Now back at home with my second cousin's letter greeting my Chicago autumn, I'm unable to silence a keen sense that all cheap versions of immortality—that highly prized headiness of making good arguments, that arrogant analyticity of philosophy—somehow offend the dead. At the end of that topsy-turvy summer, philosophy bereft of taste and flesh—expounded professionally yet without existential spice—becomes insufferable. This gutturally spiritual distaste decisively ends my second period of *religiously* held atheistic beliefs. I begin to drink from yet-to-be-begotten loves and chew on unanswered questions. *At which feasts do children of survivors nourish themselves? To whom do they return from diaspora? How does a child of silence speak to oneself?*

Eating Kosher in Bratislava

Three rescuers of Slovak Jews were born at the turn of the twentieth century in what was then the Austro-Hungarian monarchy. Their lives pass through the time frames of this story. Gisi Fleischmann was born in my native Bratislava in 1892, twenty years after my maternal great-grandfather Jakub and seven years before my grandfather Nathan. The Orthodox Rabbi Chaim Michael Dov Weissmandl was born in Debrecen in 1903, studied at the yeshiva in Sereď, and became a major force in the daring rescue of Slovak Jews. The Bauhaus-trained architect and secular Jew André (Andrej) Steiner was born in Dunajská Streda in 1908, four years after my grandmother Ilonka and twenty years before my mother.

Gisi grew up in an Orthodox Jewish home. Her parents ran a sought-after Julius Fischer kosher restaurant, hotel, and theater on the Kapucínská Street in Bratislava. Gisi and her two younger brothers became Zionists; Communists and Zionists believed in a more rational form of life. My mother followed Karl Marx's universal idea of social justice for everyone, while Gisi followed Theodor Herzl's idea of a Jewish homeland. Even before Slovakia became Hitler's puppet, Gisi's two younger brothers transformed their parents' kosher establishment into a hub for Zionists.[4]

On March 14, 1939, the Slovak State established itself as a German ally, and the next day, Hitler occupied Czechoslovakia and Moravia. That first divorce of modern Czechoslovakia occurred before my birth. On September 26, 1940, the *Judenrat* (Jewish center) *Ústredňa Židov* (UŽ) replaced all Jewish organizations in the Slovak State. On February 12, 1942, the Slovak police began to register all Jews born between 1897 and 1926 in order to establish their "work capacity"; this task was to be accomplished within about one month. Reb Dov advised the yeshiva students not to register and called on all Slovak Jews to prepare bunkers and hiding places.[5] He survived in one of those bunkers at the end of the war. Sometime between 1941 and 1942, Gisi joined with Reb Dov, Andrej, and others within *UŽ* to form a secret Working Group," a Slovak shadow government. Gisi commanded the respect of rabbis and Jewish leaders and became the backbone of the Working Group, and Reb Dov convinced Andrej to become their spokesperson.[6]

In the 1940s Gisi, Andrej, and Reb Dov became the light in the Slovak darkness; the Working Group developed audacious plans to bribe the Nazis in order to save the Jews.

No photographs of the Julius Fischer kosher restaurant and Zionist hub in Bratislava survived.[7]

2

DIASPORA

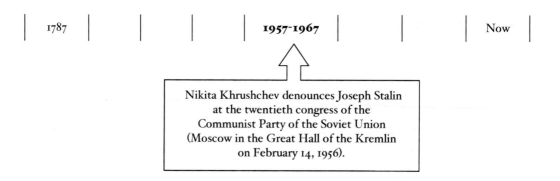

| 1787 | | | | **1957-1967** | | | Now |

Nikita Khrushchev denounces Joseph Stalin
at the twentieth congress of the
Communist Party of the Soviet Union
(Moscow in the Great Hall of the Kremlin
on February 14, 1956).

My birth is framed by the fall of Stalin (1956) and the divorce of my Communist parents (1959). My mother never told me of my Jewish origins and hid from me the impact that the Holocaust had on her life. I live in a triple diaspora: severed from my Jewish origins, thrown into the political cataclysm of the Cold War era, and affected by my unstable home life.

My Communist Parents (1948–1956)

Nikita Khrushchev's 1956 party congress destroyed the cult of Stalin, whose humongous statues would have crushed me as they fell to the ground all over the Soviet bloc, but I was born in Bratislava, the provincial capital of Slovakia, before the greatest of Stalin's memorials, the saint of the era gazing from the Letná Plane in Prague, was dynamited into a thousand pieces. Like many in that insane twentieth century, I was an issue of passionate if not fundamentalist believers in a better world.

"She must have abandoned her childhood identity in those mountain nights she spent with partisan comrades-in-arms," I tell Patricia. We're sitting in our Chicago flat at the turn of the twenty-first century, four years after I received the letter from my cousin Gary in Sydney. "Humanism promised to dissolve all singularity in the melting pot of secular universality. Socialists believed this just as much as the multiracial North Americans."

"Or perhaps your mother severed part of her Jewish self after the Slovak National Uprising was defeated in nineteen forty-four, when she struggled for her mere survival," Patricia speculates. We have no way of knowing.

In their postwar East-Central European cohort, my parents can be counted among the true Communist believers. This should be as uncontroversial as my writing, "My parents were true Baptist believers from the American South." Early memory populates my freshly pledged North American head with parallels, analogies, allegories, and metaphors drawn from my totalitarian experience. I practice an imaginary transference of the Communist period by projecting smells of homegrown rotten tomatoes onto anything that resembles their decay in the promised land. Memory mercifully forgets some of the worst, holds unrelentingly on to the future even while not forgiving the past, and remembers what appears deceptively near in the nostalgic or longing present.

I am remembering events I've never witnessed yet know to be my reality.

My parents were young and passionate about their beliefs. My father, Radislav, was born in the Moravian village of Čejč in 1929. Mother met him when he was studying art history. She didn't ask her parents whether she could marry a goy boy. He was a bit younger, tall, articulate, and very handsome. They gravitated toward each other as two enthusiastic leftist youths, two secular intellectuals taken up by the political climate ushering in the Communist age. Their generation welcomed the Soviet liberation in 1945 and spearheaded the Communist takeover in February 1948.

5. Magda Beck's food-stamp card in Myjava; June 30, 1946

6. Radislav Matuštík in Prague after 1945

A child caught between familial dislocation and political turmoil, I was cooked up in a world colliding with itself. Like many offspring of those with a religious upbringing, I learned to come to terms with the native atheism to which my nation, schooling, and home adhered. Since the demise of Stalin, the Letná Plane welcomed Pope John Paul II (riding his bulletproof Papa-mobile under the watchful eyes of

Communist agents); witnessed the largest demonstration of the Velvet Revolution in 1989, when a crowd of more than a million rattled keys to end the Communist regime; and also hosted the largest concert of the Rolling Stones 2003 worldwide tour, when Mick Jagger celebrated his sixtieth birthday with President Václav Havel.

Following the wishes of her physician father, Mother tried her fortune as a medical student, but when a new dramaturgy department opened at the Comenius University in Bratislava, she enrolled as a freshman. She became a part of the burgeoning Communist literati. My father followed in the footsteps of his own father, a hardware-store owner who became a founding member of the Communist Party in Čejč. Mother wrote plays, some of which, such as *Kristina,* were performed to wide acclaim in Slovakia in the early 1950s. Father was appointed as an assistant professor of art history at Comenius University in Bratislava. Gradually becoming a leading critic of contemporary art, he influenced the new generation of art-history students and artists in Slovakia.

Thanks to Stalin's death, I was born when the love my parents baked in the revolutionary socialist fervor for a better world suffered its first drastic deflation and had to be devalued to ensure their survival. I don't know whether political or erotic infidelities broke up their marriage. My parents divorced when I was two, and Mother and I began to commute between Prague, the Bohemian capital of Czechoslovakia, where she moved after her divorce, and Bratislava, the Slovak capital and the city of my birth. Czech-speaking Radislav, who planned to work in Prague, became a leading art historian of contemporary Slovak art; Magda continued to speak and write in Slovak about Slovak themes even after she and I moved to Prague. After the Czecho-Slovak state divorce in 1992, Father opted for Slovak citizenship to avoid losing his pension and his access to the Slovak art world.

The Lost Child (1957)

I was born under a sign I couldn't find on the zodiac, and this hole in my mythology signaled my first identity crisis. I would have gotten motion and national-identity sickness had I not adopted Czech as a second native tongue and Prague as my intellectual and spiritual birthplace. While Czechs and Slovaks can understand one another, the two nations have distinct histories and cultures. The Slovaks are more Catholic and pastoral, emotionally uncomplicated; the Czechs boast strong

Protestant, heretical, and atheistic traditions. They're more cerebral, and because of the lineage of Bohemian kings, they enjoyed sustained political and even economic stability. Czechoslovakia was grafted out of the decaying Austro-Hungarian monarchy as a multicultural Central European hybrid in which the Slovaks always felt less at home than the Czechs. I could pass for a Czech or a Slovak on either side of the divide, which had its diplomatic advantages, but also I experienced the emotional fragility of someone who could not easily profess primary allegiance to either ethnic world.

As Father and Mother plunged into various love affairs, their distance grew, and I was conceived when they no longer even ate together. Father was doing his army service, which meant there were fewer physical occasions when my parents could have concocted the recipe. Mother mentioned definitive intimate occasions, though Father suspected assistant cooks in Mother's kitchen. Well done, I was two weeks overbaked.

I often question my fated origins like an unsuspecting Oedipus. *Does this calculation of my birth according to the gestation cycle express my unwillingness to enter the twentieth century?*

"Does the calculation provide some real basis for my father's doubts about me?" I ask Patricia.

I could have been conceived during Radislav's home leave, which he spent with Magda. Playing it safe with the gods, I chose April eighth for my birth, which usually falls on the holidays of Passover and Easter. On birthdays I eat greasy *bramborák*, painted Easter eggs, and paschal lambs coated in confectioner's sugar. I console myself, thinking, *The reign of Aries—"Beran" in Czech and "Baran" in Slovak—would seem the best time to suffer the trauma of my birth. With a movable high holiday, I sail safely between my tragic family origins, its hybrid heritage, and the world's historical circumstances, sequestered to my corner of the universe.*

My Immaculate Conception and Virgin Birth

Mother's secularism and Father's absence created fertile grounds for private mythology and an imaginary midrash. But one must not conflate an immaculate conception (being untouched at birth by original sin) with a virgin birth (a birth by parthenogenesis, in which offspring—e.g., among komodo dragons or hammerhead sharks—are produced without fertilization by males). As I was haunted by the unspoken shadow of my origins, the Holocaust towered as the mortal sin of Mother's era. Protecting me from the unforgiven, she anticipated some great dangers.

She erected a safe zone, a bubble at my conception; I would imagine my special safe place. I don't recall my father's presence in my early life, which explains my virgin birth. Mother's lovingly anxious silence cradled my birth.

Conceived by a Slovak mother and a Moravian father sometime during the year when Grandpa Nathan died, I was shuttled between Bratislava and Prague in the country once called Czechoslovakia. To speak about this immaculately virginal myth of my lost origins is to betray its silence. As a child I harbored early messianic ambitions, for I often called my alienated father "Uncle Radislav." *She launched me in a mysterious virginal bubble. My silent mother said yes to the gift of my life, and my prodigal father consented to lend me his name.* Those were my self-created creation myths.

My midrash also would ward off my family's never articulated but deeply held myth about the elephant in the corner—my bastard origins. Perhaps that mythology was born with my father's desire to shirk the responsibility of caring for another child when he already had decided to leave our home. Mother never questioned his earthly paternity, only the fact that he didn't take care of me. Later I would be unsure whether Father's absence should be traced through my biological lineage rather than the diaspora. Father's ambivalence about me made it perhaps easier for him to abandon us shortly after my birth. *Did Mother's twin secrets—her silent hiding of our origins, then hiding her reasons for hiding those origins—make it easier for her to care for me?*

7. Martin Matuštík as a young Pionýr (pioneer) in Prague, before 1968

My Rebellious Boyhood (1966–1968)

When I started third grade, Mother and I finally settled into a seemingly stable life in Prague. She enrolled me in a selective language-oriented primary school at Lupáčová Street in the Žižkov part of Prague. Jan Žižka was a Hussite rebel leader, famous for his military victories over the Crusaders sent by Rome to crush the first Protestant heresy in Bohemia a hundred years before Martin Luther. Under Communism this district became home to poor workers and Roma. My proud grammar school still stands, repainted after the collapse of Communism in Czechoslovakia in November 1989. Žižkov gradually turned into a Czech SoHo, with hip clubs, art galleries, and an alternative scene with cafés, youth hangouts, and brothels. Across the street stands a long building where Hungarian billionaire George Soros housed his Central European University right after 1989. When the former prime minister and second Czech president Václav Klaus angled Soros out of Prague, and after Professor Ernest Gellner's sudden death in Prague on November 5, 1995, this fabulous institution and its modern library, the only one of its kind in Central Europe, moved to Budapest. The Soros Central European University became the Hotel Olšanka. In 2001 I started to bring US students to Prague for summer school and housed them in the same neighborhood.

From third grade on, I had daily Russian and English lessons. Focus on languages made up part of the special curriculum in arts and humanities. Russian was a required subject. We were part of the empire and had to learn the language of the colonial power shared by Slavs and the other tribes within its borders. In my school I had to take more Russian subjects than I would in a regular school. My reward for putting up with Russian was learning the language of the imperialists: English. In addition I became natively bilingual—speaking Slovak at home and Czech at school—and tasted the flavors of the two warring empires.

When I recently visited my primary school, I realized how poorly I fared in my first three years there, how precarious for the rest of my future those fragile schoolboy steps were.

I lived in a dreamy world, half aware of myself and the adults around me. I came out of my boy shell as a disobedient, unfocused, rebellious pupil.

"Martin never will amount to anything," my grammar-school teachers concluded. "He is definitely on the path to delinquency or some such trouble."

In fact I drove most of my teachers totally crazy. "He can't sit still!" they exclaimed, as I ran around in the classroom, enjoying all kinds of commotion.

"He never can complete a simple task by doing it the way one asks him to do," they repeatedly complained. I always had to add something to the assignment just to provoke the teacher. Teachers in socialist countries demanded conformity and discipline, as those were the prized marks of reliable citizenry, so they constantly griped about my misbehavior and disobedience.

"There's no way we can discipline this boy!" they proclaimed, and finally gave up on me.

Like Pink Floyd later proclaimed about so many of us, I was "just another brick in the wall." Michel Foucault's study of the Panopticon prison architecture in *Discipline and Punish* reminds me of the long school hallways with a Big Brother guarding me at all times. I once made a cute socialist starlet in my preschool years then turned into a *Pionýr* schoolboy. I'm not sure whether I liked or pretended to like the prescribed uniform (white shirts and red kerchiefs), salute, and oath: "*Pionýr* pupils protect the truth and keep their given word; they work hard and learn well; they are friends of all children; they are brave, comradely, and helpful to others; they are honest and just; they protect nature and all life on earth; and they love their country."[8] Given my early antiauthoritarian streak, I later wasn't sought out for the Czechoslovak Socialist Union of Youth (SSM) or the adult Communist Party of Czechoslovakia (KSČ).

"There is an insolent twinkle in this pupil's dark-brown eyes!" a teacher proclaimed one day, revealing the deep secret that never has entirely left the world's perception of me, all the way to my adult job-performance reviews written by my superiors in the United States.

I was distinguished in receiving lectures behind the principal's doors, as I was getting poor grades in all subjects. To add to the disaster, I earned at first a B and then a C for "bad behavior." When we received final grades for conduct, mine was judged to be unbecoming of a good citizen (read: "unpatriotic," "un-socialist," "un-Soviet"). With poor grades and complaints following me home, I was on a fast track for expulsion or placement in a "special" school that Mother didn't intend for me.

"Martin needs to be reeducated, made into a real patriot and socialist," faithful functionaries of the State recommended. They saw a danger to the order in my insubordination, and they were ready to take revenge. Mother's high standing in the Communist Party had some mitigating effect, but that ended after the Soviet invasion in 1968 when she became disloyal to the establishment.

Mother's Ghosts in the Pantry

Surviving as Mother's wanted child, I imagined I was saved by the slave masters who found me floating down the river. I had stronger ties early on to female teachers and surrogate mother figures, and at the time, I didn't know Mother's ghosts in the pantry. The ingredient that endowed my conception with an aura of immaculate origin was articulated later by Mother's first secret, her silence about the Shoah. The postwar Communist vision of social justice was to sweep the pantry clean and elevate communal life into a larger holy family. This desire formed her into a radically liberated, pro-choice woman—she chose *my* life and clung to directing it as long as she could take care of me. Years would pass before I discovered that not one but two ghosts haunted the pantry. Her choice of socialism distracted me from searching for her personal reasons for keeping silent about the annihilation of our Jewish kin structure.

Could it have been the Holocaust that caused her haunting silence, and was this the reason that stopped her from aborting me in the midst of our collapsing family life? Was she compelled by that very silence to love and choose life against terrible odds for my existence? Or was there still another ingredient that cooked up my innocent birth and kept the pantry blessed?

In my adult years, I would try to account for the nature of her secret in the absence of spoken answers. And then, after finding the public and historical keys to her silence, I had to come to terms with *her* survivor guilt and *her* reasons for living in the midst of universal human cataclysms and breaches. When I began my search, I hardly could imagine what would be required of me in mending the world by giving birth to my meanings for living.

Even if Father's biological cooking could resolve the genetic search for a "historical me," he could not love me well while his Communist holy family and kitchen were falling apart. After our parents' divorce, my brother, Pavel, spent most of his school years with Father in Bratislava, while I spent mine with Mother in Prague. Although I have sketchy memories of growing up with Pavel in Prague, this period left a deep bond of brotherly affection between us.

My Siblings

On one of our returns from the United States to their native country, Pavel and I took a new Škoda car rental through the Bohemian countryside and exchanged insults of endearment.

"I contributed to your intellectual genius by tipping you out of the baby carriage onto the cement sidewalk," Pavel boasted of his role in my life.

"I'm proud of hitting your head with a wooden stick, thus contributing to your leadership genius," I replied with laughter, as if I were his Zen teacher. "I wonder why our father kept marrying and divorcing rather than just having as many lovers as he desired," I added.

"He probably did have more mistresses than wives, but he could love art history as his one and only spouse," Pavel replied.

My father and a Jewish friend of my mother's conceived Kyra two years after I was born. I don't know the exact chronology of these events, but it matters little, since in this part of the world, married and divorced partners often make up an extended family circle. Mother continued her friendship with Kyra's mother and in turn continued to see Father even after they divorced. Kyra was rejected by Comenius University, where she wanted to study studio art. With Father's surname, after he was expelled from the Communist Party in the aftermath of the Soviet invasion in 1968, she was marked as persona non grata. In the end she earned her degree in Budapest and later struggled as a young artist and teacher at a Bratislava high school. Kyra was hidden from me until later years, when we would celebrate Passover together in Bratislava and Pavel and I would share with her our wider Jewish ties.

Father had Nina with his fourth and last wife. As a teen Nina discovered Bratislava's youth subculture, and against Father's intellectual dominance, chose a path of economic security and enjoyment. Born late in Father's life, she became his darling. She rejected his intellectual loves, including his youthful socialist dreams and art history. Echoing Nietzsche, Nina completed Father's value nihilism by stripping it of all speculative baggage. The Wild West markets and the unfettered pursuit of money were the name of the game in the post-Communist Wild East. In the years following her mother's premature death and then the Velvet Revolution of 1989, Nina married a jazz musician who worked in Bratislava as a taxi driver and later operated a private foreign-exchange currency outlet. He used to walk around with bags of cash and bodyguards with loaded guns for protection against gangs. After their divorce Nina successfully ran a small café while her ex-husband opened a fourth exchange booth.

"Love without a family burden would seem a good deal cleaner for a secular humanist like him," I proposed to Pavel on our car ride.

"Dad married four times and had children with three wives," Pavel said.

"Without having time or patience for any of them," I replied, adding moral judgment.

"Father enjoyed his children when they loved him, but often the burden of caring for them distracted him from his intellectual life."

"We all seemed to struggle to win his love," I said, identifying with my siblings.

"He cared for his world of art history more than anything else."

"Yes. His passion for it remained more constant and faithful than for food, women, friends, or children," I concluded, suddenly ending our exchange.

In that conversation, I must have finished the rest of my thoughts in silence. I often thought of Father as one of those species that does well alone without suffering paralyzing loneliness. Pavel never took Father for granted, although as his firstborn, my brother had received Father's first love.

Café Steiner in Brno

Brno is the second largest city in the Czech Republic. Pavel spent his happiest young-adult years there; his first daughter was born in Brno; his first grandchildren live in Brno; and most of his university friends come from Brno or Moravia. Pavel studied theater and art history there. He shared a university room with one of his lifelong friends, Petr Oslzlý, who became Václav Havel's presidential advisor in 1990. Before I fled Prague in 1977, I forgot a pair of socks at Petr's home. My brother's friend kept that pair of socks for my return, wearing them from time to time, thinking of my wanderings. Petr became a famous theater director in Brno and one year invited me to speak about Fyodor Dostoyevsky after a staging of *The Brothers Karamazov*.

Café Steiner opened in 2003 on Gorky Street in Brno in the corner store of a functionalist tenement apartment building commissioned by Hugo Hecht and designed by Andrej Steiner from 1937 to 1938. The café hosted an art show about Steiner on August 20, 2008—his centennial birthday; he lived for almost a year after that. In

2012 New York, Tel Aviv, and Brno hosted the exhibition *Brno—The City of Bauhaus*. Café Steiner's designer, architect Petr Mutina of Brno's RAW studio, received the Interior of 2003 award from Brno Design Center's professional jury.

Andrej Steiner studied Bauhaus architecture at a German technical school in Brno from 1925 to 1932 and completed his internship in the studio of Ernst Wiesner. After opening his studio in 1934, he designed functionalist commercial and apartment buildings in Bratislava and Brno and published the architectural journal *Forum* in Bratislava. In March 1939 Andrej was imprisoned because his father-in-law, the head of the Czechoslovak Jewish Agency, had fled to London in advance of the invasion of Hitler's armies. Andrej, however, was released on March 14—a day before Hitler reached Brno—to finish an important architectural commission for a Brno apartment house. That same day, Andrej fled with his wife Hetty Weiner and young son Peter to his native Slovakia just as it converted itself into one of Germany's axis states.

In 2003 Andrej Steiner was awarded an honorary doctorate from Brno's Masaryk University. My brother received his degree in theater and art history from the same university. After the Iron Curtain fell in November 1989, Pavel returned to Brno, his intellectual birthplace, before he eventually stayed in Bratislava, just as I returned at first to Prague. We share ambivalence toward Bratislava, the city of our birth. Next year in Café Steiner! My pair of worn-out socks is still in Brno.

Loving Pravda

Mrs. Purple ("Fialová" in Czech) wasn't very deep. She was unskilled as a primary teacher and the one teacher I loved to drive crazy. We would read and translate tedious articles from the daily Soviet newspaper, *Pravda* (*Truth*). Once one learned its basic ideological vocabulary, one would find the Orwellian speak wasn't very different from what politicians say in elections or when they go to war to promote peace. Then all the articles became collages of linguistic fury signifying nothing.

"One must adopt the practice of speaking and writing like they do *Pravda*," Fialová insisted. "Truth speaking" was, I believe, the main purpose behind the constant language instruction in Russian.

"Soviet speech is the truth," she exclaimed with fire in her eyes. "Tomorrow means yesterday!"

The eschatological vision of the futuristic Soviet land proclaimed the Messiah who already had come. The Jewish-Christian end of time survived in atheistic Edens. Mrs. Purple's lessons served as brainwashing exercises in pseudoreligious political stupidities and secondarily taught us language. She inspired in us contempt, and little rascals that we were, we relished undoing her Russian classes about the Soviet motherland. Her raging tears held no promise of tomorrow.

I never quite learned the blanket Czech hatred of the colonizers—the Russians. There were three reasons for this. One of my disobedient school buddies was a Czech-born boy of Russian parents. He shared his given Christian name with Lenin. It was with Vladimir that I caused the most disturbances in my Russian hours. Then my first love enrolled in my third-grade classroom; she was a ten-year-old Azerbaijani beauty named Rita. She had long dark hair, mysterious black eyes, and plentiful dark eyebrows. I pursued her with such prepubescent intensity that her memory even today runs shivers up my spine. Who dares to deny children their ability to experience passion for each other even before their bodies become stirred by hormonal storms? Finally, in high school, I had a Russian teacher who was a native speaker, and she loved the great classic authors: Tolstoy, Dostoevsky, Chekhov, and Gogol. With Vladimir, I disturbed the Soviet *pravda*; with Rita I anticipated women's secrets; with the Russian classics, I learned to think. Loving the language of invaders, I drank from prohibited Russian writers, like Berdyaev and Soloviev, in the original language. I consumed Russian greats as nonviolent weapons to confront the oppressive regime.

Who's My Father? Who's My Mother?

Before I plunged into my school days, Mother and I oscillated between Prague and Bratislava. The two national capitals are seven hours apart by train and five by car. In motion I breathed echoes of my parents' first cooking. Prague and Bratislava now dominated the two divorced republics that once had formed a federation. Who actually took charge of me hardly seemed to matter amid the rising storms of my early childhood. My caretaker was the mother of a former student of my father who had been my mother's unhappy admirer. My father's student, Martin, was a young poet who committed suicide in the Prague Hotel built in Dejvice in the bombastic Stalinist style of the early 1950s. My father later told me that the walls of the hotel room where Martin was found were covered with lines of his unpublished poetry. Mother didn't attend Martin's funeral in Bratislava, even though she later placed me in his mother's home.

I don't look like anyone in the memory albums of the contemporaries of my parents, except for Mother. After her death close acquaintances reinforced the myth of my matrilineal conception.

"You are Magda appearing before our very eyes all over again!" they would say, welcoming me.

My heritage boasted one certainty: I was Magdalena's son. Silence and love, haunting anxiety, and enabling freedom—this was how I mythologized my mother's legacy.

New and Old Fears

"Mrs. Purple became incapable of teaching Russian and retired early," I tell Patricia, as we diverge from our earlier conversation about my mother. This year's Indian summer didn't last long.

"She taught you in that building across from the former Soros University?" she asks me. Our last trip to Prague triggers a string of my early-childhood memories.

"And then there was my civics teacher! He was one of few males teaching at early-grade levels. He was such a crotchety Communist, an unimaginative guardian of the state religion. Mr. Civics taught us about the main official holidays and public rituals that would replace all their religious equivalents."

"But wasn't religion more or less outlawed in your school?" Patricia asks.

"Yes and no!" I reply. "In the Communist liturgical calendar, there were feasts for welcoming new citizens as a kind of baptism or circumcision. Initiations into various youth organizations took the place of Christian confirmations or Jewish bar and bat mitzvahs. The Communist weddings and burials and a slew of rituals from 'blessing' crops to anointing military hardware to honoring flags completed the sacred rites of passage and maturity."

I relish making visible this religious zeal of the secular state. My initiation into proper flag hanging, parading, and waving was significant. We had two flags to pledge to—the Czechoslovak national flag and the Soviet internationalist flag. On major holidays, such as May first (May Day) or May ninth (celebrating Soviet liberation), we were obliged to hang flags not only on public windows and streets but also at home. The neighborhood-watch groups would inspect the windows and report those who didn't "celebrate." Mandated joy was to be spontaneous. This petty form of patriotic tyranny was followed by an almost hysterical addiction to flag-waving and flag posting and public injunctions that anyone "suspicious" (those who would not "celebrate") should be reported to the authorities. I lived with neighborhood committees at school, at work, on my street, and in public spaces such as movies, pubs, and even churches.

The idiots of propaganda, the teachers of patriotic values, were paid to addict us to fear and use it as a political and educational tool to make us more docile. We had nuclear-war drills, gas-mask drills, biological-weapons drills, and numerous patriotic demonstrations. These ranged from showing our national resolve to defeat the imperialists, to participating in flag parades, to listening to public slogans that sang from the streets' loudspeakers one could not turn off, to being bombarded with the constant advertising of state values on the radio and television, in newsreels, in the dailies, and on state-sponsored billboards.

My civics teacher taught physical education. As Foucault explains, "There is a deep connection between the immortality ideology of the state and the training of docile bodies." I owned many pairs of bright-red underwear. The red of our childhood undergarments was intended to make us patriotic in our very flesh. We were to look up to the Communist Party in the same way a man yearns for a woman. The red draping our bodies would create a Red Sea of flag-waving revolutionaries on their way to the promised land. Whereas the patriotic marchers wrapped themselves in flags, creating an orchestrated frenzy, the thousands of red pairs of underwear painted socialist solidarity in the mass gymnastic festivals called *Spartakiáda* (from "Spartacus"). Bodies lifted into the air, bodies twisted around each other, bodies elevated to cathedral heights, bodies whirling in an un-Sufi-like dance would sculpt the socialist symbols of the hammer and sickle and the five-cornered red stars, and we, the children of the Soviet future, would make Hitler's rallies and the film propagandist Leni Riefenstahl go pale with jealousy. A dance of red underwear signified the megalomania Hitler and Stalin shared in their predilection for bombastic and big in the Nuremberg or the Red Square rallies.

"When I encounter the big and the bombastic, I shudder with terror." I gesture with my shoulders as if terror were my present reality.

"Why now?" Patricia asks, trying to read my body language.

"Nine eleven?"

The warmth of the late Indian summer is eclipsed by the fire of the collapsing Twin Towers. The old and new red alerts become my poisonous bedfellows. I fear new Herods this late and far from my nativity.

"You don't mean the falling skies?" She resists connecting Stalin's bathos, with which I weave all the red silk of my youth with anything that immediate and raw as the new war on terror.

"Not far behind patriots and flag wavers follow secret agents who either trigger in us fear of the omnipresent enemy or make sure that at appointed times we will *celebrate* the prescribed joy."

"Not here, not now!" She shakes her head.

"One becomes suspect celebrating *more* than has been ordered. The singularity must never deviate from the collective." I keep steady to my train of thought that is quickly becoming my private monologue.

"Can't you see that your comparison of the Soviet state with America's response to terrorism breaks down if taken too far?" she insists.

"Only if you don't want to see how easy it is to barter individual freedom for safety."

Our conversation reveals more about me than our historical moment. Patricia doesn't disagree with what could happen anywhere, but her questioning makes me aware that I react as a survivor of the red terror.

Václav Havel's essay "The Power of the Powerless" narrates a greengrocer's refusal to celebrate May Day by not displaying the proletarian-unity mantra in his shop window. How I wanted to play a different tune in my youth! I dreamed of showing up at school one day, wearing underwear that wasn't red. But by my refusing the Soviet red under my pants or on our Prague windowsills—by going naked under my jeans or displaying no flag at all—I would have been charged with a misdemeanor if not treason.

"I desired to become underwear deviant!" I reminisce to Patricia. "We were taught not to be spontaneous about what the state already prescribed—hence the terror I caused my teachers by delivering my assignments in creative ways. Through fear we increased our production, pledged our allegiance, hung our flags, and hung the enemies of the state." I'm now going down the memorial path with some relief.

When the US president raises terrorist alerts from orange to red, there must be a danger of repeated attacks. One must not joke with the TSA in airport screening lines. Passing through the airport X-ray machine and refusing to have one's underpants inspected would raise a red alert regardless of the garment's color.

"We put on red underwear to celebrate the prescribed joy, and perhaps later even procreated in our fearful unconscious for the socialist future." I switch to a lighter tone, and Patricia laughs, imagining me as a young deviant, courting her in my immaculately bleached yet still virginally red underwear. Joking was our bread of life during the Cold War, and one also must scare away dark ages in the lands where stars and stripes drape ladies of liberty.

"These patriotic acts were funded with fear from without and introjected within. This is when it was impressed upon me what it meant to act out of fear: to hang a flag; to wave a flag; to touch the flag properly; to wrap oneself, out of dread, in the flag—the red internationalist flag most of all. Taking down an officially posted flag was risky business; desecrating the Soviet flag carried a Gulag sentence. When I see people burning flags these days, instinctively I look over my shoulder for secret agents," I say, finishing my litany.

Patricia listens to my red alerts as they run to her shores across traumatized generations; my fears are refugees from Communism, but some fears were born before my birth and had been passed on to me by Shoah survivors. Which other fears must I face now?

The First Kiss

I wouldn't go along with my teacher without asking questions during our civics lessons: "How will ducking under a desk protect me from a nuclear blast? What good is a gas mask against bacteriological weapons?" As a result I suffered ostracism from the teacher in his classroom exercises. Patriotic ideology didn't sit well in my young mind.

A common Russian grammar mistake those days was the confusion between "red" and "beautiful." In Russian *krasnyj* means "red," and *krasivij* is the word for "beautiful." In Czech as well as Slovak, *krásny* is "beautiful," and *červený,* "red," is an entirely different word. So we confused a beautiful girl (in Czech *krásná dívka*) with the Red Square (in Russian, *Krasnaja Ploscad*). We called girls in Russian the "reds" rather than "beautiful." This had its one-track male teen logic: The red girls were Communists, and never mind that they were Russian girls—if a girl could be kissed, she must be beautiful.

A Bratislava street gang initiated me in the secrets of sex, power, and violence. This was in my first two years of grammar school in Bratislava, while living with Martin's mother, Auntie Zuzana and before we moved to Prague. She cleaned offices down the street, and after her poet son took his life, I became her surrogate baby Martin. She loved me as her own, and when my mother couldn't be with me and my father wouldn't care for me, no love was insignificant. My childhood buddy, J., lived on the same block. He had an alcoholic father and lived in a small hell of a one-bedroom socialist project.

Years later J. found me in the new century on the Internet, and on one of my visits in Bratislava, we remembered our boyhood years together.

"My father lectured only ten minutes from where we lived, but he never came to see me," I said.

"I went with you to see your father at Comenius University," J. replied.

"I still think I had it easier than you did in your home."

"My father didn't give me much attention. I came from his second marriage, but unlike you I had a stable home."

My friend and I grew up fast in an unruly street gang. The group rode industrial trains across the Danube River, and we'd jump off at high speed. On one brave occasion, we swam across the dangerous Danube from the Old Town side to Lido Beach. We rummaged through car cemeteries for spare parts. I took part in not so innocent pranks that scared people in the dark alleys—often unsuspecting women—walking the streets in the shadows of night. The younger ones among us learned all about sex from teenage boys who seemed eager to initiate us into its secrets. The gang held group masturbation Olympics in order to celebrate the best "shot" of those who could produce one and to certify for the younger ones that they truly had become "men." It must have taken me several years of horsing around with the gang before my body gave evidence of my maturity.

For the longest time, I thought babies were conceived from plantlike semen passed through a kiss. In those prepubescent days, I fancied kissing as a culminating, never-ending bliss. Precociously I intimated the joy of the wedding kiss. Even after volcanic forces took hold of my adolescent body, the kiss never lost its sacred aura of eternity. I kissed first in infinitely imagined embraces; later I frustrated precocious girls by taking time with my kisses. I was wildly impressed by vividly narrated accounts of what awaited me in the arms of women, and with that vision of the prize, I promised myself that I would find a girlfriend as soon as I could.

My Teacher Protector

Alžběta, this pupil mythologized, *came to protect me from slaughter.* As the Prague Spring of 1968 was about to erupt, Alžběta captured me from her uncomprehending colleagues, who complained about my disruptive behavior in class. In their pettiness, smallness, and resentment with which the oppressive regime's bad diet malnourished them, they conspired, like so many Herods, to destroy innocence—my life—by barring all future chances for my higher education.

"She saved my life. She impressed me as Socrates did one of his pupils—becoming for me the lifetime example of a true pedagogue," I explain to Patricia.

Alžběta, my queen, arrived into the bombastic empire in which the future was yesterday's news. The myth of my birth, reinvigorated by the queen's homage to the holy bubble of my self-protective independence, transformed my unruly spirit of rebellion. I gradually hit upon the rascal living within me, and my chemistry and art teacher, Elizabeth (Alžběta) Holá, befriended him early. I graduated to Mrs. Holá's classes in fifth grade in 1967. She had grown aware of my name before she met me, for "my case" was often discussed in the teachers' kitchen. Alžběta intervened in the worst outcomes of my rebellious youth and in the turmoil that arose after my mother's death.

"I never would meet another like her among my teachers in Prague or later as a university student, not even among my university colleagues in the US academy."

I used to walk home with Alžběta from school, since we didn't live far from each other. During these walks we'd get lost in endless conversations. "Tell me about chemical elements and colors and art and life," I'd demand of my teacher. Mother carried on similar talks with me about the wonders of the universe.

"I discovered that the secret of your disturbance was never an attention deficit," Alžběta told me when I visited with her in Prague after 1989. "The trouble with you resided in the world that was failing to feed you because you craved intense creative attention."

"I disturbed my surroundings because I was hungry for a spirited, feisty, true conversation," I said, reminiscing with her, "and I was getting the bored faces of spiritless disciplinarians instead."

"I spoke to you as an adult"—she peered at me wisely from behind her spectacles—"and you would grow quiet, focused, and absorbed in thought." A large oblong mirror behind her armchair sent multiple messages. Still-life villages and the countryside glanced at us from the wall, some painted by her.

"And a miracle happened. Gradually I began to learn and show remarkable results in your class—for the first time ever!" Alžběta's chemistry and art classrooms had mesmerized me as a child.

"You weren't stupid or violent, just lost a bit." She often demurred, and at home she spoke quietly.

"Your chemistry classroom and labs were full of alchemic wonder; your art classroom was a silent mountain where gods gathered to create out of beauty; and your office was a hermitage where one couldn't enter for cocktail small talk but had to have something to say from oneself or at least pose a real question."

My student years brought new wonderment and happiness, during which Mother and the magi-queen imparted to me the legacy of open receptivity. Their feminine hands planted seeds of freedom in me. The boy stepped out of the imagined protective cocoon, transforming the inner rebel against absent fathers and wrongful authorities into a young man who had to learn to create out of threatening chaos.

Mrs. Holá never had disciplinary problems with her pupils. She would look with calm and inner silence, turning her eyes at a student who was causing a disturbance until he or she quieted down. Her classes were radically different from the chaos that had reigned in Mrs. Purple's Russian hour. Engaged pupils who can be drawn into wonder often discover an inner space of repose.

"As pupils we both feared yet were drawn to Holá's class," Radko commented in a conversation we had during our adult years when I visited him in Prague. My former classmate had gained weight and lost hair but retained irony.

"She received each of us in her classes as precious beings. As her students we were prompted to find ourselves," I said.

"What does a teacher like her teach?" Radko asked, shaking his head, as if he has never been her student.

"It wasn't primarily chemistry or drawing that she showed us—it was the path to oneself." I think I'd known that truth intuitively, even as a ten-year-old.

"She taught inner freedom and gave us an opening to any other form of liberation," Radko agreed.

"Without uttering a word about the oppressive regime in which we lived, she challenged it at its core and pointed us toward self-transformation," I continued.

"I didn't retain much from her chemistry or drawing lessons. What I did receive, however, has been guiding me to discover the rest of the world by my own light."

I continued to converse with Radko about the impact our teachers had on our lives. Ascetic cookbooks from the Communist East make us forget about the coming of magi-queens. World histories celebrating the end of the Cold War sing about the light on the dark sky of my nativity.

During the early months of the Prague Spring, Alžběta saved me for a second time. Her friend, Dr. Hrabal, was a school psychologist who taught me how to discipline myself and to study on my own. In his office I had my first encounter with Rorschach test blots. He showed me a series of abstract images then asked me to articulate what I saw in them.

"You reveal suppressed anger," Dr. Hrabal told me, as he was listening to my descriptions.

"I don't think of myself as an angry boy," I responded with doubt.

"You harbor a lot of anger toward your father, your mother, and the institutions that failed you."

I thought of my absent father, my virgin birth, and the institutions they represented.

"We have to find creative outlets for your anger. I'll teach you how to beat the system by using the best in you," he suggested.

Instead of becoming a cunning criminal or drug-addicted dropout, I was destined to grow into an overachiever in my studies. With my anger turned now against the social and political windmills, I began to earn straight A's. At the end of the ninth grade, Dr. Hrabal redesigned my imperfect birth and upbringing with a fresh dossier. My parental record was littered with their apostasy. The engineered dossier had to improve upon my own educational disasters. Dr. Hrabal retouched my bad history, and with files and the memory of parental misdeeds happily erased from my inheritance, without having to disown them or confess to a lie, in 1972, I was admitted to a secondary school where Mrs. Alžběta had teacher friends. She entrusted me into their protective care. Although we couldn't leave from behind the Iron Wall curtain at will, a tightly knit underground railroad from slavery to freedom thrived in the best of our schools. Many teachers—including Alžběta—resisted in hiding the oppressive face of regimes. Happily practicing the Socratic sin of seducing and maleducating youth into thinking, they sabotaged in us a future that could therefore never come. I never stopped addressing my queen with a formal "you," even when I called her by her first name in my later adult years.

Shoeboxes and Mute Things (1997–1998)

It is after the Chicago summer of 1997, and the letters from Sydney now prompt me to look into paper boxes that reek of old-fashioned shoes. The label announces correspondence written by Magda, a young Communist, to her lover, Radislav. The shoeboxes are packed with her unpublished writings, diaries, and copies of historically important letters. Mother used to correspond with various dignitaries and famous theater personalities. Old pieces of paper make me sneeze with sudden memory stirred up by yellow dust. Boxed air becomes stained with time. Words are torn by archival smells and fall off the crumbling pages. Reading is arrested by wear and tear.

She must have retrieved her youthful love letters when she divorced Father! The last correspondence is dated after my birth; then the paper trail stops. Mother's correspondence is a historical literary document from the 1950s. The letter lines exude intellectual passion, excitement of party congresses, creativity of writers' unions, songs of personal love, the aroma of hope for a better world. Although I look in vain for a cynical apparatchik or power-hungry Stalinist, the author of the letters is a humanist.

By the time Patricia and I moved to Chicago, besides these remnants of the Communist-era shoeboxes, I inherited several mute furniture witnesses who used to stand in Mother's home office. I have lost many clues to my past; when I do find some clues, I lack a reading key to grasp their importance. I don't recognize the odor of their varnish. As I hold archival objects for a closer inspection, the lingering snippets of memory send up my nostrils a whiff of Mother's childhood house. Things bear *objective* silences for us of the universe, which doesn't seem to answer. But like speakers becoming mute, the silence of things produces words spoken once before. The silence of Magda's shoeboxes stored the fleeting sense of time and bottled the intangible effects linked to her memory. I'm strumming on these choked, smothered, twisted vocal cords, as if all things could be strings that may be played with a tune. My uncomprehending attachment to the objecthood of witnesses from mother's Prague office decrypts dormant codes stored up somewhere deep. If the reactivated codes aren't hidden proteins in my genes, then something else wakes up within these old shoeboxes and leaps and skips the generation that used to wait in long lines for a pair of shoes. One used to rush for shoes as one did for toilet paper in lands where the future may not have them.

Could a way of reading be transmitted along with shoeboxes as if they were aged barrels whose corks once stopped distilled wine? My barrels aren't Helen Epstein's iron boxes but rather texts made of hieroglyphs. Could a tongue taste the alphabet as if words were grapes? As I inhale the stifled air of love with which Mother coveted these mute things from her father's house, her desire to embrace them shoots an unknown fear through me. *What did she love even in her silence?* I wonder.

3

VERTIGOS OF THE INVERTED PAST

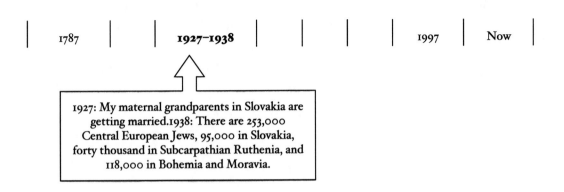

1787 1927-1938 1997 Now

1927: My maternal grandparents in Slovakia are
getting married.1938: There are 253,000
Central European Jews, 95,000 in Slovakia,
forty thousand in Subcarpathian Ruthenia, and
118,000 in Bohemia and Moravia.

In late August 1997, my cousin Gary in Sydney sends me a package of photos. I examine faces I've never known and utter names I never heard from my mother. I enter a conversation with the witnesses at my maternal grandparents wedding in 1927, two-thirds of whom perished by 1945.

Letters from the Future

Chicago

September 5, 1997

Dear Gary and other family relatives,

You have found me and my Beck lineage, and I have found you with your family and relatives of whom I had no trace until your letter! I thought for a long time that it would be impossible to locate those who immigrated to Australia and with whom those of us who stayed in Czechoslovakia never had any contact. My mother, no longer alive, is Magda Matuštíková, born Becková, alias Veselá, and her brother is Ernest Veselý, born Beck. Both are children of Nathan Beck and Ilonka Pressburgerová. The name Veselý was their chosen war pseudonym, which Ervín continued using in Sydney, whereas Béla and your oma, Etelka, did not use it.

One more twist to the story is that for some time after I began speaking about this with my uncle Ernest, I thought that only three Beck brothers survived and that Etelka died in the camp with her three sisters. This is what Ernest reported to me: see my enclosed, albeit not very legible, proto genealogy where Etelka is listed by me, wrongly, as a Holocaust victim who perished in Auschwitz. Recently I discovered that she lived, just as Béla and Ervín did, and that either she or the other two brothers had a shoe factory. I searched for this factory in the Australian yellow pages, on the websites for Sydney, and through the consulate office in Washington DC. I had no information about your surname! Ernest did not know. My mother, if she knew, did not tell me. I wrote to ten Vesely families in Sydney and to the Australian Jewish Historical Society. Their letter came on the same day as yours! It lists marriages, grave inscriptions, births, and deaths for several Becks and Vesely in Sydney, and they match your list for Béla and Ervín. Nothing appears on Etelka Beck, since she married Binetter! Women vanish in genealogies by name, and they died in the camps while brothers and husbands often man-aged to survive.

Patricia, my companion of ten years, and I went this summer to trace the ge-nealogy. I've lived in the United States since 1978 and was born in 1957. We made slides, dug up lots of data, and have many stories to exchange when we meet (we hope). So you see how happy I am that my e-mail messages did not get lost in some trash bin. Without this, Matustik and Binetter would have had a hard time discovering that they traced their origins to Beck.

I have been very interested in my Jewish background, though I was not brought up knowing about it. I was neither connected to a Jewish community nor educated as a secular Jew. I grew up in a Stalinist, anti-Semitic country and in a secular household. I went through a spiritual phase in my early teens in Prague and in my twenties while in the United States; it has been an eclec-tic religiosity of the East and West, though it was at one time also intensely Christian and Catholic. Such journeys happened to many others in Central Europe. I have been quite secular and nonreligious since my PhD studies in New York. Today I am harkening back to what I feel has been my robbed Jewish culture, family, and life. The religious side is something I remain hesi-tant about. All this explains why I started looking into my family narrative. So my case is more typical for the US Secretary of State—the Czech-born, exiled, Catholic-educated, later secular, yet Jewish in origin, Mrs. Albright, who has just recently discovered the extent to which the Holocaust affected her family. I apologize for all the factual errors about our familial Jewish story. Do you have any photos? Ours will come a bit later.

All the best,

Martin

Cousin Gary searched for his past reached across the Pacific until he stumbled over my cyberspace letter. New mail arrives from Gary.

Sydney

October 1, 1997

We read your letter with great interest....We are certainly not a religious family, but there is an attempt at tradition. Nobody keeps kosher, but Friday night is a family night, and we all make the effort to be there when we are in town.... It is almost Erev Rosh Hashana, the eve of the Jewish New Year. My parents are away overseas, so we are going to my uncle Erwin's home for dinner. The whole family is very excited to know about you, and we all wish you and Patricia, your brother Pavel, and his family all the best for a happy, healthy, and prosperous new year.

p.s. When you are able to make it here, please know that you will be welcome to stay in my home.

With best wishes and warmest regards,

Gary

Transgenerational Conversations

The bulky letter contains ancient photos that Gary's father, Emil, chose for me. He added recent photos of his Sydney family. If the first letter from Gary struck me as an apparition from the netherworld, the ancient family photos imbue me with awe. I am more moved and shaken by those photos than by anything else. I inhale a charoset mixture of the numinous, tragic, and sublime; the faces are made of bittersweet mortar. Mother's silence became my Golem rising: traditional foods take on freshness; mute faces come alive; alien witnesses begin to speak within me: *Nobody keeps kosher, but Friday night is a family night, and we all make the effort to be there when we are in town.... It is almost Erev Rosh Hashana, the eve of the Jewish New Year.* That's kosher enough for a lost Jew.

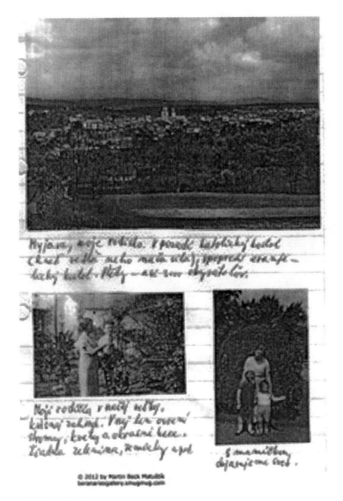

8. Myjava before 1939

I'm looking at a photo of three children and an adult woman: a boy and a girl are sitting on a blanket, while a woman next to them holds another little girl. I'm astonished by the revelation in this innocent gathering. The woman in the photo looks very much like my mother in her thirties, but unmistakably the adult is my *oma*, and the girl in her arms is my future mother. The scene takes place at Nathan's house when his firstborn sister visits him with her three children. In the photo two children are sitting on the blanket next to my *oma*, who's holding my little mother. These littles are my mother's cousins. The scene occurs before World War II in the garden of my mother's family's house. They are in Myjava, the Slovak birth village of my mother.

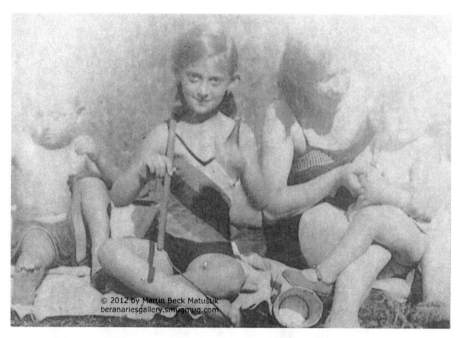

9. The Beck, Pressburger and Binetter families in Myjava before 1942

I'm transported to a slice of time from 1939, three years before Slovak Jews were expelled from schools and synagogues were closed, a life before the storm. All four persons in this photo who were visiting my mother's house in the previous photo—my *opa*'s firstborn sister and her two boys and girl—survived the Shoah. This family lived in Galanta, which, unlike my mother's native Myjava, was annexed from Slovakia by Hungary, where deportations didn't start in earnest until 1944. The boys, Erwin and Emil, were taken to a labor camp in Hungary. The girls, Olga, and their parents were deported to Auschwitz. Their father, Michael, was gassed upon his arrival in the camp. Their mother, the firstborn Beck, and their daughter were moved to a war-production camp and survived until their liberation by the Soviets. The brothers hid in Budapest thanks to false papers they obtained from Swedish diplomat Raul Wallenberg.

After 1946 Mother broke all contact with the surviving cousins from the 1939 photo of the group on the blanket in Myjava. She erased ties to her Jewish past, decided to assimilate her children, and took her secret to her grave. Not knowing the married name of my *opa*'s sister, I lost all traces that could lead me to her extended Sydney families who had left Czechoslovakia in 1946.

I pull out another photo from Gary's letter.

10. Nathan's sisters—Margit, Frida, and Olga Beck—before 1939

"Look at these three gorgeous women in their midtwenties, Margit, Frida, and Olga," I say, calling Patricia to our living room.

Each young woman, likely in her late teens or early twenties, wears a dramatic evening gown. One woman runs her long curly hair down to her waist; the other keeps hers attractively short. The third carries her hair proudly up. All three adorn their young, smiling faces and proud necks with jewelry. Wild feathers climb to heaven from their foreheads and hairdos. This was the typical fashion of the 1930s. Beautiful eyes, faces full of life, such radiant expressions—they looked as if they were ready to dance all night or sing in some performance. These young women were my *opa's* siblings, my three Beck great-aunts. Unlike their firstborn sister, they were murdered in their prime along with their husbands and young children in Auschwitz.

Another photo portrays the Becks posing with a large convertible.

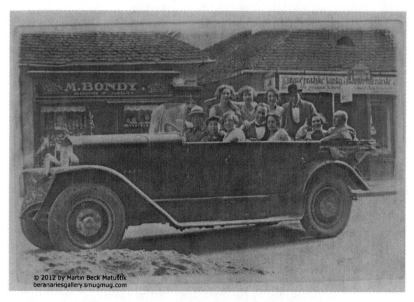

11. The Beck and Pressburger families before 1942

"Who are these other people?" Patricia asks.

There are too many names to remember, write down, and tell at once. My mother's dad had four sisters and two brothers. The brothers were taller than my grandfather, with young women hanging on their arms.

"They must either be spouses or friends or lovers." I wink at her.

The striking beauty of my great-aunts and my *oma*, who was by then either Nathan's fiancée or wife, is remarkable. I notice the firstborn Beck sister, who is now the only surviving Beck sister.

"Etelka is very much Nathan's sibling." I study her face and body build. "Sisters married earlier than brothers," I tell my wife, "for young girls couldn't be hugging their boyfriends so intimately in public in those days."

"They all married very young!" Patricia responds.

"Look at this photo." I grab a picture of a handsome gentleman. "Who is this older man?"

He stands tall, is dressed in a well-tailored dark suit, and displays a silver chain for what must be his watch.

"They used to carry their watches in their pocket. His silver chain is coming out of the right pocket," I say with excitement.

"He's smoking a big pipe," Patricia notes.

"That's not a pipe! It's a drinking cup from a spa town, probably Karlovy Vary, where Uncle Ernest lives today. That looks like a walking stick resting on his left arm. Ernest used to visit his maternal grandfather, Max, at the tobacco store in Galanta."

1930s'/Piestany? Karlovy Vary?
Max Mordechai Pressburger

© 2012 by Martin Beck Matuš!
beranariesgallery.smugmug.cc

12. Maximilian Mordechai Pressburger probably in Piešťany or Karlovy Vary sometime between the late 1800s-1930

13. Ilonka Pressburger, sometime between the late 1800s and 1930

Max is about to step out of the faded photo. He looks at me with his serious, imposing figure and earnestly carved face. I join him on the spa promenade where Goethe met his lover. Then I notice my mother.

14. Magda Beck seated on her grandmother's lap in Myjava between 1939 and 1942

"Look at little Magda sitting on her grandma's lap," I tell Patricia.

"And who are the two women behind them?"

"My mother's aunts, Fridka and Olga! Look closely at their faces in the other image." I hand her the photo of Margit, Frida, and Olga dressed for a night out. Their faces come alive, as in a darkroom.

"These pictures are from before nineteen thirty-nine," I comment, "and our families appear to be tight."

"How did it happen that your mother broke this closely held family connection?" she interrupts.

"I don't know," I say, then grow silent.

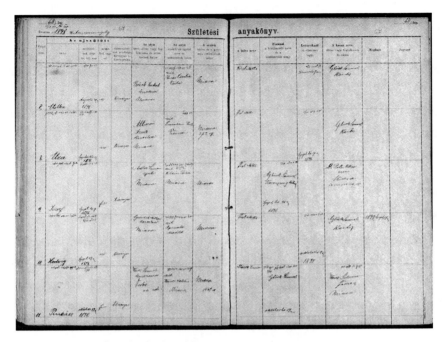

15. Birth record of Etelka Beck in Myjava

I peruse Gary's genealogy chart as my key to the tree of life. Each "great" before a name measures distances between photographic infinities. I add "great-great-great" to my *opa* to find one of my beginnings.

At one of my beginnings is Samu Beck; his son Abraham begot Jacob Beck, who begot Natan Adam Beck, my second maternal great-grandfather, who was born in 1841 in Vrbovce. This lovely Slovak village is situated near the Czech-speaking Moravian border. The two ethnic regions share the annual fall wine harvest; people toast the young wine and sing songs across today's border between Slovakia and the Czech Republic. Abraham migrated from Moravia to Vrbovce following an eastward star. Abraham's son Adam moved from Vrbovce to Myjava in 1871 at the age of thirty, and a year later he begot his last son, Jakub, who in 1899 begot my mother's dad, Opa Nathan. Names are like veils, head and face coverings, clouds of unknowing, many unnameables.

The family tree shows five lads of Natan Adam Beck; three brothers married three Reiss maidens. In Adam's home they must have spoken Slovak and Yiddish, perhaps German, Czech, and Hungarian. I imagine two families—boys and girls are Myjava's pride! Perhaps there are five Reiss sisters to marry five Beck brothers. The village doubled these pentacles with a match made in heaven. I picture the family hearths standing only a few houses apart. *The village's Broadway is a slowly crawling centipede; neighbors watch through the thin white curtains as brothers hurry up and down the main thoroughfare to court the girls. The village matchmaker seals the heaven's dictates.* I improvise screenplays for still lives: *Jakub is the youngest of Adam's five sons. He must listen to his brothers' courtly manners. The girls would not reject a mismatched suitor; the ancient Hebrew laws already allow brothers to stand in for each other at death.* I set the crucial scene in an imaginary memory lane. Then I arrest my zeal. *Down what lovers' lane do the actors memorize lines scripted in heavens yet tested by life's tragedy?*

In his solidarity with victims of history, German literary critic and author Walter Benjamin hoped that the past had not passed. If the past were closed, victims could share no future with later generations, and our remembrance of them never could become a prophetic or dangerous memory. Because memory isn't just our genetic heritage, one can remember events through which one never lived yet which one inherited across several generations. Memory grows dangerous to resist the present threats. In his most cited dictum, Benjamin insists, "It is for the sake of those without hope that hope is given to us." One who hopes against hope affirms in the present that the past will not be orphaned by our future.

© 2012 by Martin Beck Matuštík
beranariesgallery.smugmug.com

16. The Becks in Sydney after World War II

Are couples matched by their parents? I wonder. *How many families survived the war?* Still lives shiver like falling leaves. The living tree grows taller in my hands. Jakub's older brother was taken in the first wave of the Slovak transports to Auschwitz in 1942 and didn't return. *Was he murdered with his wife? Did they have small children?*

Jakub Beck and Cecilia Reiss begot ten infinities in Myjava; one of them was my *opa*, Nathan. I am here, one of the Becks who did return.

I leap in imagination to my mother's birth village. I walk up the hill to Myjava's ancient Jewish cemetery. I find the top-left quadrant. One tombstone belongs to Adam and his wife Lotte, another to Jakub, who died in 1931. His wife Cecilia is buried next to him. I gather imaginary rocks; they pray at gravestones.

Ezekiel has reserved his thunderbolt for the end. In the next photo I pull from the envelope, I see my baby mother and her brother playing together in the garden at their house in Myjava (see image 9). There's a fence, tall fruit trees, plentiful grass, and homemade blankets. Mother and Uncle appear like two cherubs turned into humans. Next to them I hear Grandpa Nathan laughing. His sister, Etelka, is playing with her three children. These three kids are the survivors Opa's firstborn sister took to Sydney. Two maids from a well-run Myjava household display layered Slovak skirts and head coverings. Their black-and-white texture is reminiscent of wedding cakes. The maids are affectionate with the children. Behold a heavenly idyll from the 1930s!

1930s/Myjava?
Ernest & Magda Beck & maid/sluzka

17. Magda Beck and Ernest Beck with their maid in Myjava before 1939

Mother appears to be very intimate with the family that survived and settled in Israel and Australia after the war, I think. Why was she silent about them if they survived? I must learn the truth. I resolve to ask about this secret when I arrive in Sydney. *What are the known reasons that motivated Jews to cut off their Jewish ancestry and origins? What were my mother's reasons?*

Witnesses from the Past: the Wedding of 1927, the Cup of 1937

The largest of the photos in Gary's packet is of the wedding party of my maternal grandparents, Nathan and Ilonka. The feast took place in 1927, either in Galanta, my grandmother's birthplace, or in Myjava, Grandpa's birthplace.[9] This year is engraved on the survivor cup that stood as a silent witness in my mother's room, was hidden in a secret suitcase during the decade of my exile, and immigrated with me to the United States upon my return home after the Iron Curtain fell. I see a scene featuring my maternal grandparents. They are surrounded by thirty guests in four staggered rows. Each guest wears a festive outfit, each standing distinguished behind the celebrated couple. Oma's warm smile and Grandpa's serious look beckon me to this Slovak village Eden. Oma Pressburger luxuriates in white, covered with lace from head to toe. Grandpa Beck is in black tie. I watch him holding Oma's wedding bouquet of white rose for the duration of the photo shoot.

18. Ilonka Pressburger and Nathan Beck's wedding in Galanta, 1927

Ilonka's face! As if she were my youthful mother! Or is she my niece at her July wedding in Los Angeles? A female trinity becomes one face. Eyes peer outward, meeting my stare:

mirrors with windows, faces with souls. Testifying to a mirror stage of which Jacques Lacan had no clue, my reflection resurrects still lives as if they were painted Jewish icons. I am drawn into vertigos of the inverted past. Mother's spirit hovers in the silence of a child wagering whether to conceive her own life. Less than a year after her parents' wedding night, Mother came into a world about which she dared not tell. She spoke not a word to me about it, but perhaps she didn't even whisper her daymares to another living soul or a diary. Would she dare to be at her parents' wedding and consent to her future? One imagines human theodicies in which G-d is begotten and then redeemed with human consent. *Gods too hope for afterlives.*

I imagine that Mother would consent to her birth even if she knew her future. I imagine her returning with me to the wedding scene before her birth, saying, "Let it be." Mother's figure is cloaked by a shawl of the tragic silence of her having survived her birth. The guests are vanishing from this photo—so many infinities erased from this picture of the world! The wedding moment descends into the garden where the photo was taken. With Eden's inhabitants expelled before the fall for no fault of their own, the wedding trees of life grow plentiful orchards. Perhaps there is a pond or a swimming pool where children play during the feast. I ponder Mother's consent to her birth in 1927 and to mine in 1957. As we behold the garden image, Mother and I are two possibilities of saying yes to life. I enter the wedding scene from the future as a second-generation survivor of a survivor's silence.

With Nathan I count seven then-living Beck siblings: Etelka's three sisters (all three were murdered in Auschwitz along with their husbands and young children when the Germans already had lost the war). My great-aunts wink at me as they sit prettily at the end of the first row. I glance above their shoulders to Nathan's two brothers, one of whom is handsome and tall. The youngest brother, getting away with wearing a mischievous cap for the wedding, fills the open space between his sisters at the end of the second row. I later learn that the tall one used to ride an old Jawa motorcycle, became a dentist, and evaded transports by joining the Slovak partisans. The youngest brother survived on the Russian front and became a lawyer.

The firstborn Beck sister has two boys and a girl. They are too small to pose for the picture. They are awaiting the wedding party, being attended by maids. In their teens, the two boys slaved for the Nazis in Hungary before obtaining false papers from Raul Wallenberg in Budapest. Their teenage sister and their mother, my great-aunt Etelka, are the only Becks who came back from Auschwitz. Etelka's husband, as I mentioned, was gassed upon his arrival in the camp in 1944. Not knowing his face, I believe he rises from the dead in the second or third row. Etelka took her kids to

Sydney, where her two sons started a shoe business. Nathan's two surviving brothers lived in Israel until they joined their family members in Sydney. The wedding couple and their two children—my grandparents, Magda, and her brother, my uncle Ernest—spent the war on the run and with the Slovak partisans. Mother joined the postwar socialist dream and remained in Czechoslovakia.

Who are the other living faces? I know hardly anyone to the left of my great-grandfather. Are they siblings? Cousins? Nephews? Searching for my grandmother's sister, I find her in white, adorned with a stylish scarf. She's the youngest girl in the top row, counting third from the right. Her first husband never returned from Auschwitz. In this photo he places his right hand around her right shoulder.

Mother's silent witnesses testified for years in her home office. Not knowing of their plea, they accompanied me from my birth in 1957 into my young-adult flat in Prague and lived with me until 1977:

An old Czech Bible, Kralická edition from 1613, which Mother had by her sickbed when she died.

A dark-stained brass wine cup that Mother had on her writing desk.

The shoebox filled with her correspondence that I haven't yet read.

Two antique bookcases and a Persian rug.

19. Nathan Beck's kiddush wedding cup of 1927–37

I hid the Bible, the cup, and the box before I fled Prague in 1977. The furniture pieces and the ancient carpet from Mother's childhood house I left behind. I recovered the key silent survivors from their hiding places after 1989. Until this topsy-turvy summer of 1997, when messengers from Sydney reconnected me with my past, I didn't recognize these mute survivors of the Nazi and Communist eras as visitors from my Jewish prehistory. The brass cup didn't remind me of Kristallnacht; I took it for an ordinary cup. For a long time, I identified its wine with Mother's Christian confirmation communion. In the Hussite and then the Lutheran traditions, before the Second Vatican Council let Catholics do so, she could receive two kinds of communion: bread and wine, body and blood of the god-man. I examine the cup with a fresh reference to the last plague on the Egyptians. *The blood marked the village doors when the war's end passed over my mother and her surviving kin and they fled through the parted Slovak seas.* Those who were murdered in Auschwitz are not celebrated with the Egyptians who drowned in the Red Sea, yet the Shoah is recalled in secularly constructed state rituals within a calendric hiatus between several High Holy Days. One must reenact the Passover for those who are to survive this remembrance and live in our here-and-now life. *What was my mother's postwar diaspora that could explain her continued fright and flight?*

20. In Myjava before 1939; from the left, behind little Magda Beck: Cecilia Reiss (Jakub Beck's wife), Olga Beck, Ilonka Pressburger, Etelka Beck, and Nathan Beck

Eichmann in Bratislava

Adolf Eichmann visited my native city on November 4, 1938. At 8:00 a.m. he met at the Hotel Carlton, room 431, with two Slovak officials. They discussed the German blueprint for the first deportation of some 7,500 Slovak Jews without property to the territories that were to be occupied within hours by Hungary according to the Vienna Arbitration of November 2, 1938. Eichmann already had worked in Germany on the "Jewish question." His proposals were given to Prime Minister Jozef Tiso at 9:00 a.m. The deportations were intended to scapegoat the Jews for the autonomous Slovak government's failure to keep the territories.[10]

In 1942, two days after my future April birthday, Reinhard Heydrich showed up in Bratislava; he was followed by Eichmann on May 25. Both Aryans promised in Bratislava that they would treat the Jews humanly. Heydrich was one of the chief architects of the Shoah and Heinrich Himmler's right hand in Prague. Heydrich stood at the origin of the project for the Jewish Central Museum in Prague, which would have documented and celebrated the extermination of the Jewish race had Hitler won the war.

The following is an excerpt from Eichmann's trial in Jerusalem on May 23, 1961. Dieter Wisliceny was in 1942–1944 Himmler's and Eichmann's deputy in Bratislava.[11]

> THE STATE ATTORNEY BACH: Dieter Wisliceny was the Accused's representative in Bratislava during the decisive years. Here he describes in great detail how he carried out his assignment, what instructions he received from the Accused....

From Dieter Wisliceny's trial testimony in Nuremberg on January 3, 1946, page 3 and 6:

> Eichmann summoned me to Berlin [in March 1942], where he informed me that he was able to send entire Jewish families from Slovakia to Poland.... I should immediately notify the Slovak Government accordingly. On May 25, 1942, Obersturmbannführer Eichmann came to Bratislava.

On May 27, in the middle of a skittles game in Bratislava, Eichmann suddenly left for Prague because of the assassination attempt there on Heydrich by the Czech MI6 paratroopers sent from Britain. Heydrich died on June 4. Destruction of the Czech village Lidice and extermination of all its living beings mark the most notorious act of retribution for Heydrich's death. According to Wisliceny's affidavit from 1946, cited at the trial of Eichmann in Jerusalem on May 23, 1961, after Eichmann's stop in Bratislava, Wisliceny traveled to Berlin to ask about events in Poland.

> THE STATE ATTORNEY BACH: Eichmann went to his strong-box, pulled out a thin file from it, and opened it at a certain page, and then said the following: "Himmler has received orders from Hitler for the complete biological extermination of European Jewry." This was sometime in July 1942.

In fall 1942 in Bratislava, Andrej Steiner, Fleischmann, and Rabbi Weissmandl approached Wisliceny with bribes to stop deportation of the Jews from Slovakia.

From the trial of Eichmann in Jerusalem on May 23, 1961:

> THE STATE ATTORNEY BACH: [O]n page 11 of his 1946 testimony, Wisliceny talks about the efforts of the Jews in Bratislava to save themselves from being transported by paying money.... in order to induce Eichmann to put an end to a large extent to the Final Solution. He says that he gave the money to Eichmann [and] that Eichmann initially reproached him but later agreed to pass it on to Himmler, and asked for the money to be transferred to him.

Steiner's Working Group collected $50,000 from the Jewish Orthodox communities in Slovakia. He delivered the first $25,000 to Wisliceny in Bratislava in fall 1942. When the second half of the money did not come right away, the transports resumed after Rosh Hashana, followed by two more after Yom Kippur.

The following is an excerpt from an interview with Andrej Steiner by Ruth Lichtenstein titled, "The Road to Atlanta."[12]

RUTH LICHTENSTEIN: How was the $50,000 bribe demanded by Wisliceny paid?

ANDREJ STEINER: In two $25,000 installments.

RUTH LICHTENSTEIN: Where did the first installment come from?

ANDREJ STEINER: Shlomo Stern and his wife, of the [Slovak] Orthodox community. He had the money, in American dollars, buried. During the night they unearthed it and stood the whole night washing and ironing the bills so they shouldn't smell...They should look like they had come...from overseas.

RUTH LICHTENSTEIN: And after a short break in deportations, another one left after Rosh Hashanah.

RABBI PARNESS: When did the Working Group know that the Jews were going to be killed in Auschwitz? When did you realize that deportation meant death? How early on?

ANDREJ STEINER: In '42...the Slovak government called the Jewish leaders...and said that they have an understanding with the Germans to give so-and-so many workers, and they are going to pay to the Germans for every worker, I think $500, something like that.

RUTH LICHTENSTEIN: Yes.

ANDREJ STEINER: But the Slovaks told the Jewish leadership.

RABBI PARNESS: That they would be killed?

ANDREJ STEINER: Yes.

RABBI PARNESS: But it was common knowledge in Slovakia? All the Slovaks knew about it.

ANDREJ STEINER: Yes. Yes. Yes.

Between March 25 and October 20, 1942, close to 58,000 Jews were stripped of their citizenship and deported from Slovakia. Whether or not the bribes from the Working Group were the sole reason, deportations from Slovakia did stop for two years. Reb Dov knew already in November 1942 that deportation meant death. He believed that once this became known widely they would be able to collect more money.

Breaches and Repairs

Time punctuated by the number seven reaches 1997. The best time in Chicago is the Indian summer.

"The initials on the cup are N.B. The engraved year reads, '1927–1937.'" I'm holding the cup to the sunlight in our living room as I explain my discovery to Patricia.

"'N.B.' must stand for 'Nathan Beck,' your grandfather," she says, pointing to the inscription.

I'm overwhelmed with sudden awareness. "With Mother's birth in August 1928, the cup commemorates her parents' tenth wedding anniversary," I conclude. Out of its artful silence—letters and numbers—an old cup speaks as a living witness. I recite to Patricia what I hear the cup now say.

In the period of 1927–1937, I couldn't have been a Christian gift because your grandparents became Lutheran only after Slovakia morphed into a fascist-clerical state in 1939. I had to be your family's Jewish kiddush cup. They would drink from me the kosher wine sanctified for the Sabbath and Jewish holidays. I am your silent wedding and blessing guest who survived the Nazi persecution, lived past your mother's Communist dream and its disappointment, and returned to you from diaspora. With your help I hid in Prague. And now I will help you to unlock the silence and tell. Will you let me?

"I think Mother tried to scratch away the dates on the brass kiddush cup," I venture.

There's a line trying to erase the wedding and anniversary dates engraved on the wedding cup of her parents, as if this witness survived with shame. What survivor's guilt will I find when I drink from the bottom of this well? I was born thirty years after my grandparents married. The wedding photo survived for some seventy years before it broke into my life.

"I think she tried to rid herself of her origins in a moment of panic," Patricia says.

"What panic? Some Communist purges?" I'm trying to situate the origin of this visible erasure.

"We don't have a date for the scratches," she concedes, then stops her thought halfway. "But the Cold War fear…"

"And she didn't just throw the cup away either," I say, emphasizing this apparent contradiction. I assume the lines cutting the wedding metal originated in the post-war years when Mother cut off her Jewish ties.

"Your family didn't destroy it while they were on the run from the Nazis," Patricia says.

Did the cup survive the Second World War unharmed? I wonder. *Was its memory distorted in defense against the Nazi persecution or against the frost of the Cold War?* The mute guest survived my birth, escape, and return only after surviving Mother's silence. Its joy and sorrow hid all meanings, including the meaning of its shame. For whom was the erasure meant as a redemptive, saving act? Deciphering the cup's dates directed me to its Jewish holy grail: my mother's haunted, veiled birthright. And yet mending the cup's scar—healing the deconstructive lines that cross that birthright—has been left to the next generation. The wedding guests from 1927 greet me seventy years later: portraits of infinities rising in their glory, the fleshed bones of Ezekiel's prophecy, vertigos of the inverted past. Out of Mother's still life echoes that uncanny Solomon's Song "Love Is Strong as Death."

4

THE LAND WHERE THE FUTURE
MEANS YESTERDAY

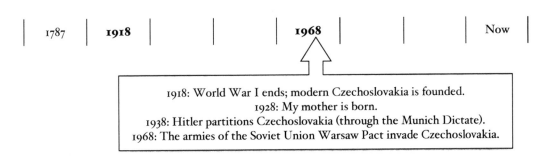

| 1787 | | **1918** | | | | **1968** | | | | Now | |

1918: World War I ends; modern Czechoslovakia is founded.
1928: My mother is born.
1938: Hitler partitions Czechoslovakia (through the Munich Dictate).
1968: The armies of the Soviet Union Warsaw Pact invade Czechoslovakia.

On August 21, 1968, I wake up to the Soviet invasion of Prague. One year later I'm shocked by Jan Palach's self-immolation in protest of the normalization regime. Just as the metaphor of "immaculate conception" describes how Mother's silence shielded her children from the original sin of her era—the Holocaust—so the metaphor of "the three queens from the East" alludes to special persons who helped this young boy survive the Herods of his era. This chapter ends with a new dramatic timeline running from 1938 to 1945, narrated through memoir letters my uncle wrote to me between 1987 and 2000.

The Fall (1967–1970)

After the Soviet Communist Party chairman, Nikita Khrushchev, brought down the cult of personality that Lenin's revolutionary successor, Stalin, had assumed for himself, and then a decade after the supersize statute of Stalin was blown up on the Letná Plane into fragments of generational betrayal, my parents rose momentarily in the eyes of the political regime they had helped to usher into Central Europe only to fall further from their youthful dream of a more just world. On that fateful morning of August 21, 1968, ominous vultures from the land where the future meant yesterday filled heavens for unfaithful sky burials. At 5:00 a.m. I saw big Antonov planes flying above Prague buildings. Something terrible was happening. When apples from forbidden Edens failed to satiate hunger, ancient trees of good and evil didn't rush seeds to spring blossoms. Which other trees would admit my parental generation's graft when later Anton Chekhov's cherry orchard must be cut down by forces stronger than youthful dreams?

Waking up Lenin

From mid-1967 to the end of 1969, reformed Communists were chasing down their youth. On the first day of the August invasion, a fourteen-year-old boy was killed by a random Soviet bullet not far from me on the main square in Prague.[13] We shared tender age, space, and time: a boy woke up, died, survived. My parents' postwar dream received a brief purchase on its postmortem during the Prague Spring, and the invasion accelerated Soviet Communism's rigor mortis. At the moment when an older boy peer was killed by an occupier's bullet, I was waking up from my boyhood. Late-summer resurrections were ripened for rape by brotherly comrades. Thrust to a larger reality, I barely could intimate in gray contours how this happening would mark my life.

I went to the kitchen situated at the courtyard side of our apartment. From the tenement on the other side of the courtyard, I heard a loudspeaker announce from a neighbor's balcony, "At midnight we were invaded by the five Warsaw Pact armies." Within hours I took the assault on my country into my body. A sixth-grader spent the summer of the Soviet invasion precociously educated by a street delirium of anger and despair, astonishment and laughter. I drank rage and sorrow

from the same cup. I sobbed and shouted. I trembled with preadolescent antici-
pations of stolen loves. Tears come out of the depths of every anniversary of this
August day. Before I met myself at forty as a survivor's child, I had to forget that
dying boy. A child of a survivor survives this boy's August death before the adult
meets a survivor child.

I went down to the Prague center and hurled my first cobblestone at a passing
Russian tank. Then there were curses, screams, and Molotov cocktails. The invasion
period played out on a dramatic stage. An existentially earnest Franz Kafka depicts
the tragic and weighty side of history. When he runs into the limits of metamorphosis, tragic Kafka meets the comic Good Soldier Švejk.

"Lenin, wake up! Brezhnev went crazy!"

"I will exchange unbound Lenin for a bound hardback of Brezhnev."

I was caught in the thrall of human closeness with total strangers. Active nonviolent resistance took many forms. People refused to serve food and water to the
soldiers; women didn't return smiles and certainly wouldn't offer more than that;
and men prostrated themselves on the roads in front of moving military hardware.
Groups organized and changed street and road signs and even printed and distributed false maps all over the country so that one army unit began to cross over to West
Germany, thereby threatening a feared (and by us hoped-for) international conflict.
Other invading units were regularly lost. Those vehicles that actively sought to round
up reformed Communists and other activists on the Soviet hit lists were publicized
with their license-plate numbers, and their efforts were actively frustrated by dem-
onstrators who followed the vehicles and obstructed their sinister intents with sit-ins
and shouting matches.

"The Soviet art of the twentieth century." Humor took various forms: written
and painted street posters, sidewalk theater and pantomime, song and dance, ad hoc
newspapers and journals, pirate radio broadcasts, alternative TV shows and films,
nonstop debating corners where strangers could say or hear just about anything in
those days, and the drinking of wine or beer or making out with a lover in front of
the occupying soldiers.

"With the Soviet Union forever and ever...in hell." It didn't take long to harness
my unrecognized inventiveness and channel my youthful rebellious and nonconformist energies to become a creative street humorist myself. I started with writing and
drawing posters. My production station was near the saint's sculpture on the top part
of Wenceslas Square.

At first I just imitated other posters I saw (I carried a small notebook and wrote down the texts of many of them as I walked through Prague), but after a short time, I created my own. Runners would come and take our creations to be published in some shop window or wall in Prague. I don't remember much of what I wrote or drew, and no one thought in those moments about intellectual property rights.

"Dubček, we love you!"

"This month's menu: Brezhnev's brains."

"Make love, not war." (This one is still current.)

"Ivan, go home. Natasha is warming up the bed for you!"

"Ivan, go home. The girls do not love you here anymore!"

With humor we made the invading soldiers cry. The powers that be and home-land-security agents continue to shake in anger and fear at such irreverence.

"For the defense of our banks, we do not need the Soviet tanks; oh, the shit we have saved that we can keep alone quite well." (This could be offered to all corrupt banks that are too big to fail.)

Not only were the young girls teasing the soldiers by showing off their "stuff" from a safe distance or by having the time of their lives with their boyfriends in front of the occupants. Not only were people withholding from the army food and drink and advice, and confusing and frustrating them whenever they could. Not only was the occupying army subject to creativity that made them look and feel ridiculous, stupid, and backward. But now people started to talk incessantly to the soldiers—growing up, we had to learn the empire's language, and now we put it to good use.

"Do you know where you are?" an old lady would question the young Russian soldier. "Why are you in Prague? What is your mission? Why did you come in tanks?"

A group of workers tried to explain the sinister nature of the Soviet presence; others told them about the Prague Spring reform, and still others insisted that the Russians needed this change at home. Students spoke reason to officers, and if that didn't work, shouted and screamed and begged them to go home.

"Ivan, go home, and never come back!"

Young soldiers would cringe and suffer psychic breakdowns, and the command-ing officers periodically had to rotate and replace the army units. Some officers suffered the same fate. Beginning in that late summer of 1968, we managed for six months to defy the occupying brothers (there were very few sisters) with active non-violent resistance.

"My little brother, close the gate. The wolf is hungry for a lamb. This night will not be short," Karel Kryl sang in a popular protest refrain.

Heretics with a Human Face

Those writers who with Ludvík Vaculík in 1967 signed the manifesto "2000 Words" inaugurated the coming of the Prague Spring. The Czechoslovak president, Antonín Novotný, resigned, and Alexander Dubček became the first Communist Party secretary. The Soviet-decorated general, Ludvík Svoboda, became president of the country. Dubček took the country on a new path of "socialism with a human face." After the invasion I connected the day of Novotný's resignation with the Prague Spring itself. On that day the debating circles spontaneously erupted all over Prague and wouldn't cease talking until the normalization of the 1970s crushed every piece of opposition. The irony is that Novotný managed to keep the Russians away from Czechoslovakia, retaining relative autonomy and even increasing openness in the late 1960s, while Dubček's innocent democratization brought their army in. Once the Soviets decided to invade and got the green light from NATO and the United States that they would respect the post-Yalta Soviet sphere, there was nothing to be done.

Our "spring" of 1968 began in January with Dubček's inauguration and lasted until December. More unheard-of books were published in Czechoslovakia from mid-1967 to the end of 1968 than in any period after 1948. It was as if all titles listed on the Communist "index" had been moved to some accelerated production stage. The word *index* comes from the list of prohibited or heretical books held by the Catholic Inquisition, and most dissidents used this very term to refer to the underground or *Samizdat* literature and art of the Soviet era. The word *Samizdat* comes from the Soviet-era Russian coinage "самиздат," meaning "made by myself." The verb *made* includes its multiple dissident meanings: "created, edited, censored, published, distributed, and get persecuted for it by myself." The Catholic list of *libri prohibiti* referred now to those authors who didn't receive the party's imprimatur.

We lived intensely, as if there were no tomorrow. New films were made and produced, plays written and staged, churches opened to liturgical experimentation. Prisons released political prisoners; borders to the West opened (though people weren't leaving the country then); and economic models mixed socialist modes of production and welfare checks and balances with an open-market economy—market socialism was introduced. Apart from experiments regarding worker self-management and open borders in Joseph Bros Tito's Yugoslavia, this was the first and only place where market socialism had been integrated into an increasingly democratic socialism. Socialism with a human face offered an attractive prospect not only for the captive nations of Communist Europe but also for many a developing nation. Ota Šik was one of the famous economists of the Prague Spring. Karel Kosík became known as the Czech phenomenological Marxist who articulated this open and viable version of post-Soviet Marxism.

The land of Jan Hus, the first Protestant heretic in Christendom (who was born about a hundred years before Martin Luther), became the land of perestroika and glasnost in 1968, twenty years before these policies and reforms arrived in the Soviet Union. The Roman Catholic Church first demanded that its Catholic priest and professor at Prague's Charles University, Hus, recant his beliefs, and when he would not, Emperor Zikmund and the antipope, John XXIII, ordered him burned at the stake in Kostnice in 1421. Also in the fifteenth century, in the South Bohemian city of Tábor, the Adamite sect anticipated the reformed commies-gone-hippies from the 1960s. The sect shared all property and one another's nakedness in open love that was deserving of the children of G-d. The Communist Party often linked its proletarian and anti-Catholic roots back to Hus, though this could work only by their severely restricting the scope of allowed heretical acts, and the Adamite way of living was not among them. The party imbibed in the worst excesses of the Roman Church and Inquisition, and so it could not claim the mantel of Hussite history with credibility.

Hus had his authentic followers in the Prague Spring as well as in all forms of dissent from the party's orthodoxy. The Prague reforms of 1968 went too far when the Prague Spring ideas and happy practices frightened the established powers on both sides of the old Iron Curtain. In the fifteenth century, Rome sent crusaders to subdue Bohemia and its rebel leader, Žižka, as well as the Hussite peasant armies of Czech heretics. Years before the Russians reinvented the heretical idea of "spring," the Soviet orthodox-cum-Roman crusaders followed the prevailing history and kept world stability by crushing those they deemed to be worse than the Adamites. The greatest sin of the Prague Spring was that people loved it and that it, like John Lennon's spirit, generated popular excitement. What if the virus of the "human face" spread into the Cold War spheres of influence? The armies of the orthodox status quo assured this would not happen.

The Empty Tomb

In 1969, not a full year after the Soviet invasion, on a cold January day, the death of Jan Palach, a philosophy student in Prague, shocked me out of my boyhood innocence a second time. One of two philosophy students who drew their lot to die in protest against the Soviet normalization, Palach was no hero. He was not a misanthrope either; he died sacrificially echoing Buddhist monks who were dying at that time in protest of the US war in Vietnam. Moved by the tragic pathos of Palach's self-immolation, I captured photograph of his last Prague procession. A funerary ode to resistance was my first publication.

PHOTO FROM THE FUNERAL OF JAN PALACH   © *Maphiy   J.B. Mikuštík*
TAKEN ON JAN 25, PUBL. IN SEDMICKA, PRAGUE, 13 FEB. 1969

21. The funeral ceremony for Jan Palach in Prague; January 25, 1969 (published February 13, 1969)

Growing up in Prague, I witnessed fresh flowers being placed on Palach's grave site in Olšany. During the 1970s the secret police moved his body to an unknown location, as the secular state was shot through with holy fear that the rebels could rise from the dead. The Palach site received a stream of silent visitors who left flowers and notes at his headstone, even though Czech secret service agents had buried a woman there named Marie Jedličková. Since no one saw relatives or friends of Marie frequent the grave, people assumed she was a person the secret service had made up. Ironically, because Marie wasn't a person who had lived, died, and been buried, people continued to honor her grave site as a sign of good news to come. Her burial was an unintended caricature of Mary, mother of Jesus, and Mary, harlot saint, the two women who had proclaimed the resurrection of the Christian Easter. Thus this invented Mary, simulating death in Palach's grave, proclaimed the kerygma of Palach's empty tomb. The state police wanted us to believe Palach's tomb was empty because they had stolen the body, but we resisted the omnipresent state by stubbornly believing in Palach's resurrection.

"What are all these churches but the sepulchers of God [sic]?" a madman in Nietzsche's *Joyous Science* cries out, implying the "death of G-d."

What was *this* grave but a sign of the Communist contradiction and fear—an overt atheism accompanied by a mighty effort to silence the spirit of the dead? The whereabouts of Palach's body notwithstanding, even assuming the irony to be true (the Communists stole the body to prevent its resurrection), Palach continued to appear in many Prague locations. Flowers and candles memorializing him increased throughout the oppressive decades. At Wenceslas Square, right in front of the proud bronze horse with its national saint who made love and not war with the neighboring Germans in the early medieval period, police would remove flowers and any signs mentioning Palach. The signs and flowers, however, reappeared without failure. Palach was no longer tied to his grave, especially if (as the police assured by its dispirited act) it were empty! The authorities decided to plant a flower garden for Nemo (from Latin, no man or no one), near Saint Wenceslaus's statue; these flowers were fenced, as the garden would receive unwelcome additions that would need to be removed. One was discouraged from celebrating May Day more enthusiastically (by wishing for a messianic age) or less fervently (by going to a beer hall or making love) than prescribed by ministers of state rites. The people's flower power interfered with the flowers from the police.

This was my first encounter with flower power. In the 1960s students offered flowers to Reagan's police and national guards in Berkeley, and the young later offered flowers to Communist agents in Prague in 1989. I chose a photo of the latter for the cover of my book *Postnational Identity*.[14] But the most original flower power infusing my life came from the many empty tombs for Jan Palach.

It is summer 2004. I bring my Purdue students to Palach's grave. The wandering protester had been reburied in Prague after 1989. The American students and a few ones from Prague are enrolled in my summer course on Czech existential literature. I look on as students stand around Palach's grave; they are as old as Palach was in his death. The young Czechs in my group know as little about Palach's story as the Americans who just arrived in town. The Prague youth are visiting here for the first time. I speak to them about having come to this grave under the threat of police arrest. The students imagine being in Palach's shoes; I am pondering my youth, which is mirrored in my students. We walk across the road to a modern Jewish cemetery. The young men put on their head coverings, and we hold our class at Franz Kafka's grave. We read from Kafka's *Metamorphosis* and Havel's "The Power of the Powerless." Palach and Kafka: two stories of revolt, two ways to metamorphosis. There used to be the Red Army Square in Prague. It was framed by Charles University, the Vltava River, the old Jewish cemetery with Maharal's grave[15], and Rudolfínum, Prague's Carnegie Hall. This site has since been transformed into Jan Palach Square.

"Nations that are too big or powerful to be invaded cannot appreciate the shock of military assault," I tell my students. "Small nations of Central Europe never had the luxury of invading other peoples; armies marched across their home territory." I'm not speaking of an aggressor who starts a war and is defeated on his home turf. Students take notes. They are growing up after nine eleven.

"The citizens of big states have little to build on," one student concedes. "We're like those who cannot easily empathize with male prisoners or women who have been sexually assaulted. It's easier to draft us to rally behind troops invading others."

"Since that awful time when the allied socialist armies came to offer us their brotherly help against the declared anti-Communist elements of Prague Spring, I've been allergic to any claim about the right to wage a humanitarian war of invasion," I continue, prodding them with dangerous memories.

"Does this history lesson from Prague return a second time as a farce?" a female student asks.

"Socialism with a human face was as dangerous to Brezhnev as the possibility of its virus becoming dangerous to the US sphere of influence." I teach my students a hard lesson to swallow. "As long as socialism could be portrayed in its sinister, evil-empire version as told by the United States, there was no danger that someone could get the idea of importing socialism into the US's backyard. Once Mikhail Sergeyevich Gorbachev came twenty years later with pretty much the same idea as Dubček—now under glasnost and perestroika—it was late to make it work. No one saved patience for experiments with a human face of socialism. The only socialism to be reckoned with, after Prague Spring was crushed in 1968, was Ronald Reagan's imaginary "evil empire."

The Soviet Shoes (the 1950s)

Shoes seem to be a theme in our family. I want to unlock Mother's secret with a few keys that she left me in a shoebox. During the heated months of the Prague Spring, Mother told me about her experiences with shoes in Soviet Russia and painted a vivid picture of the Soviet train stations on the outskirts of major cities.

"People camped out for days, even weeks, in hopes that a train to Moscow would come," she said. "And when one did, there was a general scramble to get in. If any train schedule existed, it didn't apply. At shoe stores people waited for the boxes to arrive—any shoes in any size—and you bought what you could get your hands on, and then outside the store, people exchanged the boxes for desired styles and sizes."

Mother might have gleaned the existence of the Soviet prison system, the gulags, on one of her official travels in the late 1950s. Her journalistic license allowed her to visit out-of-the-way pockets of Soviet poverty. The "Potemkin villages" were exemplary showcases of happy lives under Communism that had been set up for the eyes of foreign visitors and dignitaries along the main tourist routes, but they could not be erected everywhere.

"No visitor to the Soviet Union could travel freely," she complained. The ghosts of her youth were coming to haunt her waking hours with old nightmares.

"Soviet citizens needed internal passports to move from one region to another," she continued. "A tourist representative—a KGB agent—was assigned to all visitors. Anyone who wanted to travel by car either had to hire a driver (again, KGB) or report regularly en route at checkpoints. If a traveler attempted to visit something interesting that wasn't on the permitted itinerary, the KGB would intervene."

Mother obtained carte blanche for her travels, and for this she was expected to sing praises of the Soviet Union. If she didn't challenge the regime, a private driver, probably a KGB agent, would take her wherever she wanted to go. It would take the Soviet invasion of 1968 to compel her to quit the party; it would take the first years of postinvasion normalization to compel the party to expel my father.

Postmemory: Mother's Shoeboxes and Uncle's Letters

Three years have passed since the eye-opening summer of 1997 when I received that momentous mail from Sydney. I'm still trying to divine Mother's secret from her shoeboxes, which are filled with words on shriveled sheets of paper. I get unexpected help from Uncle Ernest, who wants me to "hire" him as a researcher. I can't imagine what kind of research for my philosophical work I can use from my uncle, who lives in Bohemia, so I decide to send him a small monthly stipend. Naturally he wishes to do something, and I figure I can draw on his memory to fill the gaps in my family saga. He doesn't really grasp the importance of my request until he delves deeply into the narrative. We've been discussing his life for some time, but it needs to be written down. Can we manage to connect the pieces of his failing memory?

My uncle, born in 1931, is my mother's younger brother. I send him a list of questions, and he sets himself to the task with a diligence that endows his last years with greater purpose; I integrate our dialogue with my story. Uncle Ernest writes a series of memoir letters to me from May 5, 2000 to October 10, 2001. His last handwritten note is dated November 20, 2001. Not long after, he has his second heart operation, after which he lapses into a coma and dies.

Just as Mother's shoeboxes do, Uncle Ernest's letters speak to my *postmemory*; I have to borrow this neologism from author Marianne Hirsch to describe my significant emotional relationship to events I've never lived through yet which I remember as if I experienced them in my own life. With this technical terminology, I attire myself with the academic armor of a respectable "postmemory" even as I unveil my identities and divulge my secrets to readers. I'm protected from my writing when it acts out or draws from deep emotional wells, or when my text violates propriety and speaks out of character. One cannot write dramatic lines for silence. Writing out of silence risks that the unspeakable or the gray zones may make themselves known. One must rely on postmemory to decipher forgotten grammars, to forge new conceptual and literary languages, to teach gray-zone ethics and literacy, to perform reading skills when the voice chokes with tears, and to hear with sense attuned out of silence.

Arriving from Sydney's shores, letters and photos from the future speak into and out of Mother's silence. Mother's shoebox witnesses are iron locked, and the missing key has been a wanderer. Ernest's letters join with Mother's brass cup and her old Bible to help create a lock combination to my past.

Ernest Vesely and Martin Matustik, Prague, 1970s

22. Ernest Veselý and Martin Matuštík in Prague, circa 1970

Letter from Uncle Ernest to His Nephew Martin

Karlovy Vary

May 24, 2000

Dear Matenko,

I was pleased that you have come up for me with some form of specific "thank you" in return for your economic help: writing the story of my family life....I do not own a video camera, and the tape recording would not have a high quality since I own only a machine with an old microphone. But that is not the main reason. I have never had ability as a storyteller. But in the written form, I can manage quite well, and I have a lifetime of practice in it. When I write I get automatically new images, thoughts, words, and sentences....I know that you are interested in the entire family; otherwise you would not have traveled to Myjava, Galanta, Komárno, Sydney, and you would not put together the names and dates of those family members who are alive and those who are dead; you would not be creating a beautiful album of photos. What is it that you get concretely from all this? What is the meaning of your satisfaction about learning in greater detail my concrete lifetime destiny and story, including thought and emotional development that accompany them? Today I am a free human being; I can testify about myself in truth and say anything—of course if I can remember it.

Karlovy Vary

May 31, 2000

The first six pages of the memoir were sent to me in a single letter. The bottom of page six reads:

In future letters I will continue with chapter one. I will always write on three such two-sided pages, which is the letter weight of about ten grams.

Remembrances of Life: 1931–1937

I will only attempt to set down the chronology of my life story. The reason is my memory.... My childhood was happy and without worries, without distur-bances from the outside world or the family events. It had lot to do with the social status of our family. Father was the only physician in Myjava and was responsible for the health of some twelve thousand inhabitants, many of whom did not even live in town but in small settlements and villages of surrounding

*hills called "Kopanice." Father and his family thus represented the genuine so-
cial elite. He finished building a large family house in the midst of the town,
and at that time, it was the most luxurious construction in the region. He was
well respected and also wealthy, and our family enjoyed a high lifestyle and
suffered no want.*

*I was surrounded by people who were for the most part sympathetic and car-
ing toward me. My mother was the closest person who cared for my needs, and
my fatherly grandmother spent more time with our family than with other
relatives. She suffered from diabetes, and Father preferred having her close to
his care. She personified peace, goodness, and wisdom. She knew an answer to
every question; she never raised her voice; and I remember her overflowing
with vitality and joy. We used to have at the time two maids—Tinka, who
did the shopping and cooking, and Zuzka, who cleaned and took care of us
children. And they were also my two good witches who were always ready to
defend and protect me.*

*My older sister, Magda, was the second-most significant person in my imme-
diate life, as she was the medium through which I experienced my larger environment. In my childhood she was my absolute authority. In her childhood
she was a definitive extrovert and leader type who attracted to herself friends
from the neighborhood. I was her younger brother. Magda often wished I
would stay at home and let her venture on her own. Father's younger brother,
Ervin, lived with us as well. My uncle, whom I called "Ervinko," studied law
in Bratislava, but he spent weekends with us in Myjava. I admired him because he rode on a big red motorcycle, and every so often, he fought in fistfights.
I respected him with fear, as he continually admonished and corrected me
whenever I did not embody his view of how I should live. Magda did not like
him—she might have even hated him—and he showed her in turn his disdain.*

*I used to walk with Grandmother, and she would always point to a distant
blue hill, beyond which lived Ervinko, because there was Bratislava. I often
observed that hill and wondered whether from its receding horizon Ervinko
might jump out and salute me.*

Remembrances of Life: 1937–1938

My father was an excellent physician, but psychology and the judgment of char-
acter were his weaknesses, and so was his upbringing of children. He wanted
me to be a fearless boy who would grow into a hard, uncompromising man
and who would never fear anything in life and would find solutions for every
situation. But his upbringing methods—his command to me that I "must" ac-
complish this or that—gradually created in me the opposite of what he desired.

From ages three to five, I recall that sometimes our relatives would visit us,
but more often we visited them. (Father owned a new Tatra car.) Father's
youngest sister, Olga Beck, lived with her very fat husband Hugo Benau in
Nitra, where he had a business in shoes and leather. They had a son, Peter, who
was a year younger than me, and so we knew how to play together. The three
of them were later transported by train from Nitra to Auschwitz, and they
never returned.

We used to visit Father's younger brother, Dr. Béla Beck, in Nové Zamky. He
was a wealthy and sought-out dentist with a modern office and good medi-
cal practice. He married gorgeous dark-haired Gizka, and they had a daugh-
ter, Viera, who was Magda's age. Their house had a large garden full of fruit
plants, the kinds of which we did not have in Myjava (peaches, apricots, and
grapes). I loved to travel there as a child, but neither Gizka nor Viera returned
from the concentration camp.

Father had two more Beck sisters—one married as Fridka Klein and the other
as Mancika Kemenyi. I remember their faces slightly, but there were no regular
family visits. They likewise perished with their entire families in Auschwitz.
Then there was the family from my mother's side. We often visited my mater-
nal grandparents Pressburger in Galanta. Grandpa had a large tobacco and
newspaper store right on the main street—I can still smell the mixture of to-
bacco, and I can see the boxes of expensive cigars. Father always said about my
grandpa that he was stingy. He was very tall, had an earnest look on his face,
and he was a tough man. He loved me very much. The grandma from Galanta

was an incarnation of goodness—and my mother inherited her looks as well as her character. Often during that time, Mother's younger sister, Erzička, and her daughter, Martha, visited us in Myjava. Her husband, Ernest Fuchs, owned a perfume store in Nové Mesto n/Vahom. He never returned from the death camp.

One more picture from my happy childhood: at that time even well-to-do families could not afford to vacation by the seaside. Father considered himself to be among the elite, and so one summer we went down to the Crikvenica resort in Yugoslavia. Our parents used to spend nights dancing or sitting in cafés and bars. I was guarded in those times by the hotel receptionist so that I would not pee in my bed, and so he would wake me up during the night in Croatian— "Hajdi Bubko pisilini"—and he would prompt me to go to the bathroom. The family of the Myjava banker, Mr. Siracek, vacationed with us, and their son, Radko, two years older than me, discovered that nude women sunbathed on the top roof of an old building. He found a spot from where we could observe them without being noticed until one of them discovered us a few days later and made a great scene.

In December of 1937, I turned six, and I began the first grade of grammar school in September 1938. That was the first time I left my family for a larger world. I had many good friends by then. My teacher, Mrs. Dugačková, used to say that I was among the most intelligent pupils in her class.

Kosher Bauhaus in Slovakia

In fall 1941 Andrej Steiner, who headed the Department of Labor and Construction for the *Ústredňa Židov* (UŽ), was ordered to build three labor camps in Sereď, Nováky, and Výhne. He insisted that only Jews could follow his architectural designs and that the Slovak government should employ labor-able Jews. Andrej had several thousand Jews working in more than one hundred workshops at the three camps, making items for the Germans, such as furniture he had designed.

Reb Dov asked Andrej, a secular Jew who didn't know much about Judaism, to design and build kosher kitchens and arrange for kosher food for the Orthodox Jews in the labor camps. Andrej recalled the first advice Reb Dov gave him: how to face the Nazi officials in charge of the camps.

"At the moment you start to speak to him you look at him sitting on a john: on a *toilette*! You know, a WC. And the very moment you look at him that way, he is the same human being as you are. You will see that suddenly you are going to dare to tell him anything you want. Don't be ashamed; you will achieve it." And so Steiner organized kosher kitchens for the Orthodox Jews in the work camps.[16]

5

WARD OF THE STATE

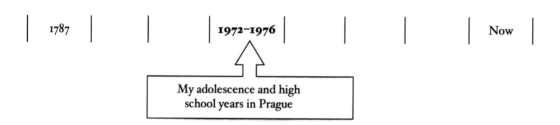

My mother died of cancer in 1972, and I became the ward of the Communist state. Shielding me from the new anti-Semitism of the Communist era as well as from my own rebelliousness against authorities, Mother "died for my sins." This image of Mother's sacrificial death borrows from a biblical metaphor through which an assimilated Jewish boy, growing up in the mixed Communist and Christian milieus of Prague, makes sense of his orphan life.

1957–1967, 1977–1997

The mail from Sydney hurries to unlock the melancholy odor of the late-summer golden sheaves. The bundles of shimmering papyrus, stuffed into fragile folders in Mother's shoebox, have been hidden since August 1977, when I buried the inherited literary treasure before my escape from Prague. The box was "buried so deep inside me that I was never sure just what it was."[17] Bristling at the slightest touch, Mother's archive mixes agitated fragrances of the Prague Spring with tender rays of Chicago's Indian summer. In 1997 my fingers run across two letters with windows opened onto 1967 to 1968. I see Mother taking stock of her life. "Dear comrade Závada," she writes about my first decade in this world:

> *Nine unthinkably hard years are behind me. I never needed to complain about my sorrows. I have displayed outwardly my "mourning" neither for my father, nor mother, nor small daughter, never for anything or anyone. I suspect that during those seven years in Prague, nobody from our party cell knew that from day to day I was actually passing through a purgatory.*

Her letter to "comrade Gregor" hints at some disfavors, but on account of what?

> *After 1960, when the play* White Road *was censored, I published really minimally. It does not mean that I have not been writing and that I remained at the level of my student or early works. It was my lot to mature out of the limelight, in the context of official disfavor and under the burden of difficult illness lasting several years. When I look back at my path, it has been almost a plus rather than a minus—in every regard.*

Orphaned (1971–1972)

"You must save him," she pleaded. The two women sipped strong coffee at Slavia. Large corner windows opened onto the National Theatre and the Hradčany, the Prague Castle that towered across the river Vltava River. "He could get lost in the world," she continued, as the other woman listened.

Four years after the Soviet invasion, Mother was in her prime. The Prague Spring had been crushed, and we lived in the period of normalization. I can picture her short, full but lean figure and broad, smiling face; she was wearing one of her many hair bands and fashionable turtlenecks. Mother was typing on an old typewriter; she never learned to work the keyboard with more than four fingers. I was fourteen, going on fifteen. Mother was alert at eight in the morning, in deep thought, gazing across her desk into Grebovka Park. It was winter, and the mixed forest trees were covered with snow. On weekends we sledded from the top of the park all the way down to the district of Nusle.

"What are you telling me?" the other woman asked, as she listened to the plea.

Mother mustered superhuman strength to undo my fated beginnings. Humans cannot cushion their offspring from their own tragic demise any more than anyone can protect another person from historical events. "I have terminal cancer," she said. "They give me a few months to live." I heard this dialogue several times years later when I returned to Prague.

Mrs. Alžběta Holá saved me for a third time after Mother approached her and placed the heavy burden of her death on her. Today I am some ten years older than Mother was when she died. I learned the full story of my teacher's interventions years later, after I visited her in Prague. My queen survived her husband's death in a car accident when she was young, and this event scarred and deformed her face for life. She never remarried and never had her own children besides us, her pupils. I became her spiritual son. She remained a star by which I navigated the night sky of adolescent aloneness.

Less than a year before her death, Mother took me for a summer vacation at a Romanian Black Sea resort. Mother must have earned enough in restaurant tips to afford us this working-class leisure. She wanted to spend some time with me before I would disappear into my young-adult exploits. That summer I was in heat with puberty and met a Romanian girl who was older and more experienced. I was content to kiss, embrace, and touch on the starlit beach.

As the Romanian language is Latin based, its vocabulary has little in common with the Slavic tongues of other captive nations (just like Hungarian, another Eastern-Bloc tongue that is closer to Finish, Estonian, Uzbeki, and Turkmen language groups). Consequently the girl and I used the hated linguistic tool of our empire: Russian. Preferably we exchanged silence for the grammar of intimate embraces. We had to learn Russian—but what a torture this must have been for Hungarians and

Romanians! Just like Latin in medieval Europe, as well as English today, the colonizing language made the empire's presence felt far and wide. It connected cultures that otherwise would have remained isolated from one another.

Isolation was the last thing on my mind as I pressed into her olive skin and drew her ripe breasts to my chest. Murmuring sweet offerings and listening to their echoes dancing back at us made us almost forget it was "Russian" we spoke. Eros *can* transform hatred—all romantics know this, at least since Romeo and Juliet defied their families. Mother watched us dance, and she seemed happy that I was facing so well the male pressures of growing up. At that beach resort, I also had my last dance with Mother. It was doubly last, because my urgent teen concerns forced a strict separation from Mother as I struggled to get other females firmly within my reach. It was at the end of that cruel weaning that the remaining vestiges of the umbilical cord were severed.

When we returned to Prague, Mother soon fell ill with digestive problems, which she blamed on the greasy Romanian diet. I assigned the unconscious guilt for Mother's ordeal to my eager ease with female tenderness. Mother's diagnosis gave way to exploratory surgery, and winter yielded its final judgment, preventing spring from arriving. Doctors discerned fates in the entrails of the operating table. What was to be done? Lenin couldn't revolutionize the forces of entropy into an electrification of eternal life. One month after the surgery, the operating physician confessed that my mother would die in a matter of weeks. Death visited from gray zones into which secular Communists wielded no charms. The state hospitals kept a respectful distance from this uncanny visitor; every ordinary death threatened the shaky paradise. Plane crashes weren't reported in the Soviet Eden. The revolutionary architecture and rituals of funeral homes consoled the survivors with a future whose tomorrow would have been yesterday.

During our last Christmas (I grew up in our atheistic home with a Christmas tree), Mother came home from the hospital. Not that she could manage on her own, but it was her wish to say good-bye. She wanted to die at home. She couldn't eat and barely managed to breathe. She shriveled with pangs of hunger and pain. In my last photos of her, Mother is an apparition of a Nazi concentration-camp prisoner suffering from extreme starvation, a Muselmann. Sitting by her bedside, I would read to her from the 1960s reprints of Martin Buber's *I and Thou* and *The Bhagavad Gita*, as well as a home typescript of František Kabelák's *The Book about Yoga*. I recited the poetry of Jiří Orten and Otokar Březina, and psalms from a Bible in her bedroom.

Mother's dying presence loaded me with a great fatigue, as if I carried Sisyphus's rock and mountain around my neck, even when I walked the plains. I would fall asleep by her bed. My visits drained all my vital energy even while I kept awake. Unlike the royal physicians who must cure all wounds of history lest they lose their heads to the wrathful king, she soberly yielded to inevitable death. Even as her body carried no shame of mortal matter, this silent witness transmitted a postmemory of cruel annihilation. Impacted by her transgenerational genetic excess coded in body languages triggered by cancer, I greeted New Year's Eve with two bottles of expensive Russian champagne.

While I drank myself into that long, lonely night without stars until I felt nothing at all, I remembered our home filled with gentle love and care. Mother had asked others to care for me after she would be gone. Unlike suffering lived to the brim when there is no instant rewind, pain honored morphine as its sole living master. Too young for her last dance, Mother slipped into an unknown eternity.

The beautiful mother's death made no sense to the tender teenage boy. There was no group for grieving teens where I could share my sorrow. Mother loved the son unto death. Leaving a parting gift, she transmitted the silence of abandonment with the silent music of loving receptivity. The boy witnessed diminishment, suffering, the death of gods on whom one depends for life. Mother's ashes carry no genetic codes for theodicies—those divine justifications that want to make sense of unlived lives, unrequited loves, loves betrayed. Codes transmitted in postmemory fail imagination (they do not descend into the archives made out of mnemonic traces or chiseled into stone by monumental historians). No instant resurrections take away fears inherited by second-generation survivors unless one finds within the ashes the keys to one's own living. Yet resurrections visit us whenever codes rush through transmitters of postmemory. Even atheists and the sorrowful G-d wrestle with love and death. The son fashioned new creation and survivor's myths; he had to exorcize the fright of an orphan life at age fourteen.

Mother too was my queen, the hierophany revealed this to the boy as a visible manifestation of the divine. He mythologized with reason against a reason that had no whys.

Mother must have died for my sins. So the boy believed and prayed. *She was my tie to life. Mater speciosa,* my beauteous mother, cut in prime by cruel furies. A woman's pieta eclipses the iconic sun of *Mater Dolorosa*. A mournful son weeps, holding his martyred mother, a sword piercing his heart.

On the morning of her death, I woke up at 5:00 a.m. from a dream in which she spoke to me. Only a minute later, the phone rang from the hospital, and the loud sobs of my stepfather resounded from the hallway. His cries of desperation struck me as more unendurable than the brutishness of the life they revealed. The remainder of January was interminably long, and these infinities aren't found in Dante's circles of unendurable time. I craved solitude to sort myself out and to question the cosmos for leaving me orphaned so soon. But more was required of this teen. I had to sign an ominous-looking book to obtain Mother's death certificate; I had to stand firm as a witness of my mother, now lying dead under a white sheet in the morgue; I had to arrange for her funeral; I had to bury her; I had to be nice to the weak grown-ups, who, feeling sorry for me, made me feel worse with their sentimental chatter. The death of another is an intimate affair. Great tragedians permit us to peek into parental cradles, lovers' beds, everyone's crypts of love.

When these same adults around me were collapsing with grief, where did my strength come from at fifteen? I wonder. Did anything in my life prepare me for this bereavement?

It was odd to see Mother's corpse in the hospital and again in the open casket before the burial. I was glad that this was my first and most dramatic encounter with physical death. In the hospital I was afraid to approach the person who was no longer; at the public display before the funeral, I kissed Mother's forehead to seal our silent parting. How intensely inward I turned! No other human could claim me better than I did to myself in the solemn parting. I had to step out more decidedly from the protective childhood bubble, even while my forced maturation brought me into a vastly expanded inward universe. Mother used to nourish this inner world in me through an upbringing based on love and freedom.

I withstood aloneness at Mother's grave because in her final departure I had not been abandoned by love. Mother's last message from her deathbed was my great, simple realization at fifteen: being orphaned meant I had to learn early the human truth that we stand alone in the world. In solitude before the cosmos, I am nevertheless not bereft of love. Tragic beauty becomes a way whereby the divine cosmos teaches love. This nodal point of discovery has been something to which I return as a source of solace, although I've forgotten the core of this epiphany many times. Human demise is not the same as lovelessness or abandonment or emptiness. If tragedy means abandonment, would not love, revealed through physical finitude and death, always be untruth? If lovelessness is the worse trigger of despair than death, then love is as strong as death.

Dying for My Sins

As a boy I committed many sins punishable in the Communist paradise, and my mother's death, while wiping her own slate clean, redeemed them all. She was my messianic Bodhisattva, a queen goddess who by her suffering charmed the dragons of the bewitched empire. As a child I took part in two mass demonstrations in 1969: the August protest against the Soviet invasion, and the victory celebration in honor of the defeat the Soviets in the finals of the world ice-hockey match that took place at the stadium in Prague. What a sweet, glorious victory over the Russians occurred that winter by the Czechoslovak team! David crushed Goliath not with a slingshot but a hockey puck. The ecstasy of the fans was instantly transfigured into a postinvasion political statement: "Russians, go home!"

I was struck by police riot gear in the ice-hockey skirmishes that erupted all over Prague, and my agitated face momentarily flickered on the TV screen in the crowd in one of those August protests. The provocative twinkle in my eyes that drove my teachers mad was clearly identifiable near Wenceslas Square. And so I again became the topic of school discussions. Then there was my photo of Jan Palach's funeral. This deed couldn't be undone even if I'd never placed it on my CV. The publication could be noted in a dossier somewhere; the photo had the capacity to destroy my life. By the time I struggled for my tenure at a US university, no one cared about such boyish publications.

As if that weren't enough, on November 2, 1970, in the eighth grade, I started a class monthly called *Všežravec* (*Omnivore*). It came typed, bound with thread and needle, with pencil illustrations, and in five homemade yet proudly official *Samizdat* copies. The journal's aim was to record the stories of the class and to publish their essays. The first issue had twenty pages of essays, jokes, cartoons (those I would borrow and copy from elsewhere), puzzles, songs, games, horoscopes, and ads. The last—blank—page was for "letters from readers" to be handwritten in pen when the issue was circulated.

For all its appearance of fun, the journal exhibited more insolence than inno-cence. It caricatured some classroom and school situations, and these stories ran in a column called, "Gossip from the School Benches." These stories detailed not only de-tailed student situations but also public teacher-student situations. More obliquely, the journal had a political subtext written all over it. This provocation came in two forms: what the journal presented in terms of content and by virtue of its spontane-ous existence. The second issue appeared on December 1. Manifestly it wished and illustrated holiday greetings on its front cover, but implied in the chosen greeting was the famous chanson by Marta Kubišová, who sang in December 1968, "*Ať mír dál zůstává s touto krajinou* [Let peace remain with this land]."

The next line of the song was the wish that the governance of the land would return to its people, and it was the wish implied on the front of my school journal in December 1970! The last issue came out shortly before the journal was prohibited by school authorities because of the implied political subversiveness of its message. On February 8, 1971, it offered a double issue, numbers 3-4. On the front cover was a quote from Ludwig Börne: "Pythagoras sacrificed one hundred bulls when he discov-ered his equation; ever since, all bulls tremble whenever a new truth is discovered."[18] This became the last bit of my early journalism. *Mother must have suffered and died for my sins so I could be shielded from the wrath of the authorities.* This made sense to me when I was a boy because we lived after the 1968 Soviet invasion of Czechoslovakia during the so-called normalization years (1970–1989), which increasingly silenced all critical voices.

The thought of Mother's redemptive suffering gave me an inner peace. Yet nei-ther Mother's ashes nor the cosmic dust would disclose ahead of their decrees the measure of their wrestling with love and death for the life of the boy. Even with my native urgency to repair—to be a healer, a teacher, a philosopher, a rabbi—would I be able to bear the truths hidden in mercy by the gods before adults can become children of disrepair, namely survivors?

A Mother dying for her son: the story of abandonment and love presented an iconic spiritual odyssey that no ordinary return home would repair. What is required by the boy's myth telling is *tikkun olam*, the mending of the broken world—a memoir in search of healing. The boy has been writing this book for a long time before be-coming a child of a survivor at forty, and the story is now written by an adult as his postmemoir.

There are empirically instrumental dimensions to the boy's myth. His mother's death ultimately protected him from the core original sin of both of his parents—their Communist heresy and consequent apostasy. In the normalized post-Stalinist justice, the hearts of the innocents weren't ripped out on the stone altar to be consumed by Chakmul, the Mayan jaguar god. Nor were the victims drowned like the Aztec virgins. Unlike in the 1950s, apostates in the 1970s weren't even hanged to appease the hungry gods of the revolution. In the years of normalization, one lived through an inverse affirmative action whereby the next generations were punished for the sins of the parents with deliberate cruelty. With the intellectual-class background and damaged political profile of his parents, the boy received poor evaluation scores, and this dossier would restrict him from all advancement in educational and later professional levels. He was a child of intellectual parents coming from a petty-bourgeois background. They rose up through high party ranks but betrayed the party from within. Such sins against "the holy spirit" could not be forgiven. With no redemption for this orphan's lineage, there was only reeducation.

Mother's Veiled Silence

At age fourteen, I was a silent witness to Mother's painful death, and she took her silence to the grave: in her dying she never spoke to me of death in Auschwitz. A lapsed Communist, Mother had arranged for a Catholic burial. A Slovak Catholic priest, Father Jan Hutyra, buried her, according to her wishes. He had survived the Nazi occupation in Slovakia and internment in the Communist religious concentration camps after 1948. Father Jan was tortured by the Communists, who forced him to stand in a pile of sand without sleep. I don't know what Mother and Father Jan discussed on her deathbed. Had she professed her Jewishness to him alone, she still did not call in a rabbi. The priest respected those boundaries as he presided over her burial not far from Palach's "empty" tomb. Father Jan did not wear his priestly vestments, and there was no mass. I imagine how in their mutual encounter of their tragic journeys, Jan symbolically could embody for Mother both a Slovak priest and a rabbi. He was to her a Slovak village priest tortured by the Communist regime on whose vineyard she had labored. She was a Slovak Jew to his Slovak Catholicism. Under the Slovak clerical-fascist regime, some of his Catholic cohorts deported Jews like her to the death camps. Their two journeys were a convergence without the erasure of memory.

From abroad, with my first earnings, I bought my mother a simple marble tombstone and had the following written in gold letters under her name and data: SHE DIED WITH FAITH IN THE EXISTENCE OF God.

Mother had met Father Jan through a Slovak nun, Sister Adéla Takáčová. She and I ran into this nun while traveling by train to Bratislava; Sister Adéla sat in our train compartment. Moved by something in my conversation with Mother, she entered a dialogue with us. It was a momentary human encounter with a far-reaching impact—she kept in touch. When Father Jan was assigned to serve the young Slovak students at Saint Salvator church opposite Charles Bridge in Prague, the nun introduced us to him. Mother kept in close contact with Jan after 1970. Following her death, until I left Czechoslovakia in 1977, Sister Adéla and Father Jan regularly helped me by making small financial contributions to my orphaned life. They were some of the many people my dying mother had asked in secret to accept me as their own.

During the 1950s the notorious Czech Communist leader and former partisan Rudolf Slánský, whose Jewish origins were unacceptable to Stalin, was executed. Faithful Communists were pursued by their anti-Semitic comrades in the entire Eastern Bloc. Anti-Semitism in postwar US culture and its various political and academic institutions barred Jews from professional advancement through rank and tenure, blocked others from memberships in country clubs, and forced still others from their jobs during the McCarthy era. The Communist revolution began to eat its creators and their children during the Stalinist purges, and even if my parents didn't actively or directly devour others, they were bystanders in danger of being consumed themselves. Mother met both Slánský and his comrade Jan Šverma in the Tatra Mountains during the Slovak National Uprising. Given her Jewish roots and Communist-intellectual prominence, she easily could have shared Slánský's destiny.

"Imagine the Nazi Sitting Nude on the Toilet"

"If there exists something like a Jewish saint, it must be someone like Weissmandl," Andrej Steiner said in his Atlanta interview. He was moved by Reb Dov's charisma, and no rescue seemed impossible.[19]

When it was time to meet Dieter Wisliceny about the bribe, the Working Group chose Steiner, a non-Orthodox, secular, confident Jew with an imposing figure, polished back hair, and articulate tongue. He went to Wisliceny, whose wife was a cousin of Heinrich Himmler, and proposed the idea of the bribe for the lives of the Jews. He remembered how he got to build those kosher kitchens in the labor camp: "And suddenly I saw Wisliceny sitting on the john!...Again, instead of being afraid, I suddenly got the courage. I told myself, *I am going to say everything [Rabbi] Weissmandl told me to say.*"[20] When Andrej arrived at the meeting, he did just that; he couldn't stifle a smirk.

Reb Dov devised the group plan with a twist in the story they told Wisliceny—the group was negotiating on behalf of world Jewry, with their world leader Ferdinand Roth based in Switzerland. This was to impress Wisliceny and make him believe there was money and power to the bribe. Roth was as fictitious as the "Mary" buried by the Communist secret service in the 1970s in Jan Palach's empty grave in Prague.

In writing about her father, a rabbi, who was killed in Auschwitz for refusing to work on the Sabbath, Sarah Kofman interweaves Robert Antelme's memoir with her story. When working becomes endless dying, one may imagine the Sabbath time while sitting in the latrines. And so "pissing" and "shitting" alongside their Kapos, the deportees found "ways of triumphing over the torturers who could not prevent these *acts* any more than they could prevent death....The joy of being in the latrines, beyond the reach of the Nazis, of escaping their power....Because there one could see them lose their pseudo-divinity and dignity."[21]

Before I learned about these strategies of confronting fear, I used to imagine the Communists or secret service agents sitting in a public WC. I later would quote to my students in existentialism the famous claim made by Michel de Montaigne that "no matter that we may mount on stilts, we still must walk on our own legs. And on the highest throne in the world, we still sit only on our own bottom."[22] Whether this toilet training of fear is part of the Jewish midrash or humor, it nonetheless empowers the powerless.[23]

My Parents Commit Apostasy, and I Assimilate

My parents' break with the party did not leave visible scars on me because as an orphan I became a ward of the Communist state. My mother and father had become active Communists and successful professionals in the 1950s, when the monster or show trials with prominent Communists had peaked in the Soviet-bloc countries (corresponding to their generational mirror in Joseph McCarthy's witch-hunts in the United States). I know little about their activities in the decade before my birth, except for journal remembrances Father published in the 1990s, or the occasional nasty article that appeared in Slovakia about his thinking during the 1950s, or his asides about youthful self-deception.

Membership in the Communist Party could be terminated in one of three ways: deletion, expulsion, or resignation. Members of any organization, religious or secular, who left the party of their own accord, were judged much more harshly—as apostates—than those who never joined. By the mid-1960s, my parents had become thoroughly disillusioned with the party, though they already must have become critical after Stalin's death. Mother saw some of the devastating effects of Soviet socialism (poverty, lack of basic goods in stores, political surveillance of dissidents) when she researched the construction of the oil pipeline in Russia as a journalist; at that point she lost all naiveté about the regime. Father's tenure at the university was restored after 1989. He taught at Comenius University in Bratislava for five years and eventually retired without being granted a full professorship. He published some writings he had completed during the normalization years, and he organized major art exhibitions at home and abroad. His one love—art history—to which he repeatedly returned with great fidelity throughout his life, and for which he even suffered, was rekindled in the twilight of his years.

The party was willing to "forget" (but not forgive) those grave sins—just as the Nazis took children away from their racially inferior parents and turned them into cute Aryans—on the condition that I would become the party's child. The fact that in the Communist heaven there was no forgiveness had to do with the nature of its particular hell. The "anathema sit!" – "Go to hell!" with which parents were excommunicated during normalization was so devoid of all spiritual meaning that even fallen angels could enjoy in their divine comedy. Devils and demons aren't atheists; they just don't accept the reality of unconditional love. Communist normalization meant a denial that such loving is even possible.

The red orgies of love for and by the party eternally bored me. The normalizers became devoid of all the passion that my believing parental generation still held for socialism. That modern hell was now nothing but the anomie of the world where slogans were uttered and marches held and discipline administered and "peace by war" preached, yet where no one had faith in the substance of any of it. The spiritlessness of this normalized hell was darker than the death of G-d announced by Nietzsche, darker than the so-called medieval *Temno* (*Darkness*), the novel by Czech writer Alois Jirásek, who describes in it the era of re-Catholicization (i.e., the normalization of Bohemia following the defeated Hussite Reformation). The Jesuits who spearheaded the post-Reformation gave Prague and the Czech landscape their glorious baroque grandeur; the post-1968 normalizers left behind only the scorched land of culture and historical amnesia.

Mother's poverty that resulted from her apostasy, along with her suffering at death and her actual death became redemptive for me in both inward and material ways. They protected me from the spiritlessness of the era and the revenge of the normalizers' hell.

Neither returning to my father in Bratislava, nor being legally permitted to live without a parent or guardian in Prague, yet practically orphaned, I became a ward of the Communist institution called the District National Committee at Prague 2. Jiří, the man Mother had dated before she became ill and married on her death-bed, became my stepfather and court-appointed guardian. Several court proceedings heard and granted the merit of my plea that removing me from the Czech-language environment in Prague to Bratislava, where my paternal father resided, would be traumatic. My Slovak was fluent because I had grown up with Mother, but my education had been in Czech. Without the court decision in my favor, I would have been shipped from Prague to Bratislava. Or had "Uncle" Radislav relinquished his legal paternal obligation to receive me after not caring for me for fifteen years, I would have been placed, like my brother had been once before by our mother, in a state home. Father, unlike my brother and uncle, neither came to see Mother in the hospital nor attended her funeral nor ever visited me in Prague. I was an orphan.

A year later, just as I began the first year of gymnasium (high school), the socialist court granted me another highly unusual arrangement. The presiding judge formally appointed my stepfather to be my foster parent. The court also appointed a legal aide from the social-work department of the District National Committee at Prague 2, a woman who happened to be one of Mother's close friends, to oversee my well-being. Under the dual supervision of foster care and Communist care, the court granted me permission to live in my own Prague flat without adult supervision. A ward of the socialist state—with the help of friends my mother bound by promise to watch over me, and with the goodwill of my Prague stepfather and the compliance of my Bratislava father—I was legally entrusted to follow my expressed wish to grow up as my own parent from the age of sixteen.

Mother's exclusive apartment in Prague was huge. We had three front rooms that overlooked the Grebovka trees and hills. From my room one walked to the middle living room then to Mother's bedroom and office. Each of the three front rooms had arched sun-filled windows. Large French doors opened up from my room to the dining room, and another door led from the dining room to Mother's room. Each room had a tall, ceramic-tile heating stove. Mine was made of beautiful green tile. In the winter we had to carry black coal up three flights from the cellar; each household had its ration of coal. One bucket of coal would give bright heat for three days and four nights. Embers remained, and we carried them down to service the frozen sidewalk. In the summer the breezes and the birdsongs came through the front windows. We had a fourth backroom and a large eat-in kitchen with a balcony that opened to the backyard. We had this flat because Mother, as a prominent Communist writer, had been granted an extra home-office space. After Mother left the Communist Party, she fought to retain her privilege to occupy a larger flat.

Mother and I had lived in spatial and aesthetic luxury envied by our neighbors, though after 1969, forced by economic hardship, she began to take renters in the backroom, the one in which I got drunk on New Year's Eve after she died. Some of the renters coincided with her more-or-less happy attempts to find a man for herself and a father for me. Having a lover must have been important to her, though in this sumptuous setting I never felt as a child the lack of a father. Her need for happiness was more crucial than my need for a new father. I never experienced our single-parent home to be wanting in love or care. I now see her inward suffering as one way in which her silence about the Holocaust spoke loudly of the wounds she had suffered in wartime.

After Mother's death I decided to exchange our big four-bedroom apartment for two smaller, separate units. I had inherited one-third of everything tangible, the other two-thirds going to my guardian and my brother, and I had two-thirds of the copyright of my mother's writings; my stepfather passing his share on to me. After my stepfather Jiří married Jaruška and started a new family—something I wished for the sake of his happiness—moving away was the one choice I found tolerable for my own happiness. I kept warm ties with them and their future children, but I was done with family experiments or arrangements made on my behalf. I wanted to begin a life that I had to steer on my own. It's difficult to say where I found the courage to think I could do this at that age. Somehow all the adults who wanted to shelter me would themselves seem too heavy a burden for me to carry. Unlike their feeling sympathy for orphans, I didn't feel pity for myself. And their pity was hard to take.

The uncanny sobriety of my burgeoning young adulthood took me out of my childhood bubble into the quiet months after the funeral. I knew with sharp awareness taking hold of me that I had to figure out what I should become, if anything at all. If no drugs or gangs or the oppressive state apparatus should claim me, then suicide might be an attractive option. These paths often appear in the dizzying freedom of spirit that the self is. *Shall I despair or hope against hope?* All these questions and ways were vying for this orphan. Once I had been thrown into the cosmic venture and repeatedly saved from early extinction by Mother—and was it not Mother G-d, Shekinah, who spoke to me and called myself out of silence through my earthly mother, queens, and angels?—no one could make my radical self-choice for me regarding whether or however I should live.

As an independent young man at sixteen, I could have taken any number of paths. A few weeks after Mother's death, some university students tried to lure me to an underground LSD party at the Strahov dorms; I can't recall why I didn't go. Did I possess a keen sense that trying drugs would lead me to a life of psychotic addiction? I could have worked for the Communist police and do their dirty bidding as a way to secure my material existence. If not debauchery, then cynicism or fear would be the demons of my era. They took many a fragile soul down those paths with them.

Leaving the party after the Soviet invasion, Mother devoted the last of her mid years to an eclectic spiritual quest made up of Eastern spiritual traditions, yoga, Christianity, Kabala, and, most significant, as I would realized in my adulthood, a return to a private practice of Judaism. This too was one of the unmarked keys she left behind. Her Catholic burial, my atheistic upbringing, our socially free and intellectually reflective milieu of my home life, all coupled with my mother's unbroken silence about the Holocaust, left me in my early teens with a mixed set of clues to my own life story. I knew Mother loved me amid all the turmoil, yet her silence haunted me; there was a lost connection to the deeper meaning of that love.

Nowhere in my dossier was there any indication of our Jewish origins. Mother succeeded in erecting a protective assimilative shield over me that for the Communist powers functioned as my immaculate conception, my birth without sin, my life purged of sins. I was born too late to directly experience the impact of the postwar and Cold War eras. But I was born early enough to inherit the dual burden of the parental passion for Communist ideals and Mother's silence about the Shoah.

Stepping into early adulthood, I learned to give up myths nurtured in the protected bubbles of imagination, fairy tales, and science fiction. I relinquished myths of my immaculate origins and virgin birth, those of the magical powers of teachers coming to my aid, and those of Mother's messianic power to bleach my original sins by her redemptive suffering. Yielding to the larger cosmologies told by historical religions and civilizations, I embraced adult myths that would shed light on the shared tragic beauty of my journey and the larger human journey of my native tribe. In a period following Mother's death and my continued Jewish assimilation, I undertook my first religious quest.

Mother's Letter to a Catholic Nun (Winter 1968)

Dear Sister,

I am sorry to answer you so late, but this was the most difficult year of my life....I have read the books you sent me, and I have also been reading marvelous works by Indian, Chinese, and Japanese spiritual writers. And since I confess in all absolute and eternal values a thorough tolerance and freedom that is based on personal sincerity, I also accept with The Bhagavad Gita *the wisdom that "all ways are My ways" and that "at the end of every way I am waiting." At this time I am reading an unpublished manuscript of the great contemporary Czech mystic, who recently died, and who has been hardly known by anyone...."Good books" are for me various books, also a book of the US bishop Robinson, or a book of the German Jew Martin Buber, or those of Zen. I do not significantly differentiate among churches. I find pointers to the Way also in ancient Egyptian or Assyrian or Indian religions (do not be annoyed with me, please, that I do not pronounce loudly the word God, as it is so often debased and so many things hide behind it) ....I hope you will not reject me, given these views of mine. I would like to come visit you with Martin sometime during the following summer....Until then I wish you peace and joy.*

Magda

6

ARCHIVES AND AFTERLIVES OF MEMORY

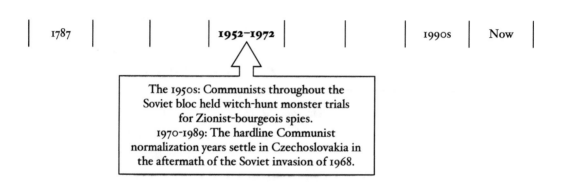

| 1787 | | | **1952–1972** | | | 1990s | Now |

The 1950s: Communists throughout the
Soviet bloc held witch-hunt monster trials
for Zionist-bourgeois spies.
1970-1989: The hardline Communist
normalization years settle in Czechoslovakia in
the aftermath of the Soviet invasion of 1968.

After the Soviet invasion in 1968, my mother writes to Premier Alexander Dubček. She still hopes to save her youthful dream of a more just future. By the end of 1969, she quits the Communist Party and becomes a pariah, and we live one step above poverty. My happy boyhood under Communism—school kitchens, communal health care, state parades, and sex education—gives way to the struggles of a young man.

My Afterlives (1928–1998)

Until the summer of 1997, I did not hone my transgenerational memory to touch the past.

"Grandpa Nathan was a village physician and Grandma Ilonka a housewife," I would say.

"Did you know your grandparents when you were growing up in Prague?" someone would ask me.

"They both died before I was born," I would respond curtly.

"Did your mother ever tell you stories about them?" They would not rest.

I have been haunted by Mother's inaudible pantry, from which I could serve but crumbs as hors d'oeuvres to my friends and colleagues; I wasn't privy to the main dish.

"Mother wasn't ready to tell me much about her life by the time she died when I was fourteen."

More than half of Mother's immediate relatives, with spouses and children, were killed at Auschwitz.

"Have you been to your mom's birthplace?"

Mother was born in 1928 in Myjava, Slovakia, to Jewish parents. With her brother and parents she survived the Holocaust. She consigned her—and thus my—heritage to a deep postwar cloaking.

"We never visited Myjava, her home village," I would admit.

Mother's maturation among the partisans formed the central part of her postwar Communist identity. The story of Jewish persecution had been touched up as a blemish in the family history.

"You should go on a search trip with Patricia and see what you find," friends would suggest.

After Gary's 1997 letter woke me up from my slumber, the shoeboxes of Mother's diaries and letters provided me with never-before-cooked recipes.

"Between my escape from Prague and the fall of the Iron Curtain, I was persona non grata. I wasn't allowed to return for eleven years." Imperfectly I would explain why until now I had missed so many clues.

Mother's silence, her death, and my exile curtained my afterlife in an archive made of a triple shroud. *Was Mother's silence motivated by the need to dissociate from the trauma of the Holocaust?* I wondered. *Was her dissociation motivated by her fearing the renewed Stalinist witch-hunt for Zionist-bourgeois spies? Or did Mother, the fashionable blonde, mask assimilation? The young Communist was afraid to mark the bodies of her sons for slaughter.* The silence of words, the muteness of things, and the shame of bodies settled me with cumulative identity crises. *Yet in this immaculate, virginal loss of my clues, was there love spoken unconditionally? By what name shall I call it when I learn its nature and fashion my adult meaning for loving?* I was wrestling with myself, with love and death, and this striving to account for myself propelled my search.

Mother spoke to me indirectly thrice: in her decision to have a child when her marriage was falling apart; in loving the old Beck bookcases, the brass cup, and the Persian rug; and in shielding her children against the Cold War anti-Semitism that infused the Communist dream. These three silences fill historical frames; the fourth, existential silence suffuses a psychological and spiritual struggle for sanity. As a teen, Mother struggled with the madness of Nazism and, as a young adult, with the madness of Stalinism, both of which had threatened to annihilate her. As a single mother, she suffered from prolonged periods of manic-depressive states.

Surviving Abandonment and Annihilation (1952–1972)

Our Bratislava flat boasted a large balcony, and the building's lobby was adorned with bright-yellow tiles; the color reminded of my oldest childhood memory, my tarot card of the Sun. Leaving her Moravian husband in Slovakia, she exchanged our big Bratislava flat for a luxurious Prague apartment, and I initially lived there with my brother Pavel. At some point Mother could no longer keep up her professional and family life in Prague, as she was often hospitalized with worsening psychiatric episodes. Consequently she placed Pavel in a state boarding home and sent me to live with Auntie Zuzana in Bratislava. Pavel must have woken up from his boyhood early, because to this day he's haunted by a vivid memory of an unstable mother and her sudden disappearance.

I don't remember Mother's episodes during my kindergarten years in Prague, but Pavel must have felt doubly abandoned—first by Father, who left home when Pavel was eight, and then by Mother, whose manic states he feared and whose depressions made him recoil. Pavel's affection for me is merged with my self-protective bubble, which allowed me to keep a distance from the psychotic mother while drawing near the loving mother. I remained for Pavel the emotional link to our loving mother. He remained for me a link to the lost father with whom he had grown up in his teens. The older brother endlessly cried in the boarding home and continued to cry for a long time, even after Father rescued him and brought him to Bratislava.

In the early 1960s, Mother was locked up in a psychiatric pavilion at Bohnice, where the doctors threw away the key, and I gradually got used to being an orphan. In my self-parenting bubble, I never doubted Mother's love for me; she joined Father in my melancholy memory of a lost Eden. Father lived not far from me in Bratislava, but I don't remember birthdays or Christmas gifts from him in those years. One day I showed up at his university office, and to add my insult to his injury, from the door, I greeted him with, "Hallo, Uncle Radek," thereby cementing for a long time our mutual alienation.

Were it not for Auntie Zuzana's care during my first year in grammar school, I most likely would have ended up in a state orphanage. She cared for me even though she lived very simply on a meager income as a cleaning lady. Mother wasn't in jail; she wasn't buried anywhere either; yet she was mysteriously gone. No one could tell me anything, nor could I visit any physical place to make peace with her absence.

I lived in my own inner-child world and, on most days after school, ran around and engaged in manly activities with the boys' gang from our Bratislava street. On Sunday mornings I listened to radio fairy-tale dramatizations; fairy tales were the happiest pastimes of my childhood under Communism.

My mother had prohibited Zuzana to ever speak about religion in my presence. I would pass the blue Lutheran church on my way to the noontime Sunday movies and make fun of my classmates who had to attend church services. I was a proud atheist who had discovered early a secret inner world in which one is saved and brought up by other forces. It never occurred to me then that it was my primordial mother and father who nourished me in my childhood solitude, enabling me to survive my house of horrors.

In the early 1960s, Mother still had powerful Communist friends and continued to be a prominent Communist as well. In one of her highly creative manic episodes, she convinced a friend to help her escape from Bohnice. The pavilion served as a de facto prison, a place where enemies of the state ended up with psychotics; it was a place of no return. Mother escaped from Bohnice after someone unhinged the doors of her building and she climbed the high garden wall. Her Communist friend picked her up on the other side and drove her to safety. After her daring escape, Mother showed up in Bratislava to visit me without explaining her long absence or her plan to take me back to Prague. She then checked us in at the expensive Hotel Devin by the Danube River. On the second evening, she forgot me in the hotel lobby and disappeared. I sat for hours in a large armchair, observing the rich and famous foreigners passing by. I was amused to see the sex workers who were there to sell themselves as much as to spy for the state in exchange for a life of relative privilege. In truth I was abandoned in the hotel lobby that night until I told someone where I lived and was delivered by Father's second wife to Zuzana's address. The next day Mother arrived at our door with two policemen by her side, claiming I'd been kidnapped.

The second manic episode, coinciding with the arrival of the Prague Spring, impressed me. I returned home from school to find a "Big Chill" occurring in all six rooms of our flat. Eyes wide shut I witnessed long-haired hippies; people on drugs; fully naked bodies coming in and out of rooms; strangers dancing on tables, singing, copulating. Perhaps the whole world of the 1960s had joined Mother in her mania. Perhaps she was always normal, and reality had only just now caught up with her. Mother decided that since we were going to paint the flat anyway, everyone could create art on our apartment walls. The walls were covered with scribbling and drawings, some nice, some obscene. No one noticed me; I connected with no one. I was a lost youth in strange world of mania and the social and cultural revolutions in progress that it mimicked.

Mother's depressive periods would arrive after a postmanic calm. Her melancholy states appeared to be saner to me because, although while in them Mother was tired and unable to perform basic human functions, she would speak to me. Attending the third grade in Prague, I learned to shop, cook for myself and feed her, clean up, and find ways to pass my rather unrestrained time. During Mother's depressions I'd get extra allowance for movies or concerts. Having no father I became mother to myself. I also played a parent to her, forcing her to get up from bed and take a walk in our park.

The veneer of depression's normality would disappear, however, with her suicide attempts. I was shaken by two failed attempts, though I learned later that there had been dozens of them. Once Mother took a dose of barbiturate sleeping pills and made her last bed by the kitchen stove with the gas fully on. Another time she tried to hang herself with a leather belt on the window ledge of the middle room that separated her office and my bedroom in Prague. After surviving the war and refusing to taste the food of despair, Mother had become a reckless, dangerous parent. Our unkosher kitchen could have exploded with deadly gas and killed us both. I was sleeping one room down from her suicidal acts. The state didn't take me from her after she managed to flee the Prague Bohnice pavilion. Mother's highly placed Communist friends secured generous literary grants for her to pay for our comfortable lifestyle. This too was possible for prominent individuals in a regime that officially had abolished all classes.

I stopped existing for Mother in her depressions. I grew aware that the son wasn't born a god to save his suffering mother. For a child, witnessing his mother's inability to live happily is the saddest thing in the world. At one point I took a series of black-and-white photos of Mother in her Prague office. These images hide words that want to emit hope. I look deeply into her eyes; they shed odorless tears containing ashes of the unnamed. She whispers her ghastly encounters with lovelessness.

If one could drink up the infinite sea of melancholy! What choice does a boy have when he bears witness to his mother's eyes after her failed suicide? Those eyes blinked with a grammar of sorrowing wells, but can a boy forgive his mother for wanting to kill herself? Even if as a child I could have let so weak a parent die, what would it have meant to do so out of love, knowing my mother was unable to live through annihilating nothingness? What would it have meant for me to be a child who out of love had chosen to be an orphan?

Kierkegaard writes about Abraham's sacrifice of his son Isaac. In an apocryphal account of Abraham's possible failure, he describes how Isaac would have lost faith if his father had despaired of the trial, if his son had caught the look of his father's despairing eyes as he was about to lift the knife to sacrifice his son. Abraham had faith, not despair, and G-d spared him from making this sacrifice. After Mother's failed suicide attempt with the sleeping pills, her head stuck in poisonous gas, I witnessed the mourning despair in my mother's eyes—I saw what Isaac must have been spared from seeing in Abraham's eyes. In aggression against herself, unlike the Greek Medea, who killed her children in political rebellion, my mother failed to ward off the horror of self-annihilation. In her return from hell, she suffered the guilt of failed love for her children. And then, a day after her return from hell, I became aware of her eyes looking at me the night before her suicide attempt. Mother's eyes were saying that she was sorry for not being able to live or die for any of her children.

Mother was among the first in Communist Czechoslovakia to have her manic depression treated in the early 1960s with experimental lithium therapy. This may have been the last "privilege" she received as a member of the literary nomenclature in the Communist Party. The miracle of my survival is that I considered myself a happy child, and I have for the most part brought joy to others who have gravitated to me. I witnessed true horrors but wasn't consumed by them. This mystery would come to reveal itself as I learned to return to my inwardness. After the Prague Spring, Mother regained the ability to lead a healthy, increasingly self-realized life. After she left the party in the wake of the Soviet invasion, she became a spiritual seeker.

I survived my mother's frightening absence and mad presence thanks to the mercy of selective memory. I collected fragments of love and sobriety and shielded myself from the rest through the art of forgetting. Nietzsche insisted on a right to forget one's origins and the weight of history. Had I found it easy to practice his joyous wisdom of forgetting, I could have taken a quicker trek to self-overcoming.

Mother's Personal Happiness and Political Passion

It is late in Chicago's summer of 1997, and with resurrected courage, I delve into the secrets of Mother's shoebox. The postinvasion correspondence reflects a world out of bounds, and Mother no longer suffered her states of mania. Geopolitics were thrown into the chaos of melancholia, and Mother won spiritual stability through the self-disciplines of yoga and meditation. I see myself back then as a boy hatching out of his cocoon; Mother had assumed a healthy presence in my life. Those five happy years between the Soviet invasion and her demise spanned a cat's infinity. They were too short on a lived human scale, yet they formed this boy's sense of love.

Springtime came into our Prague home in more than one ways. Mother launched an agreement with a well-known director, Otomar Krejča, to stage her work at the Theatre Divadlo Za Branou in Prague. She created a theater piece on the steps at the Prague National Museum, with dramatizations of classics by the likes of Dostoyevsky and Chekhov. She collaborated with other major stages—Divadlo na Vinohradech, Komorní Divadlo, and the National Theatres in Prague and Bratislava; she wrote at her desk at home. Many of her plans, like those of other progressive artists, academics, intellectuals, and politicians came to naught when my native country entered a long period of homespun freeze called "normalization."

Mother's correspondence that survived that dramatic era records a gradual change in the public mood as well as in her inward journey. Two months after the Soviet invasion, Mother wrote a personal letter to the first secretary of the Communist Party, who was the beleaguered symbol of the Prague Spring, Alexander Dubček. In her October 1968 letter, she still proudly acknowledged herself as a Communist.

"Esteemed and Dear, Dear Comrade Dubček" (October 12, 1968)

If someone could count the movements of consciousness, this would be the thousandth letter since those days after January [1968]. But it all looked as if there were plenty of those who make themselves known and to whom you had to answer. Now I am convinced that it would not be good to delay any more.

My vocation: literature, theater. My hobby: human beings and everything that concerns what is human, from the most emotional to the most rational, from the most intimate to the most public, from the most individualistic to the most social. All this together perhaps explains why I am a Communist. The second is that as a sixteen-year-old, I took part with my father, a partisan physician, in the uprising and there formed certain very strong emotional ties to an entire circle of social problems and attitudes.

I am writing you, esteemed comrade Dubček, because I want to tell you that, as an intellectual and journalist and activist, I followed from the beginning your every speech and act, and today more than ever before, I need to tell you that I support you without exception and what you do and how you lead our people. I realize the entire complexity and difficulty of your situation in the present days and weeks. I can feel in myself the sharpness of the edge on which, between what the situation demands and what people of this land need more than salt, you make step-by-step decisions, assume attitudes, and make speeches. I need to tell you, dear comrade Dubček, that the manner of your walking on this road only increases my estimation of you.

I want to tell you at the same time that I would like to be useful, and I think that I could do something. From my student years, I do not do anything other than follow and think about the crossroads and destinies of human stories, individuals, and entire social groups. Since 1960, when thanks to the intervention of V. Šalgovič, my play, Where Does the White Road Lead?, *was prohibited and when I was surrounded by several characterless primitives who gradually made it impossible for me to publish at home, I have lived in the Prague "exile." I go home as often as possible, and this possibility to permanently confront Slovakia and Bohemia, Prague and Bratislava, Orava, where I return regularly, and the native Myjava region, gives me some distance and with that perhaps some more integrated insight into numerous problems. I can see some issues, especially in culture and ideology, from other angles that are not any less serious than those of politics. I would be very grateful, esteemed comrade Dubček, if you would find a moment for me to tell you, and only you, about some problems. I can promise that this would not be lost time. If you agree, please let me know several days ahead, so that I can prepare for the conversation. I am convinced that all our problems—I think those domestic ones—are solvable and their solution lies in our hands; it is only necessary to bring all thinking heads together and all hearts that have a healthy sense for humanity, truth, justice. And of these, as we can witness especially in these recent days, we have more than a few.*

Finally I beg of you, esteemed comrade Dubček, do not think it arrogant that I append to my letter a work of one exciting September night, an updated paraphrase of an old Slovak popular fairy tale about the Garbage Man (Popolvár, *literally a Cinderella boy, collector of trash and ashes). When I was writing it, I was thinking a lot about you, estimated comrade Dubček. It is not a perfect piece of work, as it was born in the whirlwind. But the present moment conjures in life precisely this type of work.*

I hope that you will not take badly anything I wrote to you in this letter. Believe, please, without any exaggeration, that I am with you daily, as even in this moment I feel solidarity with our beautiful people and their presently difficult hours.

With warm and heartfelt comradely greeting,

Magdalena Matuštíková

I rummage through versions of Mother's curriculum vitae. All in Slovak, they're dated from the Prague thaw of 1967 to its winter of 1968. Items of her biography get accentuated then dropped. I come across a letter from April 28, 1967. Written to Comrade Závada, it intimates the wind of intellectual freedom arriving in 1968. It is indicative of that era's vital energy, and a thorough silence cloaks her Jewish origins.

Literary activity from 1945 (poems, short stories, journalism, and literary criticism):

1954, first published play, Kristina *(Bratislava, Prague, Nitra, Martin, Liberec, etc., etc.)*

1956, play, Matej Dubravec *(unpublished for so-called ideological reasons)*

1959, play, Kadial vedie biela cesta? [Where Does the White Road Lead?] *(staged in Nitra, collaborated with National Theatre in Prague with Kraus-Krejča, play forbidden in Nitra by the IV department of the Slovak Communist Party, rehabilitated in 1965. I plan to work on it with Kraus in the Theater Za Branou [Prague] this September.)*

1961, book, Mesto žije zajtra [The City Lives Tomorrow] *(awarded in the competition for the fortieth anniversary of the Czechoslovak Communist Party)*

1964, Výlet [Excursion], *full-length monologue (Prague Radio, recited by Dana Medřická, in preparation for TV)*

1965, play, Archa [Arc] *(collaborating on the play with the theater Na Vinohradech)*

1966, play, Slnovrat [Solstice] *(collaborating on the play with National Theatre in Prague and the theater Nová Scena, Bratislava)*

All above works will be ready for publication during 1967 and 1968.

In fall 1968 my mother stressed broad intellectual qualifications rather than her party work.

Theory of art, aesthetics; history of literature, theater, music, and film; philosophy; psychology. Languages: English, German, Russian, Polish, Hungarian; passively French, Italian, Spanish. Civil profile: At sixteen I took part with my father, partisan physician, in the Slovak National Uprising. After liberation I studied and from the beginning worked in the Student Socialist Union as a chair of the university organization. From 1952 I worked in the party (many committees, propaganda work, and activist). I am a member of the Czech Writers' Union. I am divorced and have two sons.

Throughout this time she kept silent about her Jewish past. In October she witnessed the rapidly collapsing cultural and literary freedom in Czechoslovakia. She tried to place somewhere her September dramatization of the Slovak fairy tale *Popolvár*. She wrote to Eva Kristinová on October 10, 1968:

In today's Sunday paper, the play Popolvár *was supposed to appear in full, a four-page insert together with illustrations—but it was not published, and I suppose that it was no longer possible. But perhaps there is some difference between the mass media and theater—at least for now. And so I beg you again: if you can, do something about this text. Not because of me, but I work now at the city committee of the party, and so I know how people are thirsty for a word, hope, any kind of minimal certainty. If you can, please, recite* Popolvár, *alone or with others, perhaps with a bit of music...in the context of any theater...And you will be doing a piece of great work.*

Mother added that she was going to write to other friends she had in Slovak television and radio, urging them to produce the text. She also appealed to Danevi Michaelli at Bratislava television.

I hope it is not too late and that you can find a way to get this thing out. It is much needed; people are hungry for "a divine word," at least in some form, and the hunger is growing by the day.

On the same day, a letter went to Gita Mayer at the Slovak National Theatre.

> *It is necessary now to hurry, as long as one can still produce things in the the-*
> *ater....In the present situation, it makes sense to show every piece which can*
> *support and strengthen people in their struggle and with conviction about the*
> *lasting existence of the moral values.*

Her third letter on the same day was to "comrade Gregor" from the Slovak National Theatre. She suddenly mentioned her Jewish past and how it cast a shadow on her career.

> *My relationship with the Slovak National Theatre has been uneven for sev-*
> *eral years...since the arrival of R. Mrlian, who was my professor and who*
> *never forgave me for several things: first of all my critical attitude toward*
> *his professional work, my attitude toward his moral character in social and*
> *political matters, and most of all, my Jewish origins—indeed, he is a faith-*
> *ful Slovak from the Liptov region. Another of your directors, Anton Kret...*
> *also had similar attitudes toward me...and even Gita Mayer had not the best*
> *relationship with me. [Mother admitted this also in the opening of the letter*
> *to Gita cited above.] And so it happened that your theater staged neither my*
> *later forbidden play,* White Road, *which without exaggeration, according*
> *to critics, is the best Slovak play of those years, nor Arc...nor* Solstice, *which*
> *I consider to be my first good play that will live up to the criteria of modern*
> *drama.* Solstice *has been accepted by the Prague theater, and if it were not for*
> *the '68 events, it would be ready for the opening. At this time of common dan-*
> *ger to all values, we must keep together. I have always had a great relationship*
> *with actors and stage directors of the Slovak National Theatre, as from my*
> *school until the staging of* Kristina *in 1954, the Slovak National Theatre was*
> *my primary stage.*

A self-proclaimed Communist in her October letter to Dubček, at the junc-
tion between October and December 1968, Mother departed from the party and
began on a fast track to her origins. She wrote to her comrades that she no longer could live by the materialist world view. She remained committed to a socially

and politically just world, yet she rejected the vanguard role of the party and the atheistic dogma that went along with it. In the 1950s she likely would have been imprisoned, if not executed, for such demonstrative acts. After the defeat of the progressive socialist reform movement of 1968, however, the Soviet occupation and the domestic normalization regime slowly destroyed her. By the 1960s Father's secular humanism had morphed into unbelieving (and later postmodern) nihilism; the party judged him to be politically unreliable; and he was deleted from Communist Party membership as a person who no longer could represent and teach its ideals. Mother elected to exit the party dramatically, while Father lapsed into passive noncompliance.

Their pariah status in the eyes of the Communist Party equally affected their children. My parents' works were removed from all libraries and bookshelves; Mother's plays were prohibited from any stage, TV, or radio productions; and their names were erased from the textbooks in which they had figured prominently in prior years. Father was expelled from his tenured teaching job in Bratislava. The intellectual purges constituted Gustav Husák's normalization period of the 1970s. Hundreds of intellectuals had to leave their posts and take up manual labor. The joke is that the Prague Metro was built by the most educated work force of historians, writers, philosophers, sociologists, journalists, artists, dissidents, and ex-Communists Czechoslovakia ever had assembled.[24] Father sued the university for several years, thus allowing him to keep his salary and his university studio apartment, the only housing he ever had. Although he continued to teach secretly from his apartment and write about underground Slovak artists, he had no hope of ever publishing those works.

My Happy Communist Homes

Palach's pieta wasn't the first political photo I took, though it was the first one I published. My first political pictures were shot at the swearing in of Czechoslovakia's president, General Ludvik Svoboda, in early 1968. My life follows a sequence of three narratives running from 1968 until 1972, and they further testify to my practice of creative remembering and forgetting: the happy moments of my life in Communism, Mother's "creative" parenting, and my inquisitive relationship to the strange and chaotic world of normalization.

Just as the Prague Spring was dawning, Mother enrolled me in a photography class at the Pioneer House (Grebovka). The party had turned this bourgeois-era estate into a multipurpose center for youngsters like me. It offered courses in many artistic disciplines, gymnastics, music, writing, and even miniature-car racing. Mother wanted me to discover myself. I could see the Pioneer House from my window through the same bedroom window from which I'd witnessed the Soviet planes fly. After trying ballet, classical guitar, piano, violin, clay pottery, and drawing, I settled for photography. Mother bought me a Russian Ljubitel (which means "lover," "fan," "admirer," and "gourmet," but in this case, it was an amateur camera), and I learned to take pictures, develop negatives, and print black-and-white photos.

Before I became a lover of wisdom, I grew up as an amateur lover of Soviet lives. The Communist state—that great Platonic parent of us, we the pioneer children— paid for it all, and I was a happy child with a red scarf around my neck. And with the state by her side, Mother wasn't a single parent after all. When the thaw of 1967 sprang into a precocious January bloom, the new president of the republic was sworn in at the Prague Castle. And I was a young journalist there to cover the event! With my Russian "lover" and my red scarf on my white shirt, I convinced the secret police agents that I was to be admitted. The young, happy pioneer covered the swearing in of the Czechoslovak president, Svoboda, in 1968 in the Vladislavský Sál of the Prague Castle. I came that close to a significant Czechoslovak presidential inauguration once more in my life—when Václav Havel was "crowned" in Prague's Saint Vitus Cathedral in December 1989. That was twenty years later.

The year was 1969. I was growing up fast; the slowness of the Communist normalization period marked the last three grades of my primary schooling. My mother became a pariah, and we were pared down to the bare necessities of the working class. Paradise without classes was supposed to come for the sake of the workers; Mother, now an ex-Communist, was punished by being forced into a proletarian life. She earned income as a waitress at the Savarin restaurant, where a museum depicting the years under Communism sprang up after 1989. She also waited tables at the Dark Beer Brewery at Charles Square solely so she could bring food to our table and pay the bills. No literary grants or publications would be forthcoming. We might have emigrated like others did then, but I became neither Swedish nor French, as Mother once again opted to stay, as she did after 1945, when I could have been born Israeli or Australian.

Even as the normalization years of revenge on the Prague Spring reformers pulled Mother into poverty, I enjoyed the benefits of free medical and dental exams. We marched from my school to the district medical office for checkups, chest and dental X-rays, a TB test, and vaccinations. The Communist "parent" took care of the bills. I can still taste the substantial meals the primary-school kitchen cooked for us after class. The luxury for the Communist elite where Mother once enjoyed the writers' castles and resorts for the party nomenclature was out of reach for us now. Only the most cynical and ardent normalizers, the hardlime career Communists and state police agents, kept enriching themselves.

Yet there still existed communal vacation spots provided by the school and the party! With my school we visited ski lodges in the northern Bohemian mountains, and in the late spring, we hiked and swam in southern Bohemia. In the fall we helped at potato or hop harvests, and once we approached the hormone zone of puberty, those communal outings opened the gates of heaven that even Communism couldn't prohibit! The state paid for all communal vacations with my classmates, and we contributed our volunteer labor for the harvest. As long as girls were harvesting the Communist production, I worshiped the party's fertility gods and goddesses with dedication.

I hardly can find an unhappy childhood memory from my normalization years. Ironically it was during Husák's ugly era that we stabilized our home life, and I don't know whether to thank Mother or the state for my happy early teens. The patronizing state, boasting socialist solidarity with arms and secret police and forced labor, was a good parent to us, both orphans and children at large.

On the Edge of Time

Science fiction, like other myths we tell, often speaks deep truths about our lives. In my college years, I discovered two feminist science-fiction novels: one by Ursula K. Le Guin, *The Dispossessed,* and the other by Marge Piercy, *The Woman on the Edge of Time.* These books often returned my thoughts to the bleak years of normalization in Prague. Le Guin's story moves with its visionary physicist protagonist between lives on two planets, Anarres and Urras. The former is home to a colony of revolutionaries who left Urras and set up a cooperative form of life under the conditions of planetary scarcity and external threat from Urras. Inhabitants on Urras are owners and competitors whose lives resemble earthly lives as we know them. Piercy's story is about a Chicana woman, roughly my mother's age, locked up in a psychiatric hospital in New York. She is, however, quite sane, alert, and prophetically open to the future with two impending alternatives for the present to consider: a wondrous, unrepressed, receptive, solitary life versus a totalitarian, repressed, inflexibly bureaucratic life. In my young-adult self-told story, I thought of normalization on Anarres with Mother who, in silence, warded off annihilating chaos and lived on the edge of time.

I must have eagerly bracketed the real political pain of the normalization era with my mother's physical and mental absence. A boy's memory testifies in the adult, I admit rather one-sidedly, to what should not be lost in the wastebaskets of history. Had I been brought up by a parent from Urras, my life would have been like the one place in Le Guin's novel that resembles our humdrum world. The totalitarian normalization that Piercy feared came from the future. But then my Communist sex educators must have been partly from Anarres. Perhaps there was pornography or deviance also on my Anarres, and there were cases of sexual abuse. There were prostitutes in socialism, and hundreds more joined their ranks after the Velvet Revolution. In my era most of them labored for the state as spies on deviant capitalist visitors from Urras, and they earned hard currency. Rape, just as child abuse, was severely punished by the socialist courts. State homes and orphanages took children away from abusive parents, not to anyone's surprise, since the socialist Platonic state already was heavily invested in our parenting. The father state loved me unto death—even if my own parents abandoned me, I never could be orphaned in socialism. Such was the love for the state that some children in the 1950s publicly disowned their anti-Communist parents.

In my normalization the state and school welfare mitigated the dual shock of my lost mother and absent father, and Communist sex education arrived early. An exemplary couple from the Communist Party headquarters explained to the blossoming pubescent youth all about the beauty of creating a socialist family (sexual techniques were part of the instruction), the low cost of available contraceptives, and the free socialist availability of abortion on demand. Two years of paid maternal leave and paid kindergarten and preschool care were standard.

"Who needs abortion in such a world but those who were raped or stupid enough to get themselves pregnant without planning?" we were told.

The Communist pair placed at our disposal a detailed how-to of socialist lovemaking. They approached us at thirteen going on fourteen without any shame about ɔf the body. There was no prudery about nakedness, and sex was em-

ι aspect of socialist family values. They instructed us regarding the

ιυυιs ι guua and safe sex and about services.

They told us:

> Every medical center has a free sexual clinic for dispensing birth-
> control pills. For those who are ready to be responsible socialist par-
> ents, the state fully pays for maternity leave. You have job security
> after the leave. The state continues to care for your family with paid
> child-care centers and preschool education. If you get pregnant and
> do not want the child, you can get a safe medical abortion free and
> on demand. But if you learn to enjoy sex without fear, you will not
> have to be pregnant when you do not want it, and there is no need to
> use abortion as a means of birth control. Some people are unhappy in
> socialism, and they resort to sexual abuse or rape, so abortion is obvi-
> ously a way to terminate an unwanted child that has resulted from a
> sexual assault.

In socialism we had shortages of toilet paper but never of birth control. On my
Anarres we did not have to ask parents or the party for permission to do sexual
things. There were homosexuals and bisexuals in socialism, as on Anarres, and we,
the youth would experiment with sexual identity. Since it was Freud and not Marx
who judged that homosexual desire developmentally fixated at an early sexual stage,
no one on my Anarres tried to "cure" gays. They would turn gays into Communists
first, if they could. Such religious tribalism gained no social currency or power over
conscience. Nor was abstinence for gays and lesbians part of a socialist doctrine.

Sometime in the 1970s, condom machines were placed at every public Prague
Metro entrance as a proud sign of normalization. The country, producing its own
exported brand, Primeros, was ready to confront AIDS even before its arrival. In a
totalitarian state where all joy except cheap alcohol was regimented and supervised,
coupling might have been the only private act we could practice at home and in numerous semipublic spaces without fear of Big Brother, who most likely was doing the
same. In the bedrooms political enemies crossed battle lines, if not at night then during a lunch break at work. The vigorous sex life enjoyed by many people, along with
nonconformist apartment gatherings, was probably the freest part of my growing up

as a young adult in a totalitarian state. Sex became a shield to the terror and nihility of normalization and generated a unique bliss one rarely found elsewhere.

On Le Guin's Anarres, partnerships and renewed commitments are valued over possessive relationships, and marriage as a patriarchal institution belongs to the latter kind. On my Anarres, family was valued for social stability but not as a means to give meaning and place to women through the men they married. Women in the great majority, like Mother, had vocations. Some didn't marry but instead had a partner while enjoying all the economic benefits of coupling. The word *partner* was in vogue in my time to designate stable heterosexual relationships long before I heard it uttered by American feminists, lesbians, and gays. Mother once invited home a gay couple who had lived for years in a stable partnership, and I knew Communists were largely tolerant of gay subculture. In the end only sexually transmitted illnesses and parental abuse would become issues that could result in teens ending up in clinics or courts. My normalization was remarkably unrepressed thanks to the social openness of the father state and the open receptivity and freedom that guided Mother's love and parenting.

Angels of My Adolescence

At fourteen, a year before my mother became terminally ill, I thought seriously, though romantically, of committing suicide. Socialism couldn't eradicate existential anxiety and questioning. Even the collective socialist destiny of a species with its sexually unrepressed regime had no good answer to human demise and death. My desire to die mirrored the hollowness of the regime. Suicide would be but another side of my rebellion, an intuitive escape of the gestating self from the *pravda* of the surrounding world and its false religion. But I was too creative and curious about the world to kill myself out of teenage existential despair, even to fight the socialism without a human face. When my interest in the opposite sex awoke, instead of lodging with death, I embraced a twenty-year-old girl.

Mother placed no age or other obvious boundaries on my exploration of intimacy with other women. With no father figures present, she talked to me openly about what I hadn't learned on my own at school. She must have read her Freud and was determined to avoid the Oedipal pitfalls that would lead me to believe in the psychoanalytic myth that it was I who had banished the father and won the mother for myself. One rule applied at home: "Do whatever you want, but never lie to me!" Although honesty and openness were the most important commandment at home, I guarded my genuine secrets and self-discovery.

My first sexual journey began with heavy necking and petting sessions. While my twenty-year-old girlfriend wanted to teach me "everything," I was in no hurry, as if in my Eden-like state, I were anticipating what many a seasoned lover finds the most strenuous: restraint. I most enjoyed inhaling the smell of her hair, speaking with her into the late-night hours, and hugging her generous breasts tightly in never-ending embraces. The street boys in Bratislava never had taught me about this bliss! The girl—curly blond hair, medium height, dark eyes, and a broad smile—was a friend of my mother's, and I first met her at home. The girl was wild and sweet and in all ways precocious, and she was one of the first angels of my adolescence. When her older boyfriend was mean to her, she would come home and "play" with me.

"You are my sweet, young Martin," she used to say. And I was glad to be that for her.

By the book I was still a virgin, though quite aware of what my body could and wanted to do. The eternity of embraces and deep kisses and touches still cast more tender spells over me than the promised intercourse. Like the early teens on Anarres, I felt unashamed and free to do "everything" with her; I explored her intricate landscapes, but I was not in a hurry to reach the summit. It was as if I intuited in this never-ending foreplay heaven's way to cheat death: "In heaven we will not marry but will be like angels."

The girl didn't seem to mind my desire to prolong the foreplay; perhaps no tender woman ever does, and after all, she had an older boyfriend who desired only one thing. Her tender visits to my bedroom were my first epiphanies of sexual intimacy. She taught me in my youth what many a woman might long for in her mature lover— that there are infinitely happy ways to be with another in total, guilt-free physical receptivity; that such embraces of enduring play can be beautiful and, as some religions boldly teach, even sacred. This angel had been sent to my sacred bubble to confirm the prototype of Mother's receptive love in ways no parent ever could reveal directly.

I don't know how much Mother knew about my secret lessons in the arts of loving.

Mother must have been a wise parent from another planet, a woman on the edge of her time, I would think regarding these times. *She cared for and nurtured my joy under the conditions of an oppressive state.*

The Holocaust Memorial Museum (1945 and the 1990s)

It is several years before Patricia and I will have moved to Chicago. I commute on weekends from Purdue to Washington, D.C., to be with Patricia, who teaches at American University. I've been teaching at Purdue since 1991. On one weekend in the capital, she and I visit the Holocaust Memorial Museum.

But she was not *Jewish,* I keep convincing myself, the boy with secrets enveloping his mother.

No, she was first an intellectual and a Communist, then a spiritualist, I assure this boy voice.

On my second visit to the Holocaust Museum, I walk to the library. I browse randomly through open stacks, where I discover a publication by the American Joint Distribution Committee, published on October 15, 1945. I examine the registry of "all persons saved from anti-Jewish persecution while living in Slovakia" between March 1939 and April 1945. My mouth soundlessly spells the letter *B*:

Beck-ová	Helena (1904) Myjava	Father, Maximilian, née Pressburger
	Magdalena (1928) Myjava	Father, Pavel
	Arnošt (1931) Myjava	Father, Pavel
	Pavel (1899) Myjava	Father, Jakob

I recognize at once Mother's year of birth and her name, Magdalena, among the only surviving repatriated Jewish persons listed in Myjava after April 1945. The rest are her family, her brother Ernest (Arnošt), her father Pavel (Nathan), and her mother Helena (Ilonka).

Who were my Jewish ancestors? I wonder. *What was their Slovak story? What was the lifeline that slept dormant in silence? Why was knowledge of their wartime persecution denied to me?*

Each museum visitor receives a passport with the story of one Jew from the time during the Holocaust. This is intended to help guests identify in a personal way with the various phases of the anti-Jewish persecution documented by the exhibition. I begin to read this museum's story as *my* story. *The stories and photos of my relatives could have been on some of these passport booklets distributed to visitors of the museum!*

At this moment I know nothing of Mother's story. I don't know that she had cousins, uncles, or aunts. On our third visit in the memorial with out-of-town guests,

I examine posters from Hitler's 1936 Olympic Games in Germany. I have grown new eyes since my last visit. I see a Jew sketched as a black man. Jews and African-American sportsmen are depicted as degenerates. Slavs are listed right along with Jews, gypsies, blacks, homosexuals, Communists, and other degenerate groups.

Years later Uncle Ernest confirmed my initial foreboding about Mother's silence: *The Holocaust marked our entire family!* The physical annihilation of my ancestors left a void, and now something new begins to live within me. I drink life with new senses—those papillae, taste buds, and microvilli that hurry messages to the brain, so that it knows whether something is sweet, sour, bitter, or salty. And for the first time, I question Mother with anger, disbelief, and horror-stricken awe.

"The Only Window to the Site of the Holocaust"

According to the Turkish Va'ad ha-Hazalah Jewish rescue committee, the daring rescue mission of the Working Group in Slovakia had been "the only window to the site of the Holocaust" during the 1940s. The apparent success of the bribery scheme by Gisi, Andrej, and Reb Dov grew into what became known as the "Europa Plan."

From the trial of Adolf Eichmann in Jerusalem on May 23, 1961:

> THE STATE ATTORNEY BACH: Wisliceny then talks about the contacts between him and engineer Steiner and Mrs. Gisi Fleischmann in connection with the negotiations to save Slovak Jewry...the whole of European Jewry.

From the trial and testimony of Dieter Wisliceny in Nuremberg on January 3, 1946:

> LT. COL. BROOKHART: Will you describe to the tribunal the approximate periods and the different types of activity?

> WISLICENY: Until 1940 the general policy within the section was to settle the Jewish question in Germany and in areas occupied by Germany by means of a planned emigration. The second phase, after that date, was the concentration of all Jews, in Poland and in other

territories occupied by Germany in the East, in ghettos. This period lasted approximately until the beginning of 1942. The third period was the so-called "final solution" of the Jewish question—that is, the planned extermination and destruction of the Jewish race; this period lasted until October 1944, when Himmler gave the order to stop their destruction.

7

CONVERSION AND DISSENT

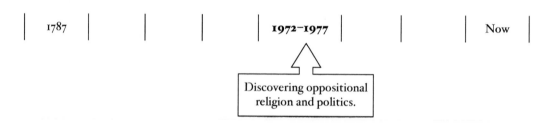

| 1787 | | | | 1972–1977 | | | Now |

Discovering oppositional
religion and politics.

After my mother's death, my newly discovered religiousness becomes a springboard for my dissent. I become involved with an underground Catholic church and meet students of the Czech philosopher Jan Patočka, who in 1977 issued with Václav Havel and Jiří Hájek the manifesto for human rights *Charta 77*. Cunning as I venture through the Communist windmills, I live through the moral gray zones between collaboration with the regime and the loss of my future and ultimately survive while losing my adolescent innocence.

My Catholic Passions (1972–1977)

I can't pinpoint how in 1972 I first tasted the excitement of the Prague Catholic underground. I discovered it neither through my high-school teachers nor Mother's friends. The MJ family boasted eight children, with two more on the way. My adopted Catholic mother took me in as her eleventh, and at fifteen I became a regular guest in the MJ family house. I cherished the classical music they played at home; I admired their Christian antiques; I partook in the intellectual debates. The clandestine atmosphere was thick with an incense of dissent. Even under Communism, Catholic life flourished in such cultured homes. And grown children imitated their parents by having children. Life was to be lived and celebrated! Catholic family structures would become effective shields against the ever-present Communist state and omniscient secret police.

Not knowing of my mother's Jewish origins, I converted to Catholic life through the MJ family's matrilineage. My Catholic conversion would take place within this marvelous environment. My new way of life became intertwined with the loves of sophisticated culture and Christian care. And my love blended with great fondness for the teenage daughters whom I met too late in life to be able to think of them only in a brotherly way—as just my Christian sisters. Female figures populated my adolescence—faces of divine kindness, the guardian angels that life sent in my direction. Three MJ girls stirred my passion: the guitar player, the biologist, and the educator. I dreamed about all three as each came of maturity, but I secretly loved the one who played classical guitar.

I was baptized in Prague. As if to reinforce the maternal epiphany of G-d, I was flanked by two godmothers at my side, Mother MJ and K., a woman who figured into the life of the MJ family as a spiritual visionary. I held secret admiration in my heart for the three eldest daughters, but I had no godfather, save for the one I sought in heaven.

I call my conversion a "doubly dissenting" religiosity because its practices challenged both the Communist and religious establishments. The state power forced on churches the pledges of allegiance to the regime through clergy who wanted to retain certain privileges. *Pacem in Terris* (Peace on Earth) was a group created to provide a "Communist" affiliation for the clergy, as they couldn't belong to the party. For different reasons than in Latin America's liberation theology or the worker-priest movement, the Vatican threatened to excommunicate priests who affiliated with the

party. Eventually a truce evolved, and many priests joined the state religious grouping in order to have parishes. The Vatican, concerned for the survival of the Church,
justified its acquiescence. Those priests who joined the organization were dubbed
"*Pacáci*" (short for "*Pacem in Terris*"). One would accept from them public sacraments
but perhaps not a confession that in some cases could have been just as well made to
the secret service.

During the Cold War, the Vatican began to secretly ordain bishops, who would
go on to secretly ordain priests. The underground church flourished alongside the
official one, and many innovations in liturgy, forms of life, Christian pastoral care,
and theology emerged in the structures that for reasons of its clandestine operation
had little Vatican oversight. After 1989 it became difficult to integrate the Catholic
underground back into the church structures that until then had collaborated with
the regime. Those priests who under Communism happily embodied various "irregu-
larities" posed a problem to the Church, which couldn't just shun the clergy that
suffered because of their faith. Yet how could the Vatican accept what it deemed to
be unorthodox forms that mutated in anti-Communist incubators? These mutants
were the Catholic priests and nuns who became too ecumenical and open to other
religions, bishops who secretly ordained married men and, in one known case, who
secretly ordained a female Catholic bishop who secretly ordained female priests. The
Church could neither uncreate these mutants who had received indelible ordination
oils nor simply invalidate the oils, succession rituals, and their sanctifications.

Religion was exciting under Communism because living it in any form posed
dangers to the state power. To be into things "religious" meant being heroic. What
young man would not dream of that? Being brought up in a proudly atheistic state,
I hungered along with others for great metaphysical questions. *What is the origin of
the universe? Does human life end with the death of the body? Is the positivist-materialism of
Marx, Lenin, and Engels, in which all mental and spiritual reality reflects self-evolving complex matter, the final answer to the origins and ends of existence?*

Instead of going out with me on a date, the guitar-playing MJ daughter I loved
decided to wed an engineer and asked me to be the man of honor at her wedding.
I never married one of the MJ daughters; one by one, each Catholic girl chose a securely established young man, each fellow coming with an implied promise that he
could support a growing family. I was a young poet/philosopher, a poor prospect for a
fertile field. My mother taught me love through the void left by her death; the Greek
god Eros taught me love by having me endure then let go of unrequited love. At the

wedding I danced all afternoon with a girl from another distinguished Catholic family. Years later I was at Christmas in Prague; my youthful unrequited love and I were now in our fifties, and she was the mother of numerous children.

"Do you know about the sufferings of the young Martin?" the Goethe within me asked her.

"I am blushing," she said with a laugh. She disappeared to another room and returned with a young woman at her side.

"But that is..." Now it was my time to blush because the girl's face was unmistakable.

"Meet my friend from America." The grown-up MJ daughter introduced us, and we shook hands.

"Martin, nice to meet you." My heart leaped with memory evoked by the daughter of the girl with whom I had danced away the best man's sorrows.

"Martin used to know your mom," my unrequited love said mischievously.

Say hallo to your mother, I blurted silently. *She'll probably tell her mom.*

After the MJ wedding party, the man of honor walked his dancer home. They kissed every few meters, all the way through the Royal Gardens at the Prague Castle, under the passage near the dark beer pub U Černého Vola, ending their tryst in the doorway to her house, over which two baroque angels still hover in welcome. They stood pressing each other for a long time in the dark corner of the entrance. It was in that tight embrace that eternity multiplied itself in intensity, as if to banish the wounded shadow of unhappy love. When his body no longer would accept postponed pleasure, and when she who actively rejoiced in it laughed with that unforgettably victorious voice of a "bad" Catholic girl who knew of her magic charms even as she protected her virginity, and when he stepped out from the dark hideout with his best man's wedding pants soiled by happiness, he no longer felt his love's sorrows.

I would meet other Catholic girls, and they gave me more of their warmth than their protected virginity could contain. I received their offerings of tenderness, letting them keep the prize for their wedding day. I didn't marry any of them. As I was first smitten by the feminine face of G-d, the spirit of the Jewish Shekinah arrived in a Christian shape. Shekinah, however, had other plans for me. On that sweetly unhappy wedding night that wasn't meant for me, two intensities—love's woes and its ecstatic embrace—melded into one. Walking home in that night's fullness, the man of honor looked up from the Loreta Monastery in the direction of the foreign ministry at Černín Palace and wondered whether the KGB had pushed the foreign minister, Jan Masaryk, from the window or whether he had jumped all by himself in those dramatic events that anticipated the Communist takeover in 1948. Years later, back in Prague, I'll walk by the Black Bull Pub. I'll see the baroque angels who survived my youthful pain and several regime changes with their heavenly wings intact. Offering thanksgiving for gifts of love, I'll greet limestone witnesses who record the passage of time.

My Life as Jaromil

During my four high-school years at the Prague gymnasium, I acquired a taste for orating poetry. The school called on me to give ornate recitations at public events. I won national prizes for my performances, and with a poet's fame, I grew long, wild, curly hair and incorporated ever-riskier authors for that era into my repertoire. I chose ideologically safe poets who wrote double-edged texts, balancing between adulating and confronting the regime. In the Russian empire, I grew fond of Dostoyevsky, Chekhov, Majakovskij, and the prohibited Yevtusenko. The true shocker arrived with my recitation of the classic Slovak poem about the local Robin Hood, Jánošík, *"Mor Ho!"* ("Get Him! Kill Him!") With that poem's declamation, I won the coveted National Socialist Youth Prize in poetry performance. Just as the Iranians on the rooftops shouted, *"Allahu Akbar!"* ("G-d is great!"), submitting while defying the clerical regime, so I cried out, *"Mor ho!"* I sent shivers down the spines of censors and teachers who didn't know how the cadence of the poem or my enthusiasm should be interpreted, sanctioned, or opposed.

Jaromil (the lover of spring), from Milan Kundera's novel *Life Is Elsewhere*, is a pathetic, young, socialist poet with romantic longings for the party, mother figures, and female bodies he never can possess. I was a bit of a failed Jaromil who rejected the early advances of the party and whose poetic pathos was suffused with antiauthoritarian sentiments. I cherished my status as a single adolescent with his own flat in Prague. I embraced becoming a young man in charge of my life, which gave me the freedom not only to host parties and secret nonconformist gatherings but also to begin dating seriously.

Gymnasium sophomores learned classic ballroom dancing. The ever-caring Communist parent—after delivering us in free clinics, vaccinating us, nursing us in preschools and kindergartens, marching us to medical and dental checkups, making us literate, feeding us at comrade kitchens, educating us about the joys of sex and socialist family planning—groomed our social skills and public manners. Oh, the Communist Party, that faithful governess who left no area untouched by its loving surveillance!

I attended yearlong dancing and etiquette lessons in the beautiful Obecní Dům, the Municipal House built in the Art Nouveau style and known for its classical-music concerts and ballroom dancing held in Smetana Hall. The inner walls of Municipal House are adorned with Alphonse Mucha's paintings, which depict the heroic history of the Czech people and the Slavic Concord. The wall panels portray Slavic youth swearing their allegiance to their mother nation. This is where many Prague high schools chose to form our souls and bodies into future citizens of the socialist motherland.

The dancing and public life of the Communist era preserved some facets of the bourgeois lifestyle of the Austrian-Hungarian monarchy and of the first Czechoslovak Republic. In the typical gray simplicity of those days, we were assigned our dancing partners for the year. We were prescribed the dancing attire from head to toe (dark suit, white dress shirt, bow tie, black dancing shoes) and were taught how to comport ourselves within this splendid architecture.

I got along with my assigned female partner, and as I moved her along on the dance floor, she was a great conversationalist. I learned my waltz, polka, *ča-ča*, and foxtrot, and after our graduation ball, my dancing partner and I decided to lose our virginity in my flat. Communist-era youths that we were, we had inherited no hang-ups. In our nakedness there was nothing hidden, dirty, or anxious, even as we knew that our first lovemaking likely would be our last night together. After I had prolonged my years of foreplay just long enough for my dance partner to melt in a young Christian convert's arms, lacking sufficient amounts of Catholic guilt, we reached our socialist maturity together. Culminating in the year in which the state had paired us up to dance, we ended our manner lessons with gusto, deliberation, and caring for each other as we stepped into free adulthood.

Along with dance and etiquette classes, we attended music-appreciation courses. Our musicology teacher was a sophisticated thirty-year-old graduate of the Prague Conservatory.

"Is she a *soudružka?*" the boys would joke among themselves, learning to use the Czech word for "comrade" in ways that carried an ambiguous aroma of intimacy and political danger. Although this comrade teacher's name has vanished from my mind,

I still see the boy who easily confused his taste for Bach and Beethoven with the sight of lean legs barely hidden from view by a miniskirt.

"She must be a *soudružka*." The sight of her skin would resolve our doubts. I append to my memory a text from Herbert Marcuse's 1969 manifesto: "And the young also attacked the spirit of seriousness in the socialist camp: miniskirts against the *apparatchiks*, rock 'n' roll against Soviet realism."[25]

Surviving the invasion of 1968 were the homegrown feminist and gay movements and, when the spring digits inverted into the velvet fall of 1989, delayed sexual revolutions. The Berlin Wall came down; Eastern European women raised the hemlines of their miniskirts; and men let their hair grow long.

In our music-appreciation classes, the front row was a privileged place for boys who could muscle their way in. Our beautiful female comrade musicologist sat sideways on the elevated theater stage where I had recited "*Mor Ho!*" and where the party delivered speeches. Seated with her chest profile proudly erect, she played fugues and romantic and dissonant tunes on an old record player and guided us through the movements of classical-music theory.

Thanks to my early language education, the Russian and English lessons became wonderful immersions in literature, history, and culture. The Russian classics inspired dissent from the Soviet empire. And when Alexander Solzhenitsyn's book *The Gulag Archipelago, 1918-1956* became available in circulated *Samizdat* editions, always for one or two nights of reading time, those Russian language skills became my prized possession. Our comrade English teacher felt comfortable using his language lessons as an excuse to bring newspaper clippings from foreign papers and magazines as well as selections from British and American literature. He dug out from somewhere an Australian native speaker who became our regular conversation guest. We also sang many English-language songs in our lessons: "My Bonny Lies over the Ocean," "Old MacDonald Had a Farm," "We Shall Overcome," and the English carol about *our* "Good King Wenceslas," which we intoned with great patriotic fervor.

My Czech Friend Is Jewish

"I didn't realize she was Jewish," I told my high-school friend Radko after the Iron Curtain crumbled and we met as adults in Prague. I knew the vague truth about my grandparents, but I had lived unaware of the Jewish origins Radko and I shared. My brother's schoolboy friend, Peter Baruch, also was Jewish. Peter and his brother were children of Holocaust survivors; their parents and our mother were friends. Both families hid the truth of their origins and persecution from their children. After Peter's family left for Israel sometime in the 1960s, my brother lost all contact with them.

Radko and I were the two boys protected by our high school principal, Marie Kubátová.

"There was a serious political crisis over my antiauthoritarian pranks in nineteen seventy-six," Radko said. "It happened during our last year, when I stopped coming to school. They wanted to kick me out right before my graduation exams because of my poem 'My Grandfather.'"

"But you won the poem competition," I said.

"The poem had Jewish overtones," he replied. "The vice principal cried when I recited it."

"Why were you called to her office?" I asked.

"She made one gesture without saying a word."

"What do you mean?" I asked.

"She silently rolled up her sleeve and showed me a number tattooed on her skin."

The principal was a survivor of the Nazi camp at Terezín, and either she had spoken with my mother or intuited more about my origins than I knew.

My Double Life

When the five-day workweek was introduced, the Communist Party turned every other Saturday into a measure of our patriotism. We cleaned up neighborhood streets or parks, helped in factories, and attended extra catechism lessons in civics. The May Day parades after 1968 became routines of discipline and punishment. The roll call would be taken in places where one worked or went to school, and one's presence in the march would be ensured for a while by the party-appointed human "sheepdogs" who herded us in, but by the time the parade reached the bottom of Vinohradská near the National Museum, it couldn't be kept together. The herd thinned out as fast as the hair receding on Lenin's head. The marching remnant calling for the victory of Communism or for eternal life with the Soviet Union, passing by the main tribune at Můstek at the bottom of Wenceslas Square, became but a lame stream of the most faithful or scared. The fake joy below the tribune showcased the convex mirror reflecting Communist gerontology's faint smiles from its main podium.

I lived a double life as a Christian religious activist and socialist orator, reciting in socialist competitions, studying sacred texts in secret. I could have blown my gymnasium diploma were it not for my Russian teacher, who skillfully stirred me from Comrade Stalin to the literary classics. I finished high school with combined written and oral maturity exams and passed with distinction. The exam subjects were Czech and world literature, English, Russian, and biology. On the same day and roughly at the same time, written exam questions were hand delivered from the ministry of education to high schools in the Czech and Slovak Republics. We tried to predict questions in relation to the main political events or anniversaries (e.g., Gagarin's space mission, the Communist revolution in Czechoslovakia, the Soviet liberation from the Nazis). In 1976 we anticipated the upcoming sixtieth anniversary of the Soviet Revolution of 1917 and the twentieth anniversary of Nikita Khrushchev's Soviet Communist Party Congress. I almost ruined my future during my oral exam in Russian when I described in great detail how at this congress Chairman Khrushchev had unmasked the Soviet Stalin personality cult. The fact was an open and accepted truth in our history books. Since the Soviet invasion in 1968, this truth became more muffled. We were reading into Khrushchev, provocatively if not prophetically, the arrival of the Soviet spring. My exams took place twenty years before Gorbachev became the bearer of the Soviet spring known as perestroika.

"Martin always has held great love for *all* Soviet Party Congresses," my teacher said, fabricating evidence for the official visitor from the ministry of education.

Like getting placed in a decent secondary school at a language gymnasium, entering higher education wasn't a foregone result of earning good grades. I couldn't count on my grades even with my highly selective language program and help from my protectors. In a letter dated May 17, 1970, written to a friend in Stockholm, Mother expressed her certainty that because of her break with the Communist Party, I never would be admitted to good secondary schools and universities.

> *Martin says that he and I live as "students"—he just bought himself a book by A. Huxley and is very focused on it and praises it very much. I am almost certain that he cannot [yet] understand it. But since, thanks to his mother, he has minimal hope for a normal course of study, let his soul take what it can and where it can.*

What she wrote about my precocious hunger for books became pronounced after her death. Unlike our peers in the free world who often dream walked through high school, in our circumstance true education was the forbidden fruit and for that reason alone a desirable one. Many young people under Communism became highly educated privately, though they never found a chance to develop vocationally acquired intellectual skills. These youngsters joined the adults branded by normalization in a period that turned the Communist dream into a vast prison-industrial society. I met friends from this early era when I returned to Prague after 1989. For many of them, it was too late to close the twenty-year gap during which university education or professional development had been denied to them.

My Teen Gray Zones

In 1976 I graduated with excellent grades from the gymnasium and was admitted to my first year of psychology study at Charles University. The bare fact of my admission to this university hid a dark secret I've never told before.

As I mentioned, entering a university wasn't a foregone conclusion of having succeeded in high school. During that time, three groups gained affirmative-action privileges during admission: children of prominent Communists in good standing, children of the working class or farm or mine workers, and young Communists themselves. Under the first category, I fared far worse than if my parents never had considered joining the Communist Party. I also could claim no proletarian roots: Father was a son of a hardware-store owner from Moravia, but given Father's own sins, it was long forgotten that his father had been a founding member of the Communist Party in his village. The fact that Mother had abandoned the party was the key issue, however, and I have no clue whether any police dossier contained information about her parents' Jewish-bourgeois household in the 1930s. Unless I dirtied my bourgeois soul with the material dust of hard labor, I would be stuck with my discredited parents in a caste of untouchables. In addition there were children of prominent parents as well as children of secret police agents who could get into the party easier than I could, had I wanted to. Since 1969 the party had ensured the loyalty of its membership ranks. Apart from joining the party or the secret service, I might have bribed someone in order to get into a university, but I had no resources to do so.

In my senior high-school year, I rented a room in my flat to a famous psychology professor, Dr. Milan Nakonečný, who had been expelled from Charles University as part of the normalization purges in the 1970s. He became one of my father figures and my private tutor. As a specialist not only in psychology but also in occult arts and Kabala, he passed on to me what he knew during our evening conversations. I read many of his unpublished works. In my senior year, he prepared me for my university entrance exams, and I scored number one out of approximately 150 applicants. I was among the top applicants in psychology at Charles University in 1976. This alone, however, could not overcome my disastrous parental dossier, as it was much more difficult to erase my family sins at the university level. The pliable intelligentsia would benefit from the regime; the cunning ones who undermined it had to be crushed.

Although I had scored number one on my entrance exams, had earned excellent grades from my gymnasium, and was an orphan with a dossier from an educational psychologist secured by Mrs. Holá, even these qualifications weren't enough in the mid-1970s to get me into the university. These were the years of the normalization purges of all suspicious intellectual elites and their offspring, and my parents had been the first victims of those purges. It immensely harmed me that I was a child of prominent, now fallen Communists. I could not bribe one, and I would not become one either. I took a riskier gamble when I had the opportunity to have sex with a highly placed Communist who significantly would improve my chances for university admission.

At age eighteen I started my university career as a one-night prostitute for the male Communist deputy to the minister of education. I have repressed memories of the details and don't recall how the priest who baptized me at age fifteen introduced me to his friend, another Catholic priest in Karlovy Vary, who then pimped me for the promise of getting me into the university. I remember that one of the priests asked me whether I was ready to go into the "lion's den" as a price for education. Not knowing the meaning of the biblical reference to Daniel's struggle with the lion, I consented that yes, I would go into that den. He then gave me a phone number to call in Prague. It was the evening after our rehearsal for the gymnasium graduation ball at Prague's ornate Lucerna Hall, which had been expropriated from the Havel family in the 1948 Communist takeover. Because of my oratory skills, I had been chosen unanimously to be the master of ceremonies for the entire gymnasium, and on that rehearsal night, I had worn a new suit I had purchased in Krakow for this special ball. I dialed the number from a booth in Wenceslas Square. I heard a man on the receiving end. I entered the lion's den in Prague 10, still not fully grasping the implications.

I was not unlike a naïve girl who was in denial as to what she was exposing herself to by consenting to visit a man alone in his home. When I arrived, however, it became clear that what the lion wanted was my body in exchange for his influencing my admission to the university. With a Faustian pact that was just as dangerous for him in Communism (perhaps not as dangerous as when homosexuals were sent to Nazi death camps along with Jews, gypsies, Communists, and the disabled) as it was compromising for me, I let the Communist deputy to the minister of education peel off my velvet suit (I wore it on the rehrearsal night) and have his way with me so that I could fulfill my higher-education dream. There was nothing particularly dangerous about his den or odd about him. His desire was just that of a homosexual man to whom the oppressive regime didn't offer opportunities to live his sexual identity openly. Using a power position to get young flesh wasn't a privileged domain of gay persons.

This was my moral gray zone: I was not raped; I consented; I sold myself in a high-stakes game; and yet in trading my future, I harmed myself. It is thanks to Primo Levi's compassion for the human worst and best while surviving Auschwitz that I found the language and courage to place my wounded deliverance on the Passover plates.[26]

Was I thinking somewhere deep in my mind that "fucking" the Communist regime somehow would be morally better than being "done" by it for life? At the time I justified my act as a rebellion. I'll never know which of the three factors ensured my university entrance: my number-one entrance scores, my special dossier and orphan status, or my giving my body for a university placement. I knew that had I been deceived, I could not protest, certainly not to my baptismal reverend father, but I could suffer harm if the deputy thought I would extort him. My vulnerability to the power for which he stood—not the extracted sexual favor—is why his lion's den had been so dangerous.

When I received my admission letter, it was a late-spring day and also the day of our gymnasium's graduation ball. As the master of ceremonies, I spoke to a full house of several hundred students and teachers. I danced that night with my classmates and favorite teachers. The night was young after the ball because we were young. I walked with my cohort over Charles Bridge in those hours when night yields to daybreak. And we sang under the baroque sculpture of the crucified. Like dancing halos, the gold Hebrew letters above the sculpture, leaped from the bridge to the castle, proclaiming messianic hope to the large medieval Jewish population that once had lived in Prague. The hope of the city belonged to us. We ended the trek in my flat, where we drank and sang until the morning hours. Still in our dancing attire, after a night of debauchery, we dragged ourselves to school. Ecstatic about my future, I soon forgot the treacherous path that had led to it. A few weeks ago, I had sold my young body for higher education. *Did I sell my soul?* That question would return in less than a year.

The Communist Windmills

In 1977, as a second-semester student of psychology, I attended several of Professor Jan Patočka's home seminars, the so-called "Jan Patočka's Flying University." I knew something was being "cooked up" in various dissident circles, but the actual nature of the planned action was kept in strict secrecy to prevent direct interference from the secret police.

Before World War II, Patočka had studied with philosophers Edmund Husserl and Martin Heidegger in Freiburg, Germany. The Moravian-born Husserl was, like Kafka, a German–speaking and writing Jew and is known as the founder of modern phenomenology. Husserl switched from math to philosophy for his doctoral studies under the influence of his Czech friend, Tomáš Garigue Masaryk, who became the first modern Czechoslovak president after the Austrian-Hungarian monarchy fell apart. Masaryk earned his PhD in philosophy in Vienna after the end of World War I and became a revered politician and influential theorist of democracy in Central Europe. A biographical-historical line binds two modern Czechoslovak president-philosophers, President Masaryk and President Havel, with philosopher Patočka as their intellectual middle term. Husserl and Masaryk weren't only countrymen by birth but also both studied with Franz Brentano and earned PhDs in philosophy in Vienna. Husserl, perhaps under Masaryk's influence, converted from Judaism to Lutheranism. After the Nazis seized power in Germany, Husserl had to give up his university post even as a Jewish convert to Lutheranism. Heidegger, one of his prized and famous students, did nothing to stop this disgrace; on the contrary, in the 1930s he became a convinced member of the Nazi party and, for a time, at the early years of the new regime, a pro-Hitler rector of Freiburg University. Heidegger dreamed, naïvely to be sure, of becoming the Führer's philosophical leader so as to guide the Nazi movement into national renewal. Soon after he discovered that the Nazis were primitive beasts bent on pure power and conquest, Heidegger retreated from Freiburg to his Black Forest hut, where he spent most of the war.

Patočka, influenced by both philosophers, learned from Husserl as much as from Heidegger, the latter's momentary political infatuation with the Nazi regime notwithstanding. Patočka created a unique Czech brand of phenomenology—a form of philosophy with ethical interest. The Czech reception of Heidegger found in Patočka and his students a humanistic stamp. On behalf of the Prague Linguistic Circle, Patočka invited Husserl in 1935 to Prague to give his famous lecture "Philosophy and the Crisis of European Man." The presentation foreshadowed the cataclysmic events that would consume Europe in World War II. Patočka attempted to find a teaching post at Charles University for his mentor, Husserl, who had been dismissed from Freiburg because he was a Jew. Husserl died in 1938, and Hitler occupied the Czech border regions, the Sudetenland. This was one year before the full Nazi occupation of Czechoslovakia, and Patočka thought he would be able to save the Husserl archives in Prague. On March 15, 1939, when Hitler's forces invaded and occupied the country, however, this became impossible, and Professor H.L. Van Breda brought the archives to Louvain, Belgium. The phenomenological movement was ejected twice from its philosophical birthplace: when the Nazis closed Czech universities, from 1939 to 1945, and with the Communist demonization of phenomenology from 1948 to 1989.

After the war Patočka taught at Charles University until 1948, when the Communist regime took over, then briefly during the Prague Spring until the normalization years put an end to his career. For the rest of his working life, he did research in archives on the pedagogical writings of Jan Ámos Komenský (Comenius) and directed private seminars.

Patočka's last public political act occurred when he showed his support of the prosecuted Czech rock band The Plastic People of the Universe and ultimately became the intellectual founder of *Charta 77*, the manifesto and movement for human rights in Czechoslovakia. The text of the manifesto was influenced by phenomenology from Husserl to Emmanuel Lévinas yet written largely by Patočka. It called on all citizens to assume personal responsibility for the state of their nation and also called on the Communist government to adhere to the human-rights declarations it had signed and ratified in various international and UN protocols and forums. The manifesto was issued in homemade editions in Prague on January 1, 1977, and signed by sixty-year-old philosophy professor Jan Patočka, playwright Václav Havel, and Jiří Hájek, the minister of foreign affairs under Alexander Dubček's government.

Some notables among Patočka's students and later signatories of *Charta 77* were the father-and-son philosophers Radim and Martin Palouš (the former was the first rector of Charles University after 1989; the latter served after 1989 as the foreign minister deputy and later as the Czech ambassador to the United States and the Czech ambassador to the United Nations under the George W. Bush administration); Václav and Ivan Havel (Ivan, a cybernetics specialist, started the Center for Theoretical Study, a think tank, after 1989); Jan Sokol (dean of the faculty of humanities of Charles University); Tomáš Halík, Pavel Kouba, and Ivan Chvatík (the latter two are philosophers and cotranslators of Heidegger's *Being and Time* into Czech).

On New Year's Day 1977, typed carbon copies of the manifesto were mailed to the central Czechoslovak government and Communist Party offices, to newspapers throughout the country, and smuggled out to papers abroad, and one copy of the Manifesto was intended for the Party secretary Gustav Husák. (As noted in chapter 4, the word *Samizdat*—"самиздат," meaning "made by myself"—is Russian because this self-made dissident form of publishing originated in Russia.) Václav Havel was arrested on the way to Husák, and his *Charta* copy was confiscated. I saw the confiscated exemplar in the 2002 exhibition at Prague's National Museum that featured *Samizdat* productions of Eastern European dissent. While the government kept silent for days about the very existence of *Charta 77*, as if hoping it would go away, the full manifesto was read on the evening of its release on Voice of America and Radio Free Europe. About a thousand people were among the first signatories of *Charta 77*. Most of them were active and established dissidents and various ex-political personages of the normalization era willing to risk persecution. Marx's claim about the revolutionary role of the proletariat, the only class that had nothing to lose but its chains, became true of Eastern European dissent, which acted as if it had nothing to lose but the state prison that held them. Had Mother been alive, she would have been among its signatories. The list of signatures grew with greater speed than the secret agents could manage to arrest people; it was a wildfire! I was reminded of the empty tomb of Jan Palach—how much this secular regime feared spiritual realities! Perhaps the militantly atheistic establishment wasn't bereft of beliefs. There was nothing remotely materialist about its fear.

Havel was arrested right away. Whenever spokespersons were arrested, died, or could not continue, others were named to replace them. The self-organized dissident movement named three new spokespersons in the fall of 1977: Christian philosopher Ladislav Hejdánek, opposition singer Marta Kubišová, and reformed Communist politician and writer Jaroslav Šabata. Creating a self-perpetuating chain of public spokespersons showed the genius of *Charta 77*. From 1977 to 1989, the regime never managed to disrupt this continuity. The state's persecution never was able to prevent this line, even with repeated and often preemptive strikes on dissidents. The government-controlled media began by condemning the extremist minority of self-invited elites, hooligans, and enemies of "the people." All media denigraded the *Charta* pamphlet yet without ever citing or publishing its text. Just as when my parents had to sign petitions exhorting the execution of Czech politician Milada Horáková on charges of conspiracy and treason, signatures were being collected at workplaces and in schools against *Charta*. Various socialist groups—from pioneers to old ladies, from comrades at cooperative farms to teachers and soldiers—competed with emotional letters against the movement, which were published and broadcast daily.

As with the state's hiding of Jan Palach's body, writing excessively about *Charta* without ever citing from the document, the state indirectly created a promotion campaign that would solidify the opposition. The official vilification never broke the dissident organization even with long prison sentences for its leaders. Václav Havel alone endured several prison sentences. In 2003 I met architect Vlado Milunić, who had designed, in cooperation with Frank Gehry, the Dancing House building near the Mánes art gallery on the Vltava River. During the *Charta 77* period, he built for Václav a special "home jail" writing room so that he wouldn't find switching between home and prison so traumatic. The real prison was no joke, but Czechs never tire of turning such burdens unbearably light.

New *Charta* documents were drafted and efficiently distributed through *Samizdat* channels. These were political, social, religious, cultural, and economic analyses of the Soviet regime and its institutions. They appeared with periodic regularity and sophistication from 1977 until 1989, thus gradually preparing the ground for a transitional government. *Charta 77* became the main dissident grouping of the late 1970s and 1980s, gathering ex-Communists; reformed Communists; anti-Communists; socialist-market economists; recognized as well as secret religious figures, priests, and rabbis of various communities; housewives; students; artists; intellectuals; and many workers. It was the only group that twelve years later would be ready to assume the leadership role in the revolutionary events of 1989. No one could even imagine this future possible in those scary, hopelessly gloomy

1970s. Just as the efficacy of the assassination of Reinhard Heydrich, Hitler's right hand in the Protectorate of Bohemia and Moravia, was often evaluated against the persecution that resulted after the act (such as the annihilation of the Czech village Lidice, which supposedly had hidden the Czech assassins who had come from Britain), so *Charta 77* was measured against what followed—increased hardship and imprisonment, ruined lives, and a new wave of exile for the various people who were associated with it.

After his long police interrogation on March 3, 1977, at the famous station Bartolomějská 10 in Prague 1, Patočka suffered a brain hemorrhage and wasn't taken to the hospital right away. Patočka died on March 13. We called his the Socratic death. Like Socrates, he chose a life of truth over protecting his own skin. Also like Socrates, Patočka was no revolutionary; he just appealed to his government to live by its already established laws and decrees. From the philosophy student Jan Opletal, who was killed by the Nazis in 1939 (this was when Patočka's career was cut short for the first time), to Palach's sacrificial protest against the Soviet occupation in 1969, to Patočka's death in 1977, there was a continuity of resistance.

In vain the latter-day Communists claimed for themselves the legacy of Master Jan Hus. In the late fall of 1989, Havel adopted the Czech heretic's motto "*Pravda zvítězí*" ("Truth shall prevail"), for his presidential campaign, and students sang, "We shall overcome." Neither of these two imperatives belonged to the regime that had presided over its thoroughly deracinated, corrupt socialist dream. In vain authorities had removed Palach's body from his grave. In vain they vilified Patočka. With the sculpture of King Wenceslas marching on his horse at the top of the square named after him, and the towering statue of Hus at Old Town Square, who could silence the underground current of peoples awakened from their oppressive slumber? These were the historical squares where the Nazis in 1939 had erected their perverted Hindu crosses of well-being, their equilateral swastikas; where the Communists had unfolded their bombastic banners in 1948; and where Soviet Marxism had placed its military hardware to make the world safer for *its* brand of brotherly democracy and *Pax Sovietica* in 1968. They were the same places where multitudes sang the end to the Soviet state's decaying power. In 1989 students from Charles University marched to commemorate the fiftieth anniversary of Jan Opletal's death. The underground spiritual stream of their predecessors in struggle gave a purchase on life to the atrophied cultural roots, and it yielded to the Velvet Revolution with Václav Havel as its spokesperson and then Czechoslovak president.

Cunning through the Gray Zones

"Mr. Matuštík, how could you embarrass the university by taking part in antisocialist activities?"

I had been brought before the academic and political authorities at Charles University in Prague. "To what are you referring?" I rhetorically asked the dean and others present.

After I'd been detained at Patočka's January seminar, I'd been arrested in March 1977 at his funeral in Strahov near a large student-housing complex. Hundreds had come to pay their last respects. The cemetery was surrounded by police using motion-picture cameras and checkpoints to intimidate and record the visitors. The low-flying helicopters made it impossible to hear the graveside speakers. I was detained, interrogated, and released shortly after the funeral. The repercussions for these sins of my own making came less than a month later. I was called to account for myself in front of the special Charles University commission composed of Dean Ráb, several professors from the department of psychology, Communist Party officials, and student leaders from the university socialist union.

"Do not play naïve. We have made a great exception by admitting *you* to study here, and you betray our trust in this way?" one of the unidentified men said. He was probably a secret service agent.

"I still don't understand the nature of the offenses," I said, still hoping to appear naïve.

"We have here two police reports on your *Charta 77* activities, and they raise serious questions regarding why we allow these kinds of individuals study at the university," another man replied, offering a gloomy face.

"What exactly did I do that was illegal?" I asked in a lawyer-like fashion.

"You took part in antistate activities, like those underground subversive seminars."

"I admit I took part in a seminar in which we discussed Socratic death. Is that subversive of the state?" I was cheeky, knowing full well that Socrates had been accused of treason against Athens.

"You're an admirer of Patočka, who was a fascist enemy of our socialist life."

I offered my counterargument. "How could he be a fascist if he was persecuted by the Nazis?"

"Do not play word games with us; we know the hostility of phenomenology toward socialism."

"How can a call to personal responsibility be hostile to genuine socialism?" I noted idealistically.

"In self-appointed activities such as *Charta 77*," one of the Communist ayatollahs declared.

"I didn't see the published text of *Charta 77*, so how can I discuss it fairly with you?"

"We don't need to discuss what is obvious to a good Communist. But we do want to give you a chance to correct your errors by distancing yourself from the *Charta* movement and Patočka."

I played for time. "What do you mean?"

"At the September student-body assembly, you will publicly read a statement in which you reject *Charta 77* and condemn Patočka."

"I don't know how to reject something I haven't read, and what's the point of condemning a dead philosophy professor?"

"If you aren't willing to comply, you don't need to return to school. And you also can get ready for two years of hard military service."

"Do I have some time to think this through?"

"Yes, we want you to come back before the start of the fall term, in August, with a written statement. Meanwhile we'd like to know your willingness to do so within the month."

"I'll get you some answers in May," I said.

"We'd like you to cooperate with the gentlemen here to help them detect other university peers who take part in antisocialist activities." They pointed to several secret service agents.

"You want me to work as a secret service informer?" I asked in disbelief.

"Don't be so dramatic! It is nothing. Just come periodically for a little chat."

"But I'm not very well suited mentally for such work."

"You want to study at the university, don't you?"

"Yes." I was sincere.

"You don't want to cause difficulties for your family, do you?"

"I would hope not," I pleaded.

"Then you must be a bit more cooperative with our socialist organizations in order to undo your transgressions. After all we're giving you a second chance."

"You're asking for too many things at once. Can I think this over?"

"Just know that if you're stubborn, the alternative is expulsion from the school and military service starting in the fall."

The verdict was final.

I was arrested twice during my first year at Charles University. The first time occurred before the funeral arrest at the cemetery. At one of the last secret seminars of Patočka's underground university, he was speaking on Heidegger and Socrates's interrogations of death and dying. How strangely wondrous that Patočka would die that Socratic death not long after this seminar! The meeting took place in the basement of the psychiatry clinic at Pavlov's Square in Prague 2. The secret police showed up in force with several arrest vans. Many were taken to the police station. I was released shortly after my data was entered into the information log. Voice of America broadcast details of the arrests that night.

Military service for me would have been with the so-called black (punitive) units; an intense indoctrination regime not only had been set in place for the rebellious minds sent there, but often dangerous or severe prison-like conditions existed. Some of these army units were sent for hard labor or to fight in such imperial ventures as in Angola and later with the Soviets in Afghanistan. Military service of two years was required for all healthy males. University students, in an equivalent of the US ROTC, could cut their service to one year after their studies, and they would begin as officers. This was a university-student privilege; not only would I lose this privilege, but I'd also endure the worst two years of military service possible.

Most of my peers considered military service a waste of time, since in my generation virtually no one with any intelligence identified patriotism with fighting for the fatherland. My generation behind the Iron Curtain acquired greater inner freedom from the stupidity of war precisely because we constantly were preparing to defend peace by waging war. The droves of doves of peace were pasted around town during May 9 liberation parades, and each dove had its native nest over a missile silo. Most young men in my time dreaded the Communist military service because of the closely felt brainwashing power it exercised over recruits for long periods of time.

There were few grounds for getting out of military service, and intelligence wasn't one of them. As early as 1974, not knowing whether I would be able to study at the university after gymnasium, I tried to avoid the prospect of military service altogether and designed a plan to obtain the coveted *Modrá knížka*, "The Blue Book," which certified one as definitively unfit for the military. Getting certified on the basis of my mother's diagnosis as manic-depressive was an option that would do it for sure, yet it likely also would pose dangers for my career. As a child I used to suffer from bronchitis, mostly because of the notoriously poor Prague air and the common practice of burning brown coal in winter. A friend told me one diagnosis the military hated was severe asthma.

To get a properly acute diagnosis, one had to demonstrate a long series of irregularly occurring attacks and procure a summer-spa hospitalization. Using my theater skills, I learned to act out asthma attacks and started to visit emergency clinics around Prague in irregular nightly intervals. I would make myself hyperventilate, and the night clinic could do nothing other than administer me with an injection to help me breathe. When I calmed down, I'd be released, each time with a prized officially stamped slip from the emergency clinic and a referral to an asthma specialist. By 1976 I was a firmly established asthmatic patient, and in the late spring of 1976, just prior to my admission to the university, I was sent for a month-long treatment at a mountain sanatorium. Had the university turned me down, I would have made myself appear more sickly to try to avoid fall conscription into the army. I planned to obtain "The Blue Book" in my second year at the university, thus freeing myself from military service altogether.

My achievements were threatened by the state authorities in 1977, since expulsion coupled with a very hard military service was one of their threats for my noncompliance. My having established a medical track record of emergency treatments proved providentially indispensable in 1977 because from the perspective of the army, I was of no great use to them. This helped me obtaining a military clearance for travel abroad prior to serving in the army.

The thinly veiled threats to my family were intimidating enough. I was even more scared of being recruited, with sticks and carrots, into working with the secret service apparatus. As soon as I had one foot in with the gang of agents, there would be no easy way out. One could only sink deeper into compromise and collaboration. Dangers grew in both staying in and trying to leave such situations. I stood before a hard life choice, one unlike any other I'd faced before.

I reasoned with myself. *Either place myself at the disposal and pleasure of the socialist state or be slowly crushed by its overwhelming, stifling, punitively jealous love! If I want to remain alive and well, then I must prostitute myself with the regime, in many equally devastating senses of the word, to save my student life, avoid direct reprisals, and prevent a premature loss of a vocation and meaningful career. To become an unknown student dissident at nineteen— how sensible would be this sacrifice?*

I thought of Jan Palach at age nineteen; I never held illusions about the extent of my political heroism. *Confronting the regime directly before having had a chance at education would usher me into a long, anonymous night with uncertain public efficacy. My saying no to the state can't be seen as being on par with Havel, Patočka, and Hájek's dissent. Wouldn't heroism in my case be what Aristotle distinguished from the virtue of courage and called recklessness? Maybe you were reckless by getting yourself arrested twice in the same year and in your first year at the university!*

Surviving My Adolescent Loss of Innocence

Origins are neither innocent nor transparent. My childhood had equipped me to become a dropout, delinquent, addict, madman. The person I have become on that staging also came out of self-choice. How would I overcome my upbringing and the social-political confusion of my origins? How would I integrate fragments of multiple worlds? These were my worlds: the youngest child of a Holocaust survivor who had hidden her tragic story in deep silence; at fourteen an orphan and ward of the socialist state; a child of parents who were at first firm then broken believers in the Communist dream; a boy born of atheist parentage and now a young Christian convert in defiance of the Communist state religion; a rebelling nineteen-year-old student who is about to flee his native country. Writing myself into this Judeo-Christian hybrid in diaspora, I am a character and a witness in my own odyssey. In wrestling with myself, I gather fragments of tumultuous origins, identity shifts, and risks posed by moral gray zones as well as discomforts of acknowledging such zones. They all form part of the journey, repair, return, and possibility. My memoirs write a literary hybrid: a philosophical remembering (anamnesis), a transgenerational homecoming, a meditation on life and death. A small life plays on a great cosmic stage of wonder, mystery, and love, contesting despair and annihilation.

The Czecho-Slovak Shoah

According to *The Slovak Jewish Records Index* (Jordan J. Auslander, 1993), the census from 1735 lists twelve thousand Jews living in Slovakia. In 1787 Jews in the Habsburg-Hungarian monarchy had to choose German family names for taxation and the draft, and in 1867, the Hungarian Diet issued the Emancipation Act, giving Jews full citizenship while abolishing residence limits and serfdom. In 1896 Judaism became equal with other religions practiced in the empire. By 1938 there were 125,000 Jews in Bohemia and Moravia and 135,000 to 140,000 Jews in the Slovak, Ruthenian, and Subcarpathian regions, and forty thousand of these lived in the territory ceded to Hungary. After the Munich *Diktat* of 1938, the Nazis seized the Sudetenland from Czechoslovakia, and Hungary annexed the Ruthenian and Subcarpathian regions of Slovakia. Between November 24, 1941, and April 15, 1945, the Germans deported nearly 74,000 Jews residing in the Protectorate of Bohemia and Moravia to a transit camp in Terezín (German: *Theresienstadt*). Before the establishment of this transit ghetto, the Germans had deported six thousand Czech Jews in six transports: five transports from Prague to the Lodz ghetto and one from Brno to Minsk. Between October 15, 1941, and October 27, 1944, the Nazis deported 75,000 to eighty thousand Czech Jews from Bohemia and Moravia to other killing centers or forced-labor camps.

On March 14, 1939, Jozef Tiso, a Catholic priest, became the president of the newly independent clerical-fascist Slovak State, and the next day Hitler declared Bohemia and Moravia to be Germany's protectorate. While some Jews fled from Bohemia to Slovakia to escape persecution (Andrej Steiner's family members, who fled from Brno, were among them), the anti-Jewish laws were introduced in Slovakia in April 1939. Only some five thousand Jews managed to leave Slovakia. By September 9, 1941, all Slovak Jews had to wear the yellow Star of David. Later Czech nationals were not allowed to reside and work in Slovakia. The first phase of the Final Solution of the Slovak Jewish problem lasted from March 25 until October 20, 1942. The Slovak Ministry of Transportation states that 57,752 Jews were deported in 1942 from Slovakia; while according to the Ministries of the Interior and of Foreign Affairs, the total is 57,628.[27] The last phase of the Slovak Holocaust took place after the defeat of the Slovak National Uprising (August 29–October 28, 1944), when Germans occupied Slovakia and some 13,500 Slovak Jews were deported to Auschwitz-Birkenau.

8

"WHAT WILL THEY DO TO US NOW?"

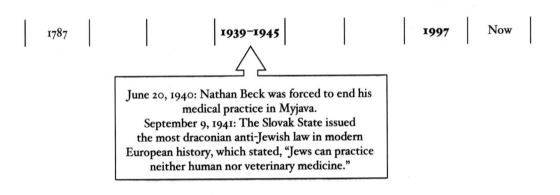

| 1787 | | | **1939–1945** | | | **1997** | Now | |

June 20, 1940: Nathan Beck was forced to end his medical practice in Myjava.
September 9, 1941: The Slovak State issued the most draconian anti-Jewish law in modern European history, which stated, "Jews can practice neither human nor veterinary medicine."

Before that momentous Chicago summer of 1997, I travel to my mother's native Slovak village—the home of her father, the family doctor Nathan Beck. I gradually uncover "Beckov's Odyssey." The lost family house, Beckov, tells the story of the Myjava Jews from 1939 to 1945. Today the building's owner is still afraid in a village bereft of its Jews: "What will they do to us now?"

Chicago, Karlovy Vary, Myjava (1997)

In the early summer of 1997, before Gary and I will discover each other in cyber-space somewhere between Sydney and Chicago, I taste silence. Patricia and I travel to Karlovy Vary, a spa jewel west of Prague, and we quiz Uncle Ernest about his childhood. Ernest is the last of my family's survivors in the Czech Republic who still carries memories of the aromas and sounds from which I was separated before my birth. *The magnitude and sudden nearness of the Holocaust shakes me. Silent mother tongues—by what senses are they tasted, told, tagged for a story?*

Ernest tells me that Nathan Beck, my maternal grandfather, was one of ten siblings. "One child died at birth, the other two during World War One because of a cholera epidemic. Their sexes and dates of birth were lost to us," he recalls, as we sit in his small kitchen in Karlovy Vary. "And of the seven living siblings, four sisters with their husbands and little children were murdered in Auschwitz."

"Who were they? My mother never told me anything about them," I say.

"My father's sister Olga from Nitra, her husband Hugo Benau, and a four-year-old son, Peter," Ernest replies, retracing his memory. "Fridka with her husband Ladislav Klein and little Viera, and the third sister, Margit, nicknamed 'Mancika,' with her husband Ernest Kemeny and daughter Klari."

"Kemeny...Does that have anything to do with Cohen?" I want to know.

"It's a Hungarian version of Cohen. They were either taken to the camp from Nové Zámky or Nové Mesto."

Ernest identifies the fourth sister, the firstborn Beck, Etelka. Like Nathan and my mother, she came from Myjava. Ernest says that she too died in Auschwitz.

"Etelka moved to the territory annexed by Hungary in Nové Zámky," he confirms.

I don't question his facts; I can't. Because Etelka's name is listed among the murdered, it closes off for a considerable time any lead I might find to my surviving relatives.

"Nathan's two brothers left Myjava before nineteen thirty-eight," Ernest continues. "Béla, whom we called 'Vojtech,' was unlike his short and dumpy siblings, Nathan and Ervin, who were tall and slim." Ernest makes fun of his own figure, which closely resembles Nathan's.

"What did Béla do?" I ask.

"He became a dentist and escaped from Nové Zámky to the Russian front." Ernest knows more than I ever imagined I could find out. "He returned home in nineteen forty-five. And his brother Ervin, a lawyer, survived until nineteen forty-four with the Slovak partisans. He evaded capture after the defeat of the Slovak uprising."

"What about Beck's name change?" I press on.

"All three Beck brothers in Myjava changed their family name to Veselý. Béla and Ervín left liberated Czechoslovakia in nineteen forty-six for Vienna and immigrated in nineteen forty-seven to Israel." Ernest was quite sure. "And they kept using their wartime alias."

"How come I never knew any of this from your sister, Magda?" I say, upset at my mother.

"We both lost all contact with the survivors. I was ill, and my memory became shaky. I don't know why my sister didn't say anything to you."

"So what happened to the Beck brothers in Israel?"

"Ervín moved to Sydney in nineteen sixty-three, and Béla joined him in nineteen sixty-five."

On this beautiful warm day before the Chicago Indian summer where my story scripts one of its beginnings, I don't know whether any of Nathan's brothers or descendants who survived the Shoah are still alive. What chance do I have fifty years later of being able to find any relatives who left Slovakia in 1946? Nathan's Myjava family remained in postwar Czechoslovakia. It is their untold story, Uncle's fallible memory, and Mother's unexplained silence that I probe with a great urgency that presses my questioning forward during this eventful summer. And this driving force feels almost inborn or perhaps inherited. This urgency, which operates without my agency—without a why—prevents me from ascribing my motives to some causal chain, a determinate personal justification, a historical or affective mnemonic map, face recognition, or G-d forbid, a theodicy. I, who wrestles with multiple selves, pulls, and identities, watch them converse as they seek an integration in me. Right now I am writing myself out of the Phoenix desert sands; they once welcomed Marrano refugees fleeing the Latin American Inquisition, later interned the Japanese families whose fathers liberated Dachau, and now erect Berlin Walls against the South.

I do not know anyone personally in Myjava; Grandpa Nathan died a year before I was born, and Mother never took me to her native village.

"Ernulo, Patricia and I should go to Myjava and find anyone who is still alive and knew our family."

"I'll give you the names of people in Myjava," he offers.

I hastily write to Ján Vrana, one of his contacts, preoccupied about my upcoming visit there with Patricia, but we must hit the road for Slovakia without waiting for an answer. Patricia and I find lodging in an old hotel next to Myjava's city hall. It was a former Communist Party establishment, and in 1997 it still exhibits vintage signs of the former architectural glory celebrated by socialist realism: red carpets and sizable rooms with malfunctioning amenities. The red hotel has the market feel of a prostitution hangout. We make the grave mistake of trying to call Ján Vrana rather than just showing up. No one answers, I later learn, because all are gathered in Ján's home garden, waiting for us that evening. They're having a barbecue celebration in our honor.

We go to the home of another contact. When we ring the bell, Mrs. Darina Rybárová, a daughter of the woman who lived in the Beck house and took care of the children, welcomes us. When my older brother Pavel was born, Darina looked after him as a nanny. Pavel knew Grandpa, but he never told me much about him. Darina's son became Myjava's first democratic mayor after 1989. Our family's village friends still have connections to important people.

"My son just celebrated his fiftieth birthday." The warm, well-built woman offers us a full plate of homemade poppy-seed-and-cottage-cheese kolacky. "Have some with tea. Careful—it's still hot."

"I want to show you some photos of Magda and Ernest. And here...my mother with your family," Darina continues. She smiles and points to a handsome woman standing behind little Mother and Uncle, both adorned with curly hair, two Semitic angels descending from a baroque church.

Darina runs out of the flat as Patricia and I leaf through her album and have our fill of sweets. She knocks on her neighbor's door and shortly returns with Olga Šikundová.

"I was Magda's classmate before the war," Olga says upon entering the room. She's in her midseventies and appears to be in good health. I imagine her walking with Mother to grammar school.

"I loved to visit with her at home and play," Olga remembers. "The Becks had beautiful toys, and our family was very poor. I loved to swim in their small swimming pool." She clearly feels fond of her childhood. "The asphalt road now covers the swimming pool, and the Communist-era apartments replaced the orchard."

This orchard resembles the one I will see in the Galanta wedding photo of Grandpa Nathan and Grandma Ilonka. Later this summer, when I receive the old wedding photo from Gary, I will learn for the first time that Etelka Beck didn't perish in the camps. She was my cousin's grandmother who came to Sydney after the war.

When Patricia and I stand up to leave, Darina turns to me. "You should visit the Borsuks." She searches through a cabinet and pulls out the address and telephone number. "Brano Borsuk is the son of the family that hid the Becks during the first part of the war. You must see him," she insists.

We return to our unclassy lodging for the first night. Ján Vrana's celebration for our return continues that night in another part of the village. The next day we abandon the Communist hotel luxury for a nearby lakeside resort. Myjava's city hall stands next to the Beck family house built in the early 1930s. There is a pharmacy on the ground floor of the house, while apartments and offices occupy the upper floors. We announce our arrival and introduce ourselves. The interesting history of the Beck house begins to unfold.

"I'm one of the grandsons of Nathan Beck, who built this house," I start. "Is it OK if we look around a bit?" The receptionist goes to fetch Mr. Valášek, the new owner.

"Where are you from?" he asks. "How often do you come back?"

We don't request any explanation, yet he commences with a story of the house ownership. "You know that after nineteen eighty-nine there were three owners who claimed the house?"

"We didn't know," I tell him.

"Ernest Veselý, the son of Nathan. Then someone came from Israel and finally Helena Karasová."

"We are coming directly from Ernest," I offer. "He didn't say anything about getting his dad's house back." I discussed the house with my uncle, but he thought there was no way to recover it.

"Podbánská 11...,." Mr. Valášek says, volunteering the contact information for Mrs. Karasová from memory. "She received this house in the restitutions of nineteen eighty-nine."

In 1997 post-Communist Czechoslovakia is still a single country. Uncle Ernest could have claimed the Slovak house as his family property even while living in the Czech Republic, but he had no papers to prove his ownership.

"Mrs. Karasová sold it to me right away." The new owner hurries up with the story. "She didn't care for the house." I'm not sure why he's offering any of this information except out of fear that Nathan's survivors may claim it.

He continues without waiting for my response. "The issue of rightful ownership has been problematic, to be sure." Patricia and I hear the same line two more times in the course of our conversation.

"But it would be nice," I suggest, "if the city placed a memorial plaque here for the Beck family. They were the only surviving Jewish household from Myjava that was repatriated there after after the war."

Apparently Mr. Valášek didn't know this. "Many different people lived in this house," he retorts, obviously not sure that he would like to have a memorial plaque to Jews on his building. He changes the topic. "Can I invite you both to lunch? You are my guests. My dad knew Dr. Beck very well." He raises his eyebrows to emphasize that connection.

In the next two days, we hear again, "Everyone expected after nineteen eighty-nine that the house would be returned to the Beck family." First we learn this from the mother of the mayor, Mr. Rybárová, then from Brano Borsuk, and finally from the man who had waited in vain for us on the first night, Ján Vrana.

Mr. Valášek takes us to the best restaurant in town, which happens to be at the resort hotel where Patricia and moved to on our second night. The Communists used to run a pioneer summer camp at the lake near the hotel, and my brother went to the lake as a child. I never came there alone or with Pavel; Mother never told me about it.

"You know, everyone in Myjava still calls the house 'Beckov,'" Mr. Valášek continues at lunch. Either he is trying to get information he imagines we have, or he wants to find out our intentions.

"One more reason to place a memorial plaque on the house, don't you think?" I seem to irritate the sensitive spot. "The city could do him this minimum honor—it would be a way to remember the Slovak Jews," I say. "The Becks were forced out from Beckov under the Slovak State. Nathan was a popular family physician. And old Myjavans still recall how some family member was cured or delivered into the world by him." I'm reciting the midrash about Nathan as I learned it recently. "If they still call it Beckov, why not have a memorial sign, even if it's a bit late to turn the house into a museum?"

"What will the Jews do to us now?" Mr. Valášek spontaneously expresses his hidden fear, perhaps the real motive for his lunch invitation. I translate the words to

Patricia; she's stunned. We've heard about the new Eastern European anti-Semitism without Jews. This was a real instance of it in 1997.

"How did Mrs. Karasová get Beckov from the state after nineteen eighty-nine?" I ask, but I don't get an answer.

Beckov's Odyssey

The following day, Patricia and I meet with Borsuk and Vrana, sons of the two Myjava partisan families who helped hide the Becks. They confirm the Beck story from their youthful memories. Beckov tells a much bigger story of survival. In 1941 Nathan already knew his family would have to struggle for their existence. Hoping to preserve something for his return, should anyone from the family survive, he arranged a transfer of the house to a well-known Prague lawyer, Mr. Karas. The falsified property books saved Beckov from the Nazis and thus erased the historical record of the original owner. Nathan had to fix the property books; as a Jew with the Star-of-David armband on his coat, he couldn't officially sell his home. Karas worked as a notary public then and rewrote the house-ownership record under his own name with the unwritten understanding that he would return it to the Beck family after the war. Who could demand proof in those times? The illegal transfer was made because of the war. If it were a sale, Karas too might have lost the house in the Aryanization of all Jewish property. The transfer of Beckov reminded me of the manner in which Communist regimes liquidated the property of dissidents who left the country. The first owner of my Prague apartment left illegally for Canada, but he transferred his property to a Communist cooperative and so retrieved some of his money before leaving the country. I took over the apartment from the new legal owner, which happened to be a Communist institution. I lost my apartment after I fled in 1977; the Communist state confiscated it as forfeited émigré's property. My brother couldn't claim it, and the state happily gave my flat as a perk to a secret agent.

Karas didn't get to enjoy Beckov for long. He had to leave the new Slovak fascist state after 1939 because he was Czech. According to Uncle Ernest, after the war Mr. Karas and the Beck family lived together in the house for some time. My father disputed a benign version of the timeline in a letter he wrote me in July 1997 after the first discovery trip Patricia and I took to Myjava several weeks earlier.

After 1945 the only inhabitants of the Beck house were Nathan and his family. After his wife died in 1948, Nathan rented the front rooms of the first floor to his maid and moved himself to the courtyard section of the house. The ground floor housed his medical office, an X-ray machine, and a patient waiting room. He rented another room in the basement to a patient survivor of rape.

My dad recalls the first years of his marriage to my mother.

Magda lived in the Myjava house after our wedding and when she was preg-nant with Pavel in 1951. Nathan drove Magda from Myjava to Bratislava, where she gave birth to Pavel. We returned with our newborn to Myjava and lived in Nathan's rooms. Grandfather occupied the bottom part of the house for nine years after the war, 1945–1954. Then, from 1954 until his death in 1956, he lived in a smaller house provided by the Myjava factory, Armatúrka. This was part of his job as an attending factory physician.

Father concludes the Beckov saga with a sense of regret about the house.

It appears that even during this postwar time Grandpa did not put his house in order.

The transfer of the registry from "Karas" to "Beck" never took place after the war, and no family members followed up regarding the property after Nathan's death. Beckov followed the path of other possessions Nathan acquired for his work, gave away, hid, or had to leave behind.

While the Gestapo enjoyed Beckov during the war, the Communists established their district headquarters there after Nathan's death. Later Beckov housed inno-cents—a kindergarten. In the 1980s Brano Borsuk attended in Beckov the meetings of an auto-moto club. Did Karas receive one hundred thousand crowns ($3,400) for Beckov from the Communists? Otherwise why would the post-Communist state re-quest this sum from the Karas family in 1989 when the house was restored to them as its last known legal owners? Myjava's city hall used it until 1989, when Mr. Valášek bought Beckov from the city only to discover that it never had belonged to the city. In 1989 Karas was the owner listed in the property books; no Beck relative had ownership papers. Jewish property confiscated prior to 1948 wasn't part of the post-Communist restitutions. Karas might have expected that the Becks never would return to Myjava after the war, and with anti-Semitism on the rise in Communist Czechoslovakia, no Beck dared to claim the house.

Helena Karasová inherited the house after 1989; the new owner bought it from her and with it everyone's guilt. While post-Communist restitutions went back only to the Communist property confiscations, not to wartime Aryanization, Valášek used Nathan's original architectural plans for the house to get its renovation approved after 1989. Mrs. Karasová must have had some fears about the material and formal basis for her father's ownership, as she sold the house almost immediately after she got it back from the State. Since our first visit, Valášek no longer owns Beckov either, and I have stopped keeping track of the most recent owners. *Does Beckov's transgenerational odyssey contain Myjava's haunted heritage?*

The Jewish Physicians in Slovakia

Hlinkova Garda (the Hlinka Guard) was a paramilitary unit that a Catholic Priest, Andrej Hlinka, created in Slovakia on October 8, 1938. The radical fascist origins of the Slovak Hlinka Guard date back to Vojtech Tuka's 1920s movement, *Rodobrana*, inspired by Mussolini's Blackshirts and the Nazi SA. The Hlinka Guard became the paramilitary arm of the Slovak People's Party (HSSP), run by another Catholic priest, Jozef Tiso, who became the president of the independent Slovak fascist state on March 14, 1939, with Vojtech Tuka as the prime minister, Alexander Mach as the minister of internal affairs (homeland security), and some sixteen other Catholic priests among members of the sixty-three-seat parliament. The Slovak State, modeling the Hlinka Guard on SS units, began to deport Slovak Jews in 1942.[28]

On July 25, 1939, Slovak State Law 184 mandated that no more than 4 percent of all practicing physicians in the country could be Jewish, and on the next day, another law prohibited any Jew from running or owning a pharmacy. But on June 31, 1939, 48 percent of all physicians in Slovakia were Jewish, so exceptions had to be granted. Despite an affidavit from the Myjava police station regarding his moral and political reliability, my grandfather Nathan Beck was forced to end his medical practice on June 20, 1940. On September 20, 1940, the Slovak Ministry of the Interior ordered all district police stations to confiscate, seal, and label the medical and dental equipment of all Jewish doctors and on September 23 at 10:00 a.m., then liquidate their medical offices. The search of the house number 1922 in Myjava, home of the Jewish Dr. Nathan Beck, who was forbidden to practice medicine in accord with Law 184, was scheduled on the same day promptly at 10:00 a.m.[29]

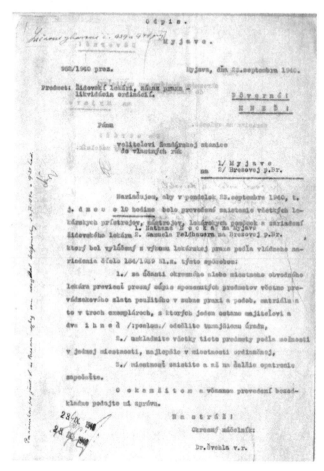

23. The search of Nathan Beck's medical office on September 23, 1940

The report of the house search notes that no precious metals or secret supplies of forbidden items, antigovernment pamphlets or flyers, or evidence of Jewish antigovernment activities were found. "Dr. Beck owns complete medical and dental equipment that he rented on December 20, 1935, to the Jew Julius Gross in Myjava. We did not confiscate the rented equipment because Julius Gross does not own his." All the equipment from Nathan's medical office that wasn't confiscated because he had rented it to Gross was listed on the same day along with the medical equipment confiscated from Nathan's house. On the following day another statement about the rental of Nathan's dental tools was signed by Gross, a dentist in Myjava. The rental agreement from December 20, 1935, is addressed to the district doctor, Nathan Beck, and signed by Dr. Julius Gross: "I accept to rent your apartment and medical office for 150 Slovak Czechoslovak crowns [about ten dollars per month] and your medical instruments for 50 Czechoslovak crowns." With another decree on April 21, 1941, the state enforced the sale of all Jewish medical equipment and offices to Aryan physicians. On September 9, 1941, the Slovak State issued the most draconian anti-Jewish law in modern European history: "Jews can practice neither human nor veterinary medicine."

One hundred one Jews were living in Myjava, according to the census from February 12, 1942. On May 15, 1942, a law regarding the expulsion of Jews from Slovakia was issued: "A Jew can be expelled from the territory of the Slovak Republic, except for those who were baptized before March 14, 1939. The expelled Jews or those who left the state territory lose the citizenship of the Slovak Republic." The Lutheran baptism that my family accepted on July 19, 1942, came too late to qualify them for this official exception, although as they had taken a new family name, it did give them a way to obtain false identity papers and pass as gentiles in areas where they weren't known. The impact of the anti-Jewish law issued by the Slovak State finally was annulled by the affidavit of Czechoslovak citizenship that Nathan obtained for the entire family from the district court in Myjava on October 22, 1946. Myjava suddenly had only three physicians.

Partisans, Lutherans, Fascists, and Marranos

The next morning in Myjava, Patricia and I arrive unannounced at the Borsuk home. As we enter the house, Brano points to a large canvas on the wall. "This painting was a gift to my father, Pavel, from Nathan, for saving him and his family during the war." He gestures toward an old wooden frame on a dark wall. "The Becks were forced to leave their house. They moved to the poor neighborhood at the edge of town. As children Ján and I used to bring them food at the new house they rented from Michal Cádra," Brano explains. "I will take you to visit Ján," he adds.

"You mean Ján Vrana? We wrote to him about our coming to Myjava," I say, and urge him to continue with the story.

"Ján and I have remained friends since childhood." Ján's parents ran a pub, while Brano's parents operated a wood mill and carpentry workshop. Nathan was their family physician.

"Did you go to school with Magda or Ernest?" I tell him about Magda's classmate, Olga, whom we met yesterday.

"No, but I know one of Ernest's classmates who is still alive." He volunteers to take us there.

We never go to meet Ernest's classmate, Ján Križka, but this is the second time I've heard his name. The first time was from my uncle. Ernest wrote in his letters to me that in the fall of the 1939 his teacher, Mrs. Dugáčková, threw him out of the first grade because he was Jewish. Not even five days after his expulsion, Ernest's Myjava buddies ostracized him. My uncle produced a still fresh memory of a shocking declaration by Ján Križka: "You are a Jew, so you no longer may play football with us!" Such proclamations from the mouths of babes must have echoed new parental and institutional imperatives. Magda also had to leave school, and she and Ernest returned to school only after the war. As if to resist hopelessness, Nathan taught them for five years at home. While they were in hiding and on the run from 1939 to 1945, he gave them daily lessons without any textbooks or school outlines. Mother and Uncle graduated from high school after the war without any loss of schooling.

"Nathan was compelled to end his medical practice, even though there were very few physicians in Myjava," Brano says, recalling what his father once told him. "While still in Myjava, Nathan worked in a locksmith workshop. Then he tended to horses."

The farm where Nathan took care of horses belonged to a family by the name of Valášek. Was the man who bought Nathan's house from Mrs. Karasová after the property restitutions in 1989 and who had invited Patricia and me to lunch to confront us with his worry about the future wrath of the Jews the son of the father who had employed Nathan at the horse farm? There are many Valášek families—was this pure coincidence?

Myjava's Beckov stands as a silent witness of the past along with the two artifacts I inherited with Mother's unspoken memory of her parents: the wedding-anniversary kiddush cup from 1937 and the baptismal Bible from 1942. *Did Mother's silence about her past echo Nathan's own postwar fear of being targeted with the survivor family as a Jew?* I wonder. *Does his silence about the house ownership hide a lost key to my story?* The lost house, the house without an original owner's key, the lost house *as a key*—but to what?

Brano takes us to an open meadow where his family's wood mill once stood. When Nathan could not avoid deportation by faking the typhoid epidemic in his second Myjava abode in 1942, the Borsuks modified their mill to hide all four Becks.

"They were in hiding the entire day, and only late at night did my dad come in secret to let them out for some fresh air," Brano explains. "In the mill father built an animal shed with two rooms. The four Becks stayed in hiding in the room camouflaged at the top. In the bottom room of the stall, my dad placed a very noisy wild horse. He housed that horse there so no one could hear anyone breathing or moving above. Many German SS and the Slovak Hlinka Guards patrolled up and down the street right near the animal shed. The staircase reached only the main room; the hiding space wasn't visible."

Brano pulls out two very old photos of the wood mill, the only ones he has. One is from winter and shows him as a young boy playing on a sled outside where my family was in hiding.

24. The Borsuk family's wood mill in Myjava, where the Becks hid in 1942

"Here, take this one to remember." He hands me the photo. "The wood mill served as a partisan center, and partisans used it to exchange and gather information there," he comments.

The first saviors of my family came from the Slovak resistance. Myjava had an active network of those who had decided right after the declaration of the Slovak State to work in clandestine opposition. Pastor Cibulka, who baptized the Becks with the Vrana and Borsuk families as witnesses, was part of the resistance network. Nathan was most likely privy to the start of the Slovak National Uprising because of these early contacts. The Becks hid in the mill until it too became unsafe.

"Somebody betrayed the hiding place," Brano says with some excitement. "My parents knew the person whom they suspected and questioned after the war."

"Who was it?" I ask.

"The daughter is still alive, and since this was never proven, I don't want to tell you the name."

"I guess not all skeletons are out of the Myjava closet," I say provocatively.

"But the captain of the Slovak police, Aujeský, warned us in time about the danger."

Uncle Ernest remembered that Aujecký was a public notary. Whatever his job was, Aujeský helped more than one Jewish family avoid transports. First he hid Jewish names from the public lists (this could explain why Ernest thought Aujecký was a notary), and then he warned about the impending "hunt for the Jews" that preceded each new transport (this would indicate his access to police information). According to available records and oral histories, no other Jewish family in Myjava except the Becks avoided deportation and extermination.

"Our parents managed to move your entire family to Kúty," Brano says. "This was a rather risky transition, as Kúty was a militant Slovak fascist region. Štefan Hačunda"—the Slovak fascist in whose Kúty house the Becks lived—"was a ranking member of the Slovak Hlinka Guard and hid your family."

"How was it possible for the Becks to survive the first Myjava transports then hide with a prominent Hlinka Guardist's family in a profascist environment?" I inquire.

"For some time, Nathan had been treating Hačunda's severely ill wife. As long as there was hope for her recovery, the Becks were safe." Brano tells what could appear to be a fairy tale about the king who calls in many healers, and as each in turn fails to cure his wife or daughter, he or she is killed. Nathan was already the most beloved physician in the region. Now he produced another miracle: he survived with his family by treating the ill wife (she neither fully recovered nor died while in Nathan's care) of a member of the Slovak Hlinka Guard and did it long enough to evade his own capture.

For one to obtain Slovak State civic papers, a baptismal certificate from Myjava wasn't enough. In gratitude the Hlinka Guardist not only protected the Becks in Kúty but also issued false papers to the entire family, which enabled them to move about and later leave the town. The papers had to read "Veselý" and indicate their Lutheran religion. After the war this high-ranking Hlinka Guardist claimed Nathan as "his Jew" to save himself, and Nathan provided such an affidavit. According to some, Hačunda was an educated man. In his letters to me, Ernest remembered that after the war Mother maintained contact with a high-ranking Hlinka Guardist who had helped the family.[30]

"There is a record from this difficult period," Brano says, "a photo of Magda and Nathan with a dedication to their Borsuk godparents." He searches for it and hands it to me, adding, "Here, look...It is signed by Magda and dated Kúty, April twenty-third, nineteen forty-three."

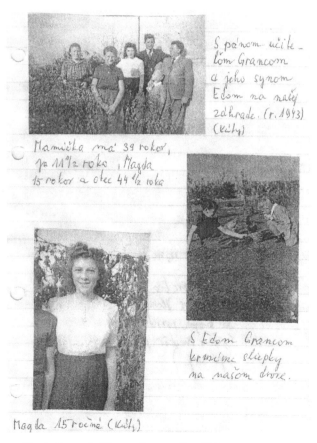

25. Uncle Ernest's "Remembrances" on Kúty, 1943-44

Brano takes us to Ján Vrana's house. Ján is very sad because Patricia and I missed his welcoming party. He's even more disappointed that we can't stay for a week, as he wants to take us on various hikes around Myjava.

"Nathan served the entire region of Kopanice, often climbing hills on foot to tend to his patients, since his new Tatra car couldn't get him to some remote houses. He would take to the road at any hour of the day or night. People loved him as their family physician. Some paid well; others gave what they could; and Nathan accepted fees for service in whatever ways people were able to pay, sometime with cheese, eggs, milk, chickens, or the homemade brews of *slivovice* or *borovička*." Ján is an enthusiastic storyteller and obviously holds warm feelings for the Beck family.

"My dad and mom were very close to your family." He offers us fresh apple cider made from her garden as we sit down at the table in his garden. Then he points up the hill behind his house. "This is the old Myjava Jewish cemetery." Taking out the gate key, he says, "You are welcome to go for a stroll."

Patricia and I walk up a rather large, steep hill, but as most of the tombstones are in Hebrew, I'm unable to decipher the inscriptions.

"Not long ago somebody arrived here from Israel," Ján calls down to us, "and knew that some of the Beck family relatives were buried in the top-left quadrant of the cemetery." He points toward four rows of approximately ten asymmetrically spread tombstones. "Perhaps they are your great-grandparents or some aunts or uncles," he suggests.

"Do you know the names of the people who visited the cemetery?" I ask, excited by the promise of some clues about the family that left in 1946. I remember that the new owner of Beckov had visitors from Israel; perhaps it was the same group.

"No, the woman and man didn't stay long and didn't leave any contact information," he says. "Perhaps we can ask the Jewish community in Senica to help you decipher the tombstones." Patricia and I don't have time to stay and pursue this research.

Ján guides us across the road to the main Myjava cemetery. The grave site of Pavel Veselý and Helena Veselá is well preserved.

Ján volunteers, "I take it as my duty and honor to take care of the grave, and I took it on from my father."

"Do you know why my grandparents were buried in the Christian cemetery?" I ask.

"It must have been either their will or the decision of their children," he speculates. "They were baptized as Lutherans; my father was one of their two godfathers.

I'm not sure whether your grandmother attended Lutheran services after the war. After the war there was no Jewish community or active synagogue in Myjava."

"Before the war Grandmother kept a kosher household, including the lighting of Sabbath candles," I say what I knew from Ernest. "The family attended synagogue, at least during the High Holy Days, until nineteen thirty-eight. Do you think her wartime Christian conversion became her reality after the war? Or was she too shell-shocked by the wartime ordeal to return to her persecuted faith?"

I question but get no answers; Ján clearly doesn't know how to reply. I hold myself back, still unaccustomed to match his discomfort with my complex identity. Naively, instinctively, I veil the part of my story he knows all too well, and I hide my broken self as the afikomen, a piece of matzo eaten in haste on the run from enemies—but I hide it for his sake, not to make myself whole in Passover to liberation. I wonder whether our family faked their Christian conversion in order to survive, though not without some internal warmth born out of gratitude toward their Christian protectors. Since 1492 Jewish conversos have survived in religious gray zones, including during the Inquisition in Catholic Spain and Portugal, as well as in the American Southwest. If I'm not a Lutheran offspring carrying my family duty, why do I feel the heat of a scarlet letter branding me as a wild boar, a pig, an apostate, a hypocrite, a Marrano?

"Did you notice that Nathan and Ilonka's headstones are turned in the opposite direction from all the other headstones in the cemetery?" I ask Ján.

He looks at me then gazes at the gravestones that read, "Pavel" and "Helena," as if he heard the Jewish names and is seeing the turned-around stones for the first time. "Perhaps this change of direction gives an indirect sign of their Jewish origin?" Ján suggests.

Or of their involuntary conversions? Or perhaps they're looking toward their ancestors buried across the road in the Jewish cemetery? I imagine how their bodies were actually laid to rest: with their heads pointing in the direction of the Jewish cemetery, or were only the headstones turned around? I wonder whether this too was a silent code Mother left *me* to decipher.

Was the first headstone for my grandmother there in 1948? I wonder. *Were the gravestones added in 1956, the year before my birth, when Nathan died? Who decided on the layout of these graves? Was it Mother in her panicked silence, or Vrana's Lutheran godparents, or someone in Myjava who never could accept their Lutheran conversion as genuine?*

My maternal grandmother died in 1948, nine months after the Communist take-over. She was young but exhausted by the war. Some villagers took her for a devout

Christian. Yet my mother's Communist conversion left no doubts that she had abandoned all religious beliefs that she might still have had in 1943 when she signed her photo for the godparents. *Did Mother's veiled silence about our Jewish origins veil another secret?* The task left to my cohort and me doesn't lie in deciphering the archives and recording their hidden memory for afterlives, as if facts alone could settle the secrets and fill the gaps.

26. Martin Matuštík with the Borsuk and Vrana families in Myjava, 1996

"Repairing the meaning of one's journey is like scripting, filming, and acting in one's own Shoah film,"[31] our Phoenix friend Rebeca told Patricia in 2013 as she was embarking on a pilgrimage to the Baal Shem Tov's grave site near Kiev.

9

ESCAPE

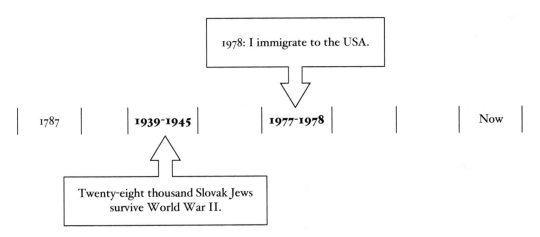

In 1977 the Communist secret service detained me at one of Jan Patočka's last secret philosophy seminars and then at his funeral. I was threatened and lured by secret agents and the party to collaborate as well as publicly condemn the dissident movement. At nineteen, then a first-year student at Charles University, I plan and carry out my quick escape from the Communist fortress.

The Communist Alcatraz (1977–1978, 1989)

By recognizing my conflict with the perverted socialist institutions as something that shouldn't define my larger journey, I confronted their ominous size as so many comic windmills. When I could neither slay their hydra heads nor fool them with native Czech humor or by quixotic sparring with windmills, I didn't aspire to heroism; with no choice left, I dared a real escape from the Communist fortress.

During my adolescent wrestling with gods and moral gray zones, I acquired a wounded kindness toward those who trade their bodies and souls for life. I learned to look with compassion on my parental generation, who bartered an entire dream of justice. I see the journeys of my contemporaries whom I left behind the Iron Curtain beset with moral minefields ripe for despair. And here I invoke again Primo Levi, who helped me once before, asking him for a bit of that humanity that breathes color into the gray scales with which so many had to paint their Communist walls.[32]

In April 1977 I gave the Communist Party and secret police my vague promise of a submission to come, but I had no intention of keeping it; I had bought myself time. Headstrong as anyone born under the astrological sign of Aries, I signed the dissident manifesto *Charta 77* but without publicizing my name on the list of the new signatories. The names of students and other vulnerable individuals were kept on hidden lists. Even though my signature was a secret one, this act granted me the inward strength to meet my situation without vacillation. There were numerous unpublished signatories whose names were reserved, not publicized, to protect their safety; many of these names appeared in print later. My name, along with my "Letter from a Young Man," was circulated in *Samizdat* (self-made) additions to *Charta 77* after my defection from Czechoslovakia. I mailed my signed letter the day I was leaving Prague, prior to my crossing the border. That was my answer to the powers that be, my last slap in the face to those who wanted to break me. This letter is something I'm sure they didn't read to that fall student assembly in 1977 at which I was supposed to make my great public confession, *"Mea culpa, mea maxima culpa."*

With devious charm, accompanied by the mystery of divine luck, I got myself out of the country before I was discovered, having received help from an unsuspecting young female admirer. She had significant prominence and contacts in the youth socialist league and the university student union. Before my troubles began, early in the fall of 1976, she had invited me to apply to a summer work camp in India, a great opportunity to spend three summer months abroad. With her blessing I received the blessing from the Socialist Student Union, and with that organization's letter of recommendation, I was accepted for this program and applied for the secret-police exit permit required to travel to the West.

Under the Communist regime, we all had passports, but to cross borders to the West, even to Yugoslavia, where Josip Broz Tito's open socialism allowed travelers free access to the West, we needed a special paper, a *zelená doložka,* a "green supplement." This prized document was issued by the special secret service branch for travel, then located in Bartolomějská street in the center of Prague. To obtain my supplement, I needed approval from the socialist oversight at the university, which I had received thanks to my admirer. I also needed clearance from the court and the military, as well as a certified promise of my having hard-currency funds that would enable me to travel—either from the state bank or a document showing that the trip had been prepaid. The Czechoslovak crown wasn't freely convertible and hard currency was purchased by a restricted bank allocation for each approved trip. Getting the required bank limit often called for other machinations and even bribes. Yet without my having the paper from the bank, the police wouldn't issue the supplement. It was a hopeless maze.

How was it possible for me to get the secret police permit in May 1977 to travel to India, Nepal, and Sri Lanka, when I had been interrogated in March and April for my *Charta 77* activities? I never will fully know. From my April decision to leave until my July 27 departure date, I lived in total suspense and terror of discovery, repercussion, and possible arrest. There were two reasons for my good fortune. First, total secrecy surrounded the closed proceedings by the Communist Party, the Socialist Youth Union, and the secret police branch against me and other dissident students at the university. Second, there was an antiquated method of keeping the lists of names of those who were under special investigation, like me, and those who applied for exit permits. This was before more efficient police surveillance and general tracking of the movement of populations became the norm for all great modern powers from China to the NSA. The police in Bartolomějská issued my travel permit, while another office interrogated me about *Charta 77,* and still another wanted me to become their spy. The offices remained inexplicably ignorant of one another other between May and July 1977, when I fled.

I neither slept with the Communist Party and its secret servants, nor rewarded my young socialist female admirer. And I also didn't suffer a guilty conscience for leading on the university authorities. Did I feel guiltier about my implied promise to have something with the socialist girl, a prize she hoped to claim after my return from India, or the repercussions she would suffer after my defection (for she was in for a lot of trouble when this whole affair came to light)? Admittedly I used her to save my skin. Under the circumstances I would have slept with her even in April in order to ensure my approval for the trip to India.

I justified to myself, *She's a young socialist careerist, and she'll survive my connivance.*

She made out all right in the end. The girl wasn't the only party affiliate at Charles University who would end up in trouble with the secret police and the upper echelons for my defection. The same professors, the dean, and even the two gentlemen who had hoped to recruit me as a spy—and who all had interrogated me in April—must have looked a bit stupid in September when I vanished. The socialist girl was just one of the faces in the chain of spells I cast on the Communist windmills.

Although the Prague gang and drug underground was flourishing in the 1970s, the chief dangers to my well-being came from the omnipresent secret police, classroom and teacher informants, and young men and women with prominent parents, such as party members and diplomats. Just as students in the West pay education costs at times by selling drugs or themselves, some of my peers started early careers as secret service agents, if not in gymnasium then at the university. Having lived on a permanent red alert until age nineteen (there never had been any other color scheme in my time), I will forever carry antibodies, accumulated and preserved for my future life, to any signs of an emerging police state. Like a child's panic after a car accident, for years after my defection, I feared all passport and border controls, and distrusted persons with guns or military outfits. My early taste of authoritarian, oppressive, ideological setups; soundings of propaganda and doublespeak or newspeak about "peace" or the "people" or the "community"; naked or outright-stupid power; portrayals of external enemies to mobilize readiness for defense; pseudoreligious babble by the secular state; and the sinister character of prisons and borders formed the basis of my deeply ingrained fear. Whenever the shape of sinister power appears, I get a gut reaction—red alert. But in place of the watchful eye and ear of the homeland security apparatus, I hear Jan Hus whisper, "One does not need to accept a corrupt authority as mandatory." The powers that be do not take kindly to this heretic's teaching.

The Heart Breaks

The socialist girl was neither an angel nor a demon of my youth, and I wonder what if anything Shekinah had to do with this particular intervention in my moral gray zones. Even so, for a long time I suffered a guilty conscience over leaving behind a Catholic girl whom I had dated for more than a year. She was the last intimate Catholic woman in my life. She came from a large family outside of Prague, and I had met her in one of those secret religious gatherings in K.'s charismatic circle. The Catholic girl and I began as friends who shared religious interests and partook in the religious underground. Our teen love grew under the cloak of ecstatic secrecy.

When it became obvious that the MJ daughters would go their own way one by one, my friendship with the Catholic girl gained in significance and became invested with hopes for marriage. I used to visit her periodically in her village—her family grew to like me very much—and she and I deepened our affection. I was an independent Prague man and a student at Charles University, while she was finishing up gymnasium. I got to know her when she was quite young, and I was the man who not only became her first serious love but also opened for her a window to the world. While our relationship grew in tenderness and warmth, however, it remained strictly platonic. Perhaps it was my respect for her firmly held Catholic values, or my awe at the prospect that taking her virginity would mean imminent marriage, but I never felt the need to question my inhibition as long as she felt secure about my devotion. When I knew my escape was inescapable, I chose to tell her half of the hard truth, which I thought she could understand and accept. I withheld the other half—the one I thought would devastate her.

"I have a vocation to become a Catholic priest. I'll have to pursue a path of celibacy, so we'd better just be friends and break our romantic relationship," I reasoned with her, without mentioning anything about my forthcoming escape.

"Are you breaking up with me because you want to marry the Church?" She understood but was crushed. Given our religious beginnings, how could she protest my choice? In my nineteen-year-old heart, I came to terms with my decision to leave home and my loved ones. I would leave the city where I woke up to the existential questions of life and death, where I had buried my mother and loved the first angels of my youth, where I had suffered my defeats. I would stake everything on this unknown quest.

Weighing all risks, I considered my life journey up until then. Having no serious bonds with my living father that would dictate my obligation to him; having come of age in my flat and at gymnasium; having learned of my intellectual abilities, which had gotten me into the university, I had nothing personal to hold me back—except my Catholic girlfriend. With her I felt a warm friendship and never expressed a promise of engagement. Our relationship came to its sudden end amid the events of 1977. *If I am to succeed with my plan,* I reasoned with myself, *I must wean B. off our bond in a way she can accept.*

I broke up with the Catholic girl two months before my departure from Prague. I was concerned that she would become so heartbroken if she knew about my plan to escape that she might prevent my leaving by committing some desperate act. In my fearfulness anything might prove to be catastrophic: from getting her pregnant, to her hurting herself, to her blurting something to the authorities.

Several years after my immigration, in the summer of 1981, the Catholic girl was allowed to travel to the West with her parents, and we met in Vienna. Ever since I had left in 1977, she had hoped to spend her life with me. I wasn't over my guilt yet, nor had I forgotten our affection and friendship. The fact that I was continuing to follow my plan to join the Catholic priesthood didn't deter her. She applied her warmth to what she must have seen as combating with the Church for my love. Nor did my plan to become a priest deter her parents, who suddenly left her in Vienna in my care and took off on their own to Rome. They gave me their blessing and said that any decision we made would be acceptable to them. I think they had been ready to say good-bye to their daughter for several years, hoping I would take her with me to the United States. Did they hope for the desired effect my spending time alone with her in a hotel room might have?

The girl and I traveled for a week, talked, and resumed our ability to be close. Immigration in those days was a one-way street. What would she do on her own if I couldn't stay with her, if I really did pursue the religious vocation? There would be no easy way back for her, and I couldn't assume responsibility for her decision. Many couples broke up in refugee camps or in new countries. Even in our cozy Salzburg room, as we slept in a tight embrace that was half our homecoming and half our sober realization of a final good-bye, I couldn't see myself taking her virginity then leaving. I knew—unspoken as it was—that in her mind full sexual intimacy would mean my inviting her to our having a life together.

There is an epilogue to this story of love unrequited in marriage yet not indifferently felt. After my departure in 1977, the Catholic girl visited many of my friends and relatives in Prague, Brno and Bratislava, collecting an oral history about me as a way to console herself. Not long after our last meeting in Vienna, she married a devout Catholic man who had been pursuing her for years. On one of my post-1989 returns to Czechoslovakia, I went with Patricia, my present life companion, to a gathering where the girl's parents showed up. They were happy to see me, yet with tears in their eyes and still heartbroken, they didn't know whether to embrace or shun Patricia for taking their daughter's place by my side.

Night Fog and Cunning

Once the decision was made and permits were secured, I had to flee Prague fast. My preparations proceeded in total secrecy because neighbors could have reported me to the police. I kept silent with my university colleagues and most friends about my having received my police permit for the summer camp in India. I knew the socialist girl wouldn't brag about it because her connection with me carried a personal—not political—prize for her. Thus I was largely able to vanish from sight on July 25, 1977.

On one occasion I ran into the socialist girl near Karlovo náměstí. A university professor who knew about my political case regarding *Charta 77*, and who kept that secret at the university, was approaching us from the opposite end of the square. He presented a clear and present danger. If the socialist girl revealed to him that I had an elaborate arrangement for student travel abroad, it could destroy my plan to get away. I was afraid the socialist girl would get a clue and become instantly terrified about my imminent flight and report my travel plans to higher authorities to avoid her complicity in my emigration. So I had to quickly prevent the three of us from having a conversation together. I grabbed the girl's hand and, as I was inviting her to have lunch with me, pulled her away. We disappeared without a trace in the recesses of a smoke-filled pub around the corner. Had the socialist girl and my professor spoken in front of me or even later about me, the simultaneous facts of my travel permit and my political case at the university could have become lethal. The interrogating university committee or the police would have stopped me from leaving, even if I hadn't revealed my plan to defect. In this volatile context, I chose to tell none of this to the Catholic girl and most of my friends and relatives.

Only my brother, father, and five close Prague friends knew, and all were crucial to the plan. My preparations included difficult nighttime liquidations of all potentially compromising materials in my flat. I had to secure a hiding place for belongings such as Mother's writings and diaries, my own diaries, and *Samizdat* literature; I hoped to recover these things some distant day. The documents and clues I cite in this memoir were smuggled out of my flat and hidden in those late-spring days of 1977. I had to plan in a hurry for life after death, as flight into exile is like death, with which one must spar for life. Mother's friend, S., hid several suitcases for me with Mother's plays, correspondence, and diaries. We removed big suitcases in the middle of the night like thieves. My friend Radko hauled some books and made arrangements to hide my other stuff after my departure. I gave him and another young man keys to the flat to act quickly after it was clear I had crossed the border. I have suffered amnesia regarding what I did with my personal diaries and notebooks. They either were lost or were taken by someone who wanted to have a piece of me in my absence; part of my story resembles "Lost Letters" in Kundera's *Book of Laughter and Forgetting*.

I had to change money on the black market for hard currency. Father would be free from six years of continuing alimony, which he was obligated to pay during my university studies, and I asked him for financial help. I don't know whether he had possessed it or borrowed it, but it must have been around ten thousand crowns ($300), which at that time amounted to almost five monthly salaries for him. This was the most significant act he had done for me since I was born, and he didn't hesitate. Not knowing that Mother's old bookcases in my flat had come from her childhood home and somehow had survived the Holocaust as well as the loss of Beckov, I left them behind to be devoured by the state. I sold the smaller antiques in order to finance my escape and initial survival. I used my meager savings to pay for my travel abroad, though closing all my bank accounts would have been risky, as it could have alerted the secret police to my planned escape. I had to leave something in the bank to camouflage my flight.

After Mother's death I drew on several income sources to support myself: a state orphan's pension, the alimony from my father, my stepfather's foster-care stipend, and the state supplement for children that Father received on my behalf. I also received monthly rent from Dr. Nakonečný, and at Charles University, I won a merit scholarship based on my grades—straight A's. My total income was about 1,600 Czechoslovak crowns (fifty-three dollars) per month, not bad for a young man living in a Communist state. My monthly cooperative apartment fee was about three hundred crowns (ten dollars); I spent five hundred crowns (fifteen dollars) on food and expenses. That left seven hundred crowns (twenty-five dollars). In those days a dollar cost thirty crowns or more on the black market, so I was able to secure $1,000 (thirty thousand crowns) prior to my escape. It was a formidable sum for any Eastern European in 1977 but a pittance to start a new life in the free world.

Every day could bring a revocation of the permit or raise suspicion that I was planning to defect. I could have been caught changing currency with foreigners or black-market dealers on the street near Wenceslas Square. Seeing me taking out my stuff, someone could ask innocently, "Are you moving?" I lived a double life, suspended between apparent normalcy by day and dismantling my entire life in Prague by night, between promising the authorities to publicly defame *Charta 77* and hoping I'd never see their faces again. By July, with my flat half empty, I was planning my funeral; only the eulogy and burial were missing. I placed flowers on Mother's grave. *Will this be the last time?* I wondered.

I placed several pairs of shoes neatly outside of my flat to signify that I was at home. I gave keys to my friends Radko and Honza; another pair went to S., who would keep Mother's private documents and writings for the next twelve years. These people would enter the flat after my departure to take what they wanted—furniture, carpets, lamps, books—before the secret service got the idea I was gone. I hoped it would take some time before the putrid "smell"—me, the dearly departed betrayer of the socialist state—would reach those who would then come and seal my flat, who would confiscate everything in it, who would strip me of my citizenship, and who would sentence me to a three-year prison term for illegally defecting from the motherland. Later, after I asked for political asylum abroad, the authorities pressured my family to write me letters urging me to return. Everyone in the family was prohibited from traveling to the West for some time, they were interrogated, and all their correspondence was read by the secret service.

I rang the doorbell at my flat in Prague in late 1989 after the Iron Curtain had crumbled.

"I expected you one day," the person who opened the door told me. "A photo survived in the flat from your primary school—I have your Socialist Youth Union membership card," he said, while pulling out the secret evidence of my past, perhaps a trophy from what was also his gray zone, which he had kept as a personal moral alibi all those years, waiting for the day of my return.

Letter from Uncle Ernest to His Nephew Martin

Karlovy Vary

January 28, 2001

Dear Mato,

On Wednesday I mailed you an envelope with the booklet "Remembrances" and today I recalled something: I do not know if you retain my "Remembrances" in the condition I mailed them to you, or you will change their appearance (size, format of the paper, etc.). But if you plan to make a copy, please make a copy also for me. I do not know now, what would I do with it, but perhaps I could have some use for it later. If I remembered if before, I would have xeroxed it myself. One more request: when you write me next, let me know the number of the last hand-written page, so that I can number them consecutively.

Remembrances of Life: 1939–1944

The disaster struck a year later, in the school year 1939–1940. On March 14 the Slovak State was proclaimed under the leadership of Dr. Jozef Tiso and the tutelage of Adolf Hitler and Andrej Hlinka's fascist Slovak Guard. Shortly after that morning, my teacher, Mrs. Dugáčková, announced to me upon my arrival at school—with patriotic light in her eyes, "Ernest, you must not return here any longer. From this day on, Jewish children are not allowed to attend school, so you should stay at home."

I did not grasp that very well, so the next day I received another rejection: at the upper part of Myjava, in front of Križka's pub, there was a small football field where we used to play every day. As usual I went that afternoon to play ball, and when the game was at its best, the fat Mr. Križko, the father of my playmates, Dušan and Jan, emerged from the pub and screamed, "Ernest Beck, I no longer want to see you or any other stinking Jews here. Neither Dušan nor Jan will be friends with Jews."

Thus ended my innocent childhood. In the days to come, I learned over and over that I could not do what was permitted for other children because I am a Jew—and a stinking one to boot. Soon after the proclamation of the so-called Slovak State, the new so-called Jewish laws were introduced. It consisted of many rules and prohibitions involving both private and public life. Father was stripped of his medical practice and his modern office with the new X-ray machine, surgery table, and many glass shelves with medical equipment—all that was confiscated. There was a real threat that our villa would be confiscated in turn, so Father "sold" it (to this day I am unsure if he sold it legitimately or just fictively transferred it to a non-Jewish ownership) to his lawyer acquaintance from Prague, Dr. Karas. Even after that transfer, we lived for some time in our house.

The time of the first transports to the camps was upon us. Father made the first attempt to save the entire family, an attempt to avoid, at least for some time, the marching orders to be the transported.

He convinced his good friend, Myjava's Lutheran minister, Dr. Julius Cibulka, to baptize the entire family. The priest risked a lot already at that time, but he baptized the Beck family with the Myjava church crowded by curious neighbors. In front of our house we had a tall iron fence set into a cement wall. In the morning after our Christian baptism, we discovered on that low cement wall a big black sign:

EVIL JEW, EVIL LUTHERAN, THE JEW IS A DOG

The sign had been painted with some advanced technology because even several coats of white paint could not cover it. When we returned after the war to Myjava, the letters still jumped out from the several layers of paint. Soon we had to leave our home, but I do not know if the reasons were economic or political. We moved to a small house called "At the Cadra" at the very edge of Myjava. I do not remember much from that period. I recall we were cramped into a small kitchen and a dark bedroom, usually with bad feelings and in constant fear. Father Nathan was unemployed; sister Magda and I were excluded from school attendance; and Mother was used to a certain standard of living, but we were now terrified by the news about the transports. All of us had to wear yellow stars, without which we were not allowed to leave the house.

Some of the Myjava Jews managed to emigrate as long as that was still possible—mainly to the United States. The remnant, about twenty families, began receiving orders to board the transports. Father made another anguished attempt to postpone the worst. Myjava now had in his place two physicians— Dr. Zeldakov and Dr. Dohnanyi. Father took advantage of the animosity between the two. He befriended the Russian, Dr. Zeldakov, [with whom] he discovered common political opinions, while Dr. Dohnanyi sympathized with the Slovak fascists. Father impressed upon Zeldakov a notion that he immediately began to plan: Dr. Zeldakov examined Mother and "discovered" that she was in the late stages of infectious typhoid. Our house doors and windows carried red signs that strictly prohibited entrance to all persons because of the dangerous infection. Dr. Zeldakov placed a notice at the city office in which the lists of transports were put together. It was all a very good idea; we survived yet another wave of the Slovak fascist insanity and avoided the deportation.

I found our new home difficult. I used to be with friends; now I was at home alone or mainly with Father. Magda helped to cook from the poor supplies and meager means we had; she cleaned, and I was to help my father. Father continued his psychological method of training to make me into a tough man: we had chickens to provide us with some food, and so we had to kill one quite often. Father knew that I could not look at the execution of these animals, at the streaming blood, and how the chicken still moved in mortal struggle even after its head was cut off by the ax, or how it would run down the courtyard even some moments after its head was severed from its body before it finally gave in to death. I would always disappear and hide somewhere so that I would not have to look. For this reason, and because the job was better done by two, Father forced me to help him. At first I held the hens with their heads on the tree stump, and Father would cut them off. Later I had to change places with him. I did not acquire an "iron" character. I would not kill a chicken now even if I were dying of hunger.

Mother's "typhoid" was not going to save us for long. The red signs disappeared from our doors and windows. By then most Jews had vanished from Myjava. Father managed another exceptional move to save the family. The anti-Jewish hysteria seemed to overcome the majority of the Slovak nation, but among the older generation, there were many individuals for whom the new ideology and party membership were mostly a means to gain social status, and their real world views did not have much in common with the fascist ideas. Father knew many such people, and he secretly continued contact with them. On the other hand, in the entire Slovak fascist hierarchy (even at the highest levels), there were people who would close their eyes to anything, even to violations of the anti-Jewish laws, to gain personally. My father took advantage of that.

Somehow he found out that the head commandant of the Slovak fascist guard, Kubala, who resided in Bratislava, had a seriously ill mother in Kúty (the village near Myjava).[33] No physician was able to help her and she had a terminal prognosis. Father utilized connections with Myjava's "good" Slovak fascists, and the Slovak guard "discovered" a miraculous physician, Dr. Beck, a Jew, who was prohibited to practice medicine (even though we were baptized by then, for everyone we were just Jews), except that he would certainly cure the deathly ill mother. The powerful could manage everything even then. So soon the Jew, Dr. Beck, moved with his entire family from the poor abode in Myjava to a small villa with five rooms and a large garden in Kúty. The entire family was then erased from the transport list, and Father was allowed a limited medical practice under the stipulation that at the top of all medical prescriptions he had to have printed the following:

✡✡ Dr. Beck, Physician-Jew ✡✡

In this town, behind the political and war fronts, I experienced two years of boyhood and early puberty. I made many friends from the farm families near us. We used to run through the meadows and forests, and we raised domestic rabbits. Uncle Ervín (who began to visit us again from Bratislava) built for them a wood hutch. Father also had a pig; the yard was full of chickens; and in the garden we grew various vegetables. Father befriended a "lukewarm fascist," Štefan Granec, an intellectual and director of the local grammar school. He arranged for me to "clandestinely" attend fourth grade, so that I was able to put some learning into my empty head.

It was August 28, 1944. In the afternoon Magda and I received an order from our father to eat and sleep because we would be traveling that night. We tried in vain to find out where we would be going and why. Everything was a great secret. With the arrival of night, our parents woke us up and dressed us in warm clothing. A covered pickup truck was waiting in front of the house. It was loaded with boxes of medicines and medical supplies (Magda and I learned all that only much later). In the very back, behind the boxes, was a makeshift bed; there we were hiding with Mother. In a hurry Father released two pigs, and about fifteen rabbits from my beloved rabbit house, into the yard, and just about the same number of chickens. He locked the house and the gate, climbed in next to the driver, and we took off. Where to? We were making yet another daring escape from our relentless persecutors.

Shoeboxes and Mute Things (1977–1988)

Lost in those hectic summer months of my 1977 escape were some of the silent witnesses Mother had preserved from Beckov. The secret police confiscated two bookcases after my departure, and someone who had a key to my flat took the Persian rug. Exile is like a journey through the underworld to resurrection: I couldn't take anything with me except the essentials for my uncertain afterlife.

But whose resurrection and which afterlife would I recognize as my own in the unknown of exile? The fact that flights into and returns from exile are like resurrections and ashes—this is what I will learn in later years, when I unearth my genealogy. These days I am forgetting the very existence of Mother's mute witnesses; their past is buried behind me in the history that unfolded in my exile from 1977 to 1988.

Good-bye, Sweet Teens

Still nineteen, with only one backpack and my resolve, I boarded the train without expecting to return to Prague or see my friends ever again. A select group of male friends—sworn to secrecy—came to say good-bye to me at Prague's Hlavní Nádraží, the main railway station. They were Radko, Honza, Dr. Nakonečný, S., and my stepfather. I finished a bottle of gin with my father in Bratislava shortly before my departure, but I couldn't see Pavel, who was in the military.

On July 25 I defected with my police permit for my route to India, Nepal, and Sri Lanka. I had secured visas to all three countries through the embassies in Moscow. I was inoculated for my travel and had my invitation letters from the Socialist Union and my papers for the work camp. I looked 100 percent legitimate: a genuine Socialist Student Union representative on his trip to do summer work in a developing country. On the inside, however, I felt rotten to the core; instead of traveling via the Soviet Union, Afghanistan, and Pakistan, as I had indicated on my request for the police permit, I took the southern route to India on the Orient Express from Vienna to Istanbul, then continued east via Iraq, Iran, Afghanistan, and Pakistan. Both northern and southern routes were still open in 1977! No agents were expecting me on the train that connected Prague and Vienna. Since the police permits didn't specify my transit countries, and my permit was as good for me as it would be for any secret agent or Communist or socialist youth using it on an official trip, me unless something compromising was found in my luggage. The secrets of any such official trips weren't available to all border agents in the paperwork at their disposal. For all they knew, I could have been a spy on assignment. When I arrived at the border between Czechoslovakia and Austria, the border patrol called some office to inquire about my permit and found my papers to be in order.

There was one dramatic moment that lasted two hours before we reached the border, when I couldn't find my police permit anywhere in my train compartment. It had fallen out from my backpack and landed behind the seat. I was truly desperate. When I found it, I felt almost as if we already had crossed the border! Then the border police boarded the train and searched everything in my backpack, including the interior of the metal construction on the inside of my pack, which they made me open. To avoid suspicion, this backpack was the only piece of luggage, besides a small satchel, that I could have taken with me on this trip. Foolish or bold, I had taken my birth certificate and official gymnasium and university transcripts with me and other crucial personal documents and held them inside the satchel, standing up and keeping cool on the outside while feeling terrified on the inside. The $1,000 I'd gathered in Prague would be delivered to me via a foreigner that fall. It was more dangerous to carry this extra currency on me than to trust a stranger to deliver a large sum to a refugee. No one searched the satchel I was holding in my right hand. I handed over my police permit and passport from this same bag and kept it unzipped in their full view. They meticulously searched everything else.

As we crossed the border to Austria, I shouted, "Freedom!" out the train window at the passing electric wires, minefields, search dogs, and border guns trained on the happy socialist citizens imprisoned in the workers' paradise. I was in no danger, and I couldn't care less about my astonished traveling companions in the train compartment.

Even though my shout of freedom was genuine, that night at the youth hostel in Vienna, I found myself the most liberated yet the most alone person in the universe. The world and my life were an open book. I had been born anew in my exile, with my future uncharted before me, and was ready to embrace an adventure for which no education could have prepared me. The very next morning, I asked for political asylum from the Austrian police authorities at the gates of the refugee camp in Traiskirchen, located about one hour from Vienna by local train.

Letter from a Young Man

(Written in Prague, spring 1977, and printed in a *Samizdat* publication after July 25, 1977.)

> *I am addressing you with my thoughts and feelings, and I would also like to tell you something. Actually I do not know where to begin—so it is best to begin from the start of this year, when* Charta 77 *appeared on public stage.*

Its thought gained my interest from the start—but mainly with the certain originality it carried in the history of our country. I think it was that thought that took root in the minds of many of our people—and it became the subject of discussions at international meetings.

I hold that human rights cannot be realized without respect for responsibility toward another human being. When Charta 77 came up with the demand to fulfill human rights, and so gave an impulse to an open discussion about the human situation in society, I realized that without the gradual change in interpersonal relationships, one cannot demand any rights from another. And because Charta 77 is not an opposition movement and has no revolutionary aims, as it said, I embrace it and place my hope in it as a movement that aims at a change of interpersonal relationships and communication, at some kind of renewal of characters, at gradual attempts for a thorough transformation of human beings. It is a historical truth and an experience that unless human relationships reach certain spiritual levels, it is impossible to speak about human freedom and rights.

I accept Charta 77 as a general appeal to everyone and, to me alone, to come out of myself and offer another the right to life and self-realization; to resist every deception around me—barbaric acts, human depravity, darkness, stupidity, ignorance—that I should see in every human a person worthy of rights and interest, that I should mercilessly resist even at the cost to me of everything that does not support life with a human face.

Charta 77 for me means an impulse for general enlightenment and a sharing of inward humanity and is the opposite of all social degeneration.

Charta 77 does not appeal to anyone else but me to live a life worthy of a human being.

Charta 77, without regard for the place of its origin, expresses a general human effort to find catharsis and renewal of life. It is a fruit of human good, and for this reason, it makes sense to further its thought as a universal solution to the crisis of humankind.

On 15.3.1977, I took part at the psychological gathering at Sokolská Street, which was visited by the state secret police. With others I followed police orders and was interrogated. On 16.3.1977, I took part in the funeral of the philosophy professor Jan Patočka. My participation was a pieta and a personal honor, the expression of a free person in a socialist state in the twentieth century; it was not a political demonstration. I was detained and interrogated by the secret service at the funeral. Because Patočka was one of the writers and first spokespersons for Charta 77, his sympathizers were followed by the state authorities. Two secret service agents took me from the cemetery with covert smiles and with these words: "Smile. Do not make any trouble. It could get worse for you." I was assured that all this was a formality, that I had not done anything criminal, and that I would not be further persecuted. I was, however, forbidden to return to the funeral.

On the Tuesday after Easter Sunday, I was called in by the dean of the philosophical faculty in Prague, Professor Dr. Václav Ráb, to a conversation at which the director of the Socialist Student Union at Charles University, Milan Vondráček, was also present. After one hour of interrogation, I was told that I had severely damaged the university and violated the constitution and admission rules by not taking as my own the scientific Marxist world view and that I did not support the political aims of the Communist Party, that I took part in the actions of Charta 77, and so I did not really have any right to attend the university. Further the dean told me directly, "To study at the philosophical faculty is an honor, and so it does not violate the human rights and the right to education if someone does not get to study there." It also interested the dean whether I knew that Professor Dr. Jan Patočka, Drsc., h.c., was after all a fascist and collaborated with that regime and, for his anti-Marxist and anti-patriotic thinking, he had to leave the faculty. Dean Ráb offered me a truce if I would bring him the next day a written statement in which I explained my motives and deeply regretted my acts. He emphasized my conscience, my youth, and that I would not live a double-faced life.

The dean was not very satisfied with my first written statement about my activities because it was more descriptive rather than self-incriminating, and it did not clearly condemn the dissidents. About a month after various prolonged delays, I had several additional "conversations" with the Socialist Student Union and the Deputy of the Communist Party, Otto Novák (in one instance they actually visited me at home). They asked again about many things , and they did not like many things: how could I honor a person, who, according to my statement, was "a fascist who collaborated with the Nazis, who wrote antipatriotic, treasonous pamphlets....And what did I think after all!" They suggested that I prepare for the fall an improved statement, suitable to public presentation—"Don't I want to study?!" The question remains what would they do with me after I threw all that dirt on my own head.

It is tragic that in the twentieth century it is possible that one can be persecuted for taking part in a funeral. It is tragic that a young man is cornered from the beginning to decide between studies, education, and work in his field or to choose moral and character depravity. It is tragic that political prostitution is the destiny of many who want to only follow their heart. It is tragic that this yearlong bending of characters is gradually changed into apathy and the inability to think and live creatively, in a revolutionary way, and most of all spiritually.

It is tragic that this society gives a person only three alternatives: submit and bear your conflicts of conscience and hope friends will understand (but even here one crosses some borders beyond which one dies inwardly); give up everything and live one's inner life surrounded by friends, work as one can, survive, do not become bitter; or leave it all behind. I decided to turn in my Socialist Youth Union member card (number 00725775) because the activities, theory, and practice of this organization no longer harmonized with my conscience. The demands placed on me and the manner in which the party representatives dealt with me violated the rights of this state as socialist principles also. The activity of these socialist organizations is limited by directives from the top, and so the creative and free work of its members is impossible. On the contrary, they use the system of coercion through regular evaluations, punishments, and cadre placements. For this reason the socialist student group is a mass institution, passively ensuring that its most active members can advance in their careers.

Furthermore I add my signature to the manifesto of Charta 77.

I testify that I believe in G-d. I want to share this with those who are open to a spiritual and universal way of thinking. I consider the greatest crime of the present regime its suppression of all spiritually thinking people of this land and of all they do for their own transformation and that of others.

I wish all well for the people of this land and the universe.

Martin Matuštík, first year student of psychology

The One Who Is Taking off—M.M. (Poem by Radko Richter)

You are taking off
So that you can go
So that a locomotive can whistle its departure
Under the modernist dome of that train station of desire.
You are taking off
So that you can shake hands one last time
So that you can show the border patrol, with a smile,
    that you are carrying nothing.
You are taking off
So that your heart can cry
As never before.
You are taking off and ask:
Where is the tombstone of your mother
When she walks in solitude
Through the dark aesthetic Canaan?
Where is the shy laughter
Laughter of your loves
Loves born so recently?
Where is that laughter

Which you photographed with your eyes in the morning?
Where did it vanish after this great flushing?
You ask then
Where is your strength
Keeping you company in lonely nights
When you read Psalms?
Where is the G-d of those flowing psalms?
Where is your home G-d?
Did G-d move already
 to Vienna
 New York
 Geneva
 Toronto
 or perhaps Jerusalem?
You are taking off
And you go at first to the one
Who knows only one's own page.
You are sitting here
 and after your desperate and nervously twisting and wall-scratching
 bowel movement
You distance that moment when you have to flush it all once and forever.
You are taking off and then
Never, never, no—you understand?!
You are taking off and you walk through Prague
In order not to miss the train.
People stare.
They pray to themselves.
A girl with beautiful breasts is thinking
Someone is going on vacation
And it is not worth it to flirt with him.
Then comes the train conductor
And you give him your last ticket
And he checks it and moves on.
The train goes through the tunnel
And Prague will no longer be.

(You will hear Czech for three more hours.)
You are taking off
And when you are there
Sometime at night
You will dream that your small Jewish soul,
Persecuted by pogroms,
Crucified, Burnt, Shot,
Wants something entirely different.
(Perhaps it is not true!)

—*RR; July 21, 1977*

Written by Radko Richter before my departure from Prague, the poem survived, hidden with my notebooks, until I returned and claimed it and other belongings in 1989. My gymnasium soul mate, through what he sensed about my mother, had more sense of my Jewish heritage and his own Jewish descent than I did after my Catholic conversion in Prague.

Stateless on the Danube River

In the spring of 1938, Jewish refugees from Austria began to stream into Slovakia. Refugees from Burgenland, Austria, lived in horrible conditions on the deck of a boat on the Danube. Under Hungarian and Slovak guards, yet stateless, they had been expelled from Austria. Saved and brought first to Slovakia, many left for Palestine. Gisi Fleischmann began her rescue work for these Jews in Bratislava.

After I fled Prague in 1977, I became a stateless refugee. Once I was in a refugee camp, I would look from the other side of the Danube in Vienna toward Bratislava. In 1986, before I was allowed back, I met secretly with my father in Budapest. I passed through Bratislava on board a Danube cruise from Budapest to Vienna. If the boat had made an emergency stop in my native town, I would have been arrested.

10

KAFKA IN AMERICA

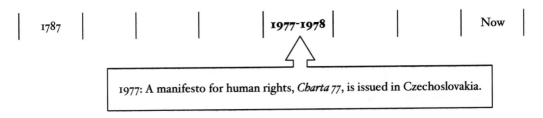

1977: A manifesto for human rights, *Charta 77*, is issued in Czechoslovakia.

Once a "Prague boy," I venture alone into the world beyond the Iron Curtain with a backpack and some cash. After eight months in an Austrian refugee camp, I discover America. This chapter presents readers with a Kafkaesque impression of my promised land; ignorant of my origins, I desire to become a Catholic priest. I discover America on my way from Prague to India and land in Santa Monica, California.

The Path of No Return (1977–1979)

I was a young man who had embarked upon a Columbus-like voyage from Prague to India but en route discovered America. Having been a ward of the socialist state, as a young dissident, I metamorphosed into a refugee Kafka. In this part of my story I have Franz Kafka write about my twentieth-century experience. Kafka, who was less heroic than the Italian sea voyager Columbus, describes for me an archetypal Central European figure of New World discovery and Jewish wandering.

"*Ich bin aus der Tschechoslowakei und ich bitte für politische Asyl,*" he uttered in broken German after he took the Vienna city train to Traiskirchen and showed up at the refugee camp gates. He repeated, "I am Kafka from Czechoslovakia, and I ask for political asylum," as if the indifferent guards never had heard someone asking for political asylum in German with a heavy *tschechische* accent. He was led to the third floor of a large building. Someone asked for his green Czechoslovak passport, and after that August summer of 1977 he never would see it again. Kafka became a stateless citizen of the world. He wasn't permitted to leave the building until his identity was verified.

My Silences, Veils, Personas

Franz Kafka was a Czech-born, German-educated Jew living as an expatriate in his hometown of Prague. As he was homeless at home, Kafka's promised land may not resemble Ulysses's Ithaca, Oedipus's Colonus, or Moses's Canaan. He has been claimed and dispossessed by his Czech, German, Israeli, philosophical, and literary circles to this day. Milan Kundera, another literary expatriate about whose fame Czechs remain ambivalent, wrote in "The Tragedy of Central Europe":[34]

> No other part of the world has been so deeply marked by the influence of Jewish genius. Aliens everywhere and everywhere at home, lifted above national quarrels, the Jews in the twentieth century were the principal cosmopolitan, integrating element in Central Europe: they were its intellectual cement, a condensed version of its spirit, creators of its spiritual unity....The novelistic visions of Kafka speak to us of a world without memory, of a world that comes after historic time.

I claim Kafka as a literary persona for my refugee self: In my story, Kafka is free from the guarded and mined fences of his disenchanting Garden of Eden. Communist agents confiscate his possessions. A different paradise awaits him in exodus. He is genuinely on his own in a wide-open world. Wandering for eight months on the other side of the barb-wired Danube River, in the wilderness of the Austrian refugee camp, waiting for his refugee asylum as if it were a never-arriving Godot, the young man makes his way across the Atlantic and arrives in the promised land. He crashes in a college dorm among his peers, and the urgency of escape recedes into the background of the City of Angels.

"Kafka" is also a bird; the *Corvus monedula* (jackdaw, *kavka* in Czech) was used by Hermann Kafka, Franz's father, as a business logo. Kafka's birdsong has a lingering taste of transgenerational memory. As an immigrant in my story, Kafka became a pawn of the Cold War.

Murmurs in a young man's heart: *Did I embark on a twenty-year-long detour, following Columbus en route to India and landing in the Americas? Did I leap across generations back to the future on a journey home but furthest from my still unknown origins?*

Quarantined

Kafka, my refugee persona, came to know Vienna from an angle not offered to ordinary tourists. For all practical purposes, he was considered a foreign Communist spy until proven innocent.

"You will be quarantined until we can write down your story and check its accuracy. You are to have no contact with anyone, and no newspapers, no phone, no TV." These were the instructions the interrogating asylum officials gave the young Czech man in the refugee camp in Austria.

The young man was fed and housed and questioned as a prisoner. He didn't know how long he would be there or what his outcome might be. He had to explain his life history in detail, along with the reasons for his escape, and give names and references, which they checked with their spies. They were suspicious because he wasn't a typical signatory of the dissident *Charta 77* who showed up as a refugee. Some well-known dissidents had been issued exit passports to Austria; in effect they were kicked out of their countries. Kafka was not one of them.

"Why did not you come to Vienna the same way as the dissident immigrants who signed *Charta 77*?" he was questioned. How could Kafka prove his unlikely story?

Suspicions followed one after another: "Were your parents not prominent Communists? Weren't you speaking regularly to the Czech secret service? They must have recruited you for their services! Are you not their spy sent through the camp to infiltrate immigrant circles abroad? How did you get into Charles University?" He couldn't tell them his undiscovered, still unmastered story because he didn't know it himself. *What shall I know when I know myself?* I now think. *I still empathize with the young man's blindness.*

"How did you manage to get a police permit to the West, given your detentions by the secret police?" This made as little sense to them (they were secret service agents) as it did to Kafka and the many to whom he would later repeat the story. He spoke of the socialist girl. They chuckled. Did they believe him? How would they find out whether Kafka had dated the girl? He had brought his birth certificate and transcripts, but they would be useless until he received a security clearance.

Kafka's refugee story was corroborated by three factors. The first was Voice of America's report of his Prague detention in January 1977 at the underground seminar of Patočka's Flying University. This was the initiating scene for the young man's dissident troubles with secret agents and the Communist administrators at Charles University. Some of the spy agencies in the West had obtained a list of detained persons from dissident events. The second was his signature of *Charta 77*. There also was his letter in support of *Charta 77,* which he wrote before his Houdini act in which he flew out of the cage as *kavka*. The third was the MJ family in Prague, who were well known in dissident Catholic circles.

For all his self-evidence, my Kafka self suffered an identity crisis that lay deeper than Oedipus's willed ignorance of his parental generation. Had Kafka boasted Jewish genealogy (but in my story he is still blind to his Jewish origins), he would have been placed not only in a different narrative context but also in a different refugee camp. The three proofs of his story and identity—but especially his significant Catholic connections from Prague—further distanced him from his mother's Jewish origins. Kafka's declared religious vocation to the priesthood proved to be another decisive factor in his quick release from political detention in the camp. The Catholic Charity was among the largest and most respected of refugee relief organizations in Traiskirchen, and he signed up with them for all his refugee needs. Kafka's Catholic leanings, quickly satisfying the investigating agents in the refugee camp, parted the Red Sea to his safety of political asylum in Austria and guided his later exodus to the promised land.

Breaches and Disrepairs of Memory

Etelka was the firstborn sister of my mother's dad, Nathan. After I learned her first name, I didn't know she had lived through Auschwitz because Uncle Ernest's faulty memory led me astray. Etelka guided the surviving Jewish lineage out of the Old World to Sydney. Ernest wrote to me while I was in the refugee camp and, wanting to help me out, sent me Martha's address in the United States. He never quite explained how Martha was related to us, and he never used to identify himself to me as being Jewish. He suffered from an involuntary version of Mother's silence. Martha was the daughter of Elisheva (she went by the diminutive "Eržička"), who in turn was the sister of my maternal grandmother, Ilonka. Martha was my mother's cousin and peer. She left Czechoslovakia with her mother, Eržička, in 1946, and they lived for some time in Israel and later moved to the United States. Martha continued her mother's Jewish life. It seemed of no importance to Ernest for him to tell me any of that when he sent me Martha's address.

The Refugee Camp

After two weeks of initial isolation, I shared a room with several other asylum seekers. We were, however, still isolated from the general population of the camp. My days in group quarantine were filled with my wild speculating about my future, enduring procedures to get asylum and immigrate somewhere, surviving camp life or figuring out how to slip out of the camp to the city, and coming up with myriad ways to scheme and make money. If the quarantine were prison isolation, camp life had all but the most brutal characteristics of prison conditions. I didn't live in a maximum-security lockup, but I had no means or identity papers to allow me to lead a normal civilian life in Vienna. The camp was a mixture of prison and military barracks. Three daily meals were taken in a big "dining" hall. Refugees lived on bunk beds in rooms with twenty or more refugee "inmates." The camp was guarded twenty-four hours a day. After the period of quaranteen ended, refugees could leave and return using a simple sign-up sheet, yet all had restricted movements.

Eventually I received a worthless piece of ID declaring me an asylum seeker. I couldn't get a regular job with those papers. I couldn't travel to another country, and ordinary citizens of Vienna would suspect me as if I were an escaped criminal. The Catholic Charity gave me a monthly stipend of sixty dollars for personal items. The rest of my means would come either from personal savings, or I could be hired out for day labor. As migrant workers, like undocumented Mexicans in the United States, refugees waited for trucks to pick them up outside of the camp gates. In this spirit of struggle for bare survival until some free country would accept us, I stayed in one of the smallest of rooms in the barracks for six months. During that fall of 1977, I worked on wine harvests and studied English, and as I had in the chaos of my youth—but now in the camp and out of the motherland's protective bubble—I tried to remain sane and alive.

On the False Trail, on the Right Trail Falsely

I had no clue that my Jewish relatives who had survived the war had passed through Vienna en route to Israel and Australia in 1946 and 1947. I had no inkling about the existence of any Jewish family members living in Sydney. That path would lie buried for the next twenty years, ten of which I'd spend in an intensely religious, largely Catholic quest, and ten in a philosophical-political, largely atheistic quest. But the young man who fled Prague in 1977 inherited his mother's phone book, where he found the addresses of two relatives that he took with him. These were the same relatives whose names Ernest had sent to him in the camp. Mother's phone book told no more about them than Uncle did.

Useless Violence

The fact that life in the camp wasn't something to be taken for granted became apparent when a gang of frustrated Albanian refugees stormed into my small room with open knives and tried to force all the inmates to jump from the third-floor windows. A man had been killed a few nights before in a similar incident. Communist Albania was one of the most oppressive regimes, and the most primitive brutes had been released from that country's jails into the camp. If cultivated Albanian citizens existed, then the camp had no blessed Mother Teresa among them. Perhaps Albania was following the example of Fidel Castro, who once emptied his jails and dumped them on Miami. Albanians were roaming the camp that night, and there were no phones or guards within the camp buildings. That frightful night had long moments of terror, and then with a slow, deliberate, almost surreal philosophical plea, I talked the Albanian squad out of stabbing or defenestrating the inmates. I made gangsters grow weary with highly speculative, religious, and Kafkaesque discourse. They wanted a fistfight; instead they received my homily. When their agitation lost its steam, they suddenly left the room the same way they had appeared. Totally shaken I tried to forget the night during which I could have suffered a useless death in a G-dforsaken hole of the world not far from my native land.

Political Asylum

The Austrians considered the refugees a burden and a danger they had to suffer because Austria, after the Soviets had left Vienna, were the most "Eastward" asylum state in the West. The Viennese tolerated Czechs and Slovaks more than they did the "darker" populations from the East and Africa. Czech and Slovak Roma were treated as badly as African-Americans had been during the Jim Crow period. Refugees were seen as thieves and treated with disgust, suspicion, and the sort of fear one witnesses with regard to white America's relations to its minority populations. Even if I were to receive political asylum in Austria and manage with that my right to work and study, it would take a long time for me to integrate into Austrian society. An immigrant's difficulty settling in Austria also existed in other European countries because of Europe's general history of ethnic conflict. Many Eastern European immigrants in the United States, as if to deflect ostracism from other Europeans, often outdo North American whites in their prejudice.

After three months in the camp, I held in my hands a most intriguing passport: a UN travel document. Others treated the owner of such a document with the same respect and disdain as the United Nations itself. The UN document states that it holds no prejudice concerning the holder's country of birth or nationality. Just as after my mother's death I became a ward of the Communist state, now I was a stateless ward of the United Nations. In the world Immanuel Kant imagined in his essay "Perpetual Peace," the UN travel document would have been the ideal League of Nations document. In the real world, however, I held Kafkaesque travel identification. I needed a visa for every country, even for transit through them, and I not only had to demonstrate that I had sufficient means of subsistence for every visit, but I also had to provide proof of a return ticket to Austria. With Austrian political asylum, I was eligible to immigrate elsewhere or apply to the university in Vienna and resume my psychology studies. Austria financed higher education as a general entitlement for those who qualified, so I would not have to pay for mu studies.

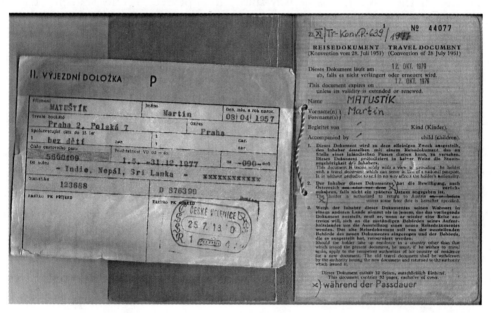

27. Martin Matuštík's Czechoslovak exit permit to India and refugee stateless passport, 1977

As a Kafka self, I decided to make a more radical break with my past and leave Europe for the New World, even though the United States offered no help to new immigrants, much less the cost of attending college. With my Kantian futuristic passport, I applied for immigration to another country. After considering Canada too cold, Australia too far, South Africa too racist, and most areas of Europe inhospitable, I applied to the US embassy in Vienna for immigration papers. As a stateless refugee with political asylum in Austria, I would receive preferential treatment under the US numerical quota system for immigrants. I would have to wait several months to hear from the embassy, and then there would be new interrogations about my story, followed by more waiting and more red tape.

While waiting to hear from the embassy, I took a short Christmas break from the camp and explored the possibilities of settling in other European countries, for instance in Scandinavia or Italy. I visited Norway, where my maternal cousins, Ivo and Vlado, had lived with their mother since 1968. She left with her two young boys without saying a word to their father, my uncle Ernest. It took years before Uncle got to visit them in Norway. They had some contact with our Sydney relatives, but because of Ernest's sporadic communication with his uncle Béla, this fact never was brought up during my visit. Ernest never mentioned it to me either. Mother's friend František lived with his gorgeous young wife Irina in Stockholm, and they were willing to take me in. František had met my mother during the Prague Spring when she began reading spiritual literature. When František left Prague shortly after the Soviet invasion of 1968, Mother briefly considered joining him. *What would my life have been like if I had become orphaned in Sweden?* I often wonder.

Kafka's Columbus Journey

My dramatic persona, Kafka, crossed the Atlantic, and his stateless UN document was stamped with a US immigrant visa. Two years later his UN passport was replaced by a white US travel document that identified him as a stateless person while always allowing his return to the United States. The new document made it easier for other countries to grant a travel visa to anyone as suspicious as Kafka from Central Europe. No one would want to risk that he may overstay his welcome and never return to the USA.

Getting placement on an immigrant flight was easier if one had lived in the camp, as expediting the refugees' trips made space for new arrivals. I was coming out of this hole alive and well, and I realized how privileged I was in the eyes of those who had waited for more than a year. At the charter rates in 1978, passage from Traiskirchen by bus to the Schwechat airport in Vienna and then on to New York and by a regular flight to Los Angeles cost a total of $190. None of my roommates was on that refugee flight. I boarded the luxury bus in the dead of winter, wearing a heavy coat and a blue scarf knitted by my mother. But I was going to Santa Monica, California, the land of sun and bronzed girls I had learned about from the Beach Boys. My US sponsor,

Doug, a computer science student at UCLA, put me up for three months. With a big smile on my face, I was starting another chapter of my adventure.

Not having been transplanted to a Czech community—as happens with many who come with spouses or who are sponsored by Czech-American families—I was surrounded from the start by other young Americans and was compelled to immerse myself in American culture. I must have struck my American peers as an alien on the "third rock from the sun," a character whom my persona, Kafka, would recognize as his alias in 1996 in the John Lithgow TV comedy about aliens transplanted into human bodies. Watching that show with true delight late after my naturalization, I decided to introduce myself to others as the "alien from the third rock." The cultural bridge provided by Lithgow's character did more for me than many a storytelling had in the past. An entire pantheon of cultural characters and TV shows had formed my American peers, and I had to engage their imagined adventures in ordinary conversation. *Leave It to Beaver,* portraying an all-American family with happy values, was the exact the opposite of my Kafkaesque childhood, and perhaps for this reason, I preferred *The Addams Family.* Then there were the Lone Ranger and Tonto, Lassie and Superman, and many cartoon characters, from Popeye to Daffy Duck to Mr. Magoo, whose cultural context would escape me for years in conversations.

While I had expected America, unlike Canada or Australia, to exert this pressure on a newcomer who had to learn how to swim alone, life there was much harder than I'd imagined, and I had to learn how to live from scratch. *I could actually drown,* I thought.

Learning to Tell My Story

In my rendition of "Kafka in America," as a new immigrant, I embraced exile as my metamorphosis and postmortem birth. Even now I travel through parallel infinite universes. I've been writing my way through life ever since "Kafka" at twenty landed in America. In my first US conversation about who I was and how I got here, I'd respond seriously, as if people really wanted to locate me, my native land, my future. Their mental maps became my generational matrices. In storytelling I rocked with the nursemaids of long bygones. In the weeks, months, and years to come, my story kept evolving and mutating. At times the telling was terse and at others more literary and then like a lullaby. I retold my story over and over, like an actor becoming hungrier than ever for waves of applause and roses, then unmasking in his dressing room. I made editorial changes and adjusted the narrative to this or that listener's interest.

In the 1960s Prague filmmakers invented a theater where viewers returned to watch different versions of the same film. The story line to be seen on any night was decided by the audience. Everyone voted by pushing red or white buttons that were attached to their seat. The majority would determine how to unfold the film story. Several votes would be taken at different points in the film. No one knew how many versions of the film existed. People, in search of the infinite, imagined and returned to watch the same film from the beginning. One needed only one film, a single love relationship, one life to live, one pair of shoes to buy and exchange in barter.

Memory dreams through imagination, and fiction longs for roots. Joy becomes one with creative fiction, as so many subjunctive and future perfect truths that could or will have been. A philosophical memoir reaches out to imagine a nearly completed future. *Can I live everywhere at once if I'm to be genuinely mortal among mortals?* If time could earn its own merit by healing all of the wounds of history, if fiction could make us believe that metamorphoses are bereft of loss, if memoirs could overreach to imagined future perfects that never again have to struggle with memory, then irreparable breaches within and among generations would not haunt our silences and words. I struggled with this discovery before I reached my conclusions, integrated my faces and personae, and bowed as myself with the curtain up.

As a new immigrant, I often had intimates and friends tell my story at gatherings. With them I could gaze into the prehistory that rises from the dead. I would listen to find out, as if for the first time, who I was and whom I would become. I would be "born again" with each more profound retelling. When Patricia became my witness, she reedited the untold segments as if they were unwanted deletions made by a harsh self-editor. She would wake up unaware of my half-told truths. And I would attend to her narrations as if a new person had come into existence. My literary characters annihilated and resurrected one another. I cooked up and penned many a heroic, humble, nostalgic, exotic, mundane version of myself. As with a Photoshop project, I could sharpen the sketches with moods, contrasts, tones, and inflection.

Does midrash cease to be creative nonfiction when it is written into life? Hidden subtexts would become freed from stone as sparks of profane illuminations. Which stories of repair could I promise to past and future generations? Which promises of repair could I give myself? Did I not unearth both breaches and repairs in the silence with which Mother cloaked her story? I would have to interrupt her silence; I would repair by editing her life story, which she would have preferred been left untold behind the double walls of her screen memories. In the present, I could not remain silent and hidden as the unmoved mover; I needed to wrestle with my gods, demons, my own discomforts and cloaks.

Love holds one another's stories without end. A closed universe would be kitsch. Open memoirs are universes whose futures may still remember disrepair. In living memory one is never a single version of oneself, nor can one be reborn by an erasure of one's past. Remembering isn't the same as finding a treasure. For this reason, just as there can be no compelling proofs for or against G-d's existence, so there is no canonical version or proof of oneself. There is but one'sawareness of the now.

What would it mean to ask myself, Do I exist? *And then to try to prove it?* Yet without such proofs, how false would it ring if I said, "For this reason I do not exist, and I may not become a self." Life would be a despairing affair in a linear universe, and love would be impossible. If destiny were fated, there would be just one telling, one canonical version of (my)self, one doctrine of the universe, and no possibility of change.

I would imagine who I could have become had I stayed in Prague, and those who stayed would freeze me in their memory of the future. Can one emigrate from one's life story? Pushing buttons on one's seat becomes more than imaginary. If reality so often poorly matches imagination, only existential decisions and flesh-and-blood encounters reveal the essential contours of the life story. That sought-for second-degree infinity is no longer an arbitrary game.

Singular shapes emerge in each earnest storytelling. *Are such shapes finite in number or variation, or are they like the buttons on one's seat with which one edits the script? If we imagine that destiny is like a snowflake, and one's life is like a singularity captured by a snowflake, then what is the meaning of one's life? Is it the script one can narrate in a memoir or produce for a film, or is it more like the spirit that underlies all variations in infinite retelling?* "What is self?" asked Søren Kierkegaard at the beginning of *The Sickness unto Death*, and he answered, "Self is spirit," and then he asked anew, "But what is spirit?" Self is a relation to the infinite in oneself; it is not any one thing that one can tell in a story—this or that memory. *How can spirit's freedom be shaped by infinite possibility yet achieve the finite singularity of a snowflake? Is a life story like a sonata's variation with its second-degree infinity? How can destiny be recognized as one's singular path yet something freely lived rather than fated?*

Midlife Crises

It is the summer of 1997, and choking on midlife, I break Mother's silence to taste ancient foods. It would take ten more years until I tasted a *bramborák* as a Hanukah latke, before I would be able to mix and cook all the facets of my life without fear that some relative or friend would reject some part of the dish. Cuts define a lived story, each break reshaping the historical present. I was born into an atheistic Communist home; I converted to Christianity as an early teen; I chose to be religious in my midtwenties; a second atheistic period would parallel my path of becoming a professional philosopher; and when I thought I had it all made and figured out, in my early forties, I discovered my lost Jewish story and had to retell everything I knew or thought I was: atheist-Christian-philosopher-Jew.

This has been my Kafkaesque discovery: until the late 1990s, no one in the United States and virtually no one who knew me in my native land identified me as Jewish. I was at first Catholic. Then I became what I thought I was at my birth: an atheist. Those who knew of my Jewish past were either dead or silent or lost to me. Once my Jewish past emerged out of Mother's silence, however, I had to tell my story.

Martha

When I left Prague, my aunt Martha lived in Connecticut. Her mother's last address was in Tel Aviv. With a vague intuition of their importance in my kin structure, I wrote to Martha and her mother, Eržička, from the refugee camp. I introduced myself simply: "I am a son of Magda. I am your distant family relative in his twenties; Ernest was my uncle. I want to meet you. I don't know of any other family members abroad. Perhaps you would sponsor my emigration."

These two women responded with interest in my situation. But then Martha received a letter from the Catholic Charity in Traiskirchen; the charitable institution was following up on her interest to sponsor my immigration. She shrank in horror because I was associated with a Christian relief organization. I wrote Martha another letter. My handwritten pages opened aromas of enthusiasm for religious repair. I had no clue of our Jewish connection and in fact longed to become a Catholic priest. I was finally coming home. Without my realizing it, my letter's religious zeal stretched disrepair across three generations. I may have been smudging my words with ignorance and naïveté, but my Christian psalmody dried up even the fresh ink of Kafka's irony. Words sounding true and sincere veiled my mother's story with a personal detour longer than Columbus's journey to India. I suffered from a generational blindness.

Letter from the Refugee Camp to My Stepfather

Vienna

October 1, 1977

I decided to stay. I received political asylum, which is also an important legal protection, and soon I will obtain the new Austrian-issued UN passport. If I knew German, I could start at the university later this October with the basic scholarship of three thousand Austrian schillings. After thinking about it, I decided to leave Europe and petitioned for immigration to the United States. My knowledge of English is also decisive for the United States, even if the possibility to study there will be more difficult, and everything is different over there than in Europe. People here come with varied destinies and by various means, some directly over the electric wires but mostly over the mountains from Yugoslavia. Refugees come from all Eastern Bloc countries but also from Chile and Bangladesh. I cannot imagine at all that I would return [to Prague]. Not at all! I am having typical emigrant dreams: I am back in Czechoslovakia with only one half of my secret service exit permit, and I am unable to go back, in vain explaining to the border guards that I am supposed to be on the other side. I am most concerned that I will hurt some people by my departure. I assume that they have already sealed my flat in Prague and that in about six months I can also expect the court sentence.

All the best, always,

Martin

Solomon's Prayer

As one makes choices, even in the worst of them, surviving any ordeal well testifies to the human spirit. The Germans knew in 1944 that they had lost the war, yet they still believed in the Final Solution. The Becks—saved from the first transports in 1942; protected by Lutheran baptism, their new name, and the false papers then betrayed by an informant; sheltered by friends and foes—had to fight for their survival until the spring of 1945. As I consider the sheer size of the annihilation while standing in the early summer of 1997 in the shadow of its emptiness, Auschwitz is nothing like what I have seen in films. Shivers of Mother's silence run through my body. I hear my mother's family humming with Solomon, "May love be strong as death."

II

OUT OF SILENCE

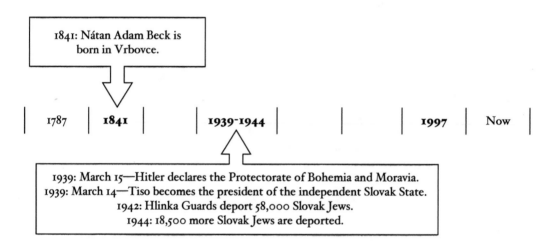

1841: Nátan Adam Beck is born in Vrbovce.

| 1787 | 1841 | 1939-1944 | | 1997 | Now |

1939: March 15—Hitler declares the Protectorate of Bohemia and Moravia.
1939: March 14—Tiso becomes the president of the independent Slovak State.
1942: Hlinka Guards deport 58,000 Slovak Jews.
1944: 18,500 more Slovak Jews are deported.

I now join the linear narrative of my life with the dramatic discovery of my lost family in 1997 with which I opened my story. At this juncture I am still to meet the Sydney survivors of Auschwitz and their children. I'm about to learn the first secret veiled by my mother's silence. Why did she hide the truth of our origins?

Myjava (1997, 1841–1956)

The early summer of 1997 tastes of brush fires, and I feel that my personal story and public history will meet in some new awareness. My Jewish origins are no longer capable of keeping my generation's silence. Patricia and I travel from Myjava to Auschwitz. The journey takes us via Kúty to Banská Bystrica, covering open regions and mountains. One by one, Jewish families vanished from Myjava, Kúty, and other villages of the Slovak State. Altman, Grünwald, Haberfeld, Kohn, Rosenzweig, Weisz...Myjava's Jewish registry of births lists ancestors and contemporaries of my grandparents.[35] *How long could the Becks avoid their deportation?* I wondered.

"The Kohn family lived near us, next to the belt makers," Brano Borsuk says, "and after the war, only their daughter showed up and left." The Kohns and Rosenzweigs are listed as witnesses on Jakub Beck's Myjava birth certificate, dated November 22, 1872.

"There were no Jews in Myjava after the war"—Ján Vrana looks at me—"except the Becks. The Communists demolished the synagogue."

Hope tastes stronger than death. With their new identity papers, their escape would be safer once they left the home region where Nathan was widely known by patients. The Becks were in flight—having lost their home, hiding place, friends; bereft of the comforts of their Tatra car, income, and possessions.

Many mythical family sagas abound regarding the wealth Nathan accumulated from the 1930s until he had to give up his practice. He was the first of the Beck siblings sent by their parents to get a university degree, followed by his two brothers. Nathan was expected to return to Myjava after his studies. His family came out of poverty. His parents, Jakub Bäck (1872–1931) and Cecilia Reiss, and grandparents, Nátan Adam Bäck (1841–?) and Loti Habersfeld, were merchants trading at local markets the wares they produced at home, be they shirt buttons or knitting supplies. Family savings paid for Grandpa Nathan's medical degree, and his future earnings were a family hope for raising everyone's standard of living. When Professor Brázda offered Nathan a prestigious research assistantship at the university in Bratislava, he turned it down and opened his practice at home in Myjava. Part of the Myjava myth about Nathan's proverbial wealth begins with the Nazi persecution. He is reported to have hidden gold Swiss Rolex watches either in his old house—having buried them in the garden—or around town, while placing cash amounts, precious metals, textiles, and other items in safekeeping with friends. No hidden Beck treasures, however, ever were found or returned by anyone in Myjava.

"Every year on All Saints' Day, someone places fresh lilies on your grandparents' grave, but we've never been able to find out who it is," Ján says. His parents owned a pub, Hostinec u Vranov, but the Communists nationalized it and paid the family five hundred Czech crowns.

A secret gratitude? I think.

The Beck's Oak

Nathan grew rich again in 1945 after the Becks returned to their house, where he resumed his private practice. Ján used to get his medical checkups at Beckov after the war and his friend Dano had his baby teeth pulled by Nathan.

"As children we played in the sand behind Dr. Beck's house. There was a one-hundred-twenty-year-old tree, which we called the Beck's Oak," Brano recalls.

Both Uncle Ernest and my father told stories that after Nathan's wife's death in 1948, their housekeeper spent anything he might have recovered from before the war or earned after it. She disappeared with the rest after his death in 1956. Nathan never trusted banks or insurance companies, nor seemed to care to save and grow rich, whether before the arrival of the Nazis or after the war. As a humanist he was too impractical to be an enterprising capitalist and too people oriented to become an ideological Communist after the war. He wasn't particularly religious either. He loved people, and they repaid his care with money and barter. A parallel saga about his abundant sexual energy and numerous extramarital liaisons has been told—many women offered their treasures for his charm and vitality. Nathan did make money, not because he charged more than people could pay, but because he was a hard-working and popular physician. The money went the same way the money came, and whatever Nathan earned in the three years after the war's end, the Communist takeover in February 1948 took away. Nathan never thought of keeping his prewar earnings in a Swiss account or in life insurance. He kept most of his cash in socks or pillows or in drawers hidden around the house.

Uncle Ernest told a tale about my father prompting his young fiancée, my mother, on a visit in Myjava to "borrow" some cash from one of the many hiding places Nathan kept around the house. Nathan never could tell whether the cash had been taken from a sock or drawer. Father, young Communist though he was, must have imagined that he was marrying into relative wealth. Mother, young Communist though she was, must have exhibited even after her war ordeal the flair of a Jewish millionaire's beloved daughter. While Father had been as careless about money as Nathan was, he never saved enough to support his lifestyle or build economic security, or even land an apartment that didn't belong to the university or one of his four wives, or in his old age, his youngest daughter. If Nathan had wealth—and judging by the Beck house, the new car, expensive textiles, and his energetic practice, the Becks were among the most well-to-do families in town—their fortune would have been stored in ways that even detectives might never find. Nathan, trusting life to always provide enough to live well and survive, wasn't even as money smart as a squirrel is storing nuts for a harsh winter.

The Europa Plan

Two million dollars was a significant sum in the 1940s; two dollars per person was a bargain for infinity. According to Reb Dov Weissmandl's "divine arithmetic," there were about one million Jews left in Europe in 1942 outside of Hungary, Poland, and Germany. The Europa Plan would have saved one million Jews—two dollars per Jew to stop all deportations from occupied territories. From the beginning of 1943, Gisi Fleischmann and Andrej Steiner conducted direct talks with Dieter Wisliceny in Bratislava. During these negotiations, the Nazis agreed to stop deportations in Europe.[36] Wisliceny was to take the plan to Himmler who is said to have agreed.

When Wisliceny informed Fleischmann that one thousand children had been transferred from the Bialystok ghetto to Terezín, Steiner proposed to Wisliceny to save these children for $100,000. This was to be a test for the Europa Plan. The Children's Rescue Plan was originally initiated by the leaders of the Yishuv (Jewish residents in Palestine before the establishment of the State of Israel), who proposed transferring five thousand children from Holocaust areas in exchange for German prisoners. At the end of August 1943, Eichmann ordered that 1,264 children ages six to twelve and at least twenty adult caretakers be taken by train from Bialystok to Terezín. They remained there in special barracks until October 5, 1943. During this time complex negotiations took place to save these children through exchange and transfer via Switzerland and Slovakia to Palestine. The children received medical care and were fed, but when the Working Group failed to raise the $100,000 for Wisliceny, the children and their adult caretakers were taken to Auschwitz, where they were gassed and burned on Erev (the eve of) Yom Kippur, October 7, 1943. The Europa Plan was dead.

From "The Road to Atlanta," an interview with Andrej Steiner by Ruth Lichtenstein:

> ANDREJ STEINER: It was [Rabbi] Weissmandl's plan to give such big bribes that the Germans would halt their destruction of Europe's remaining Jews. I took the Europa Plan to Wisliceny.
>
> RUTH LICHTENSTEIN: What was his answer?
>
> ANDREJ STEINER: He was willing to present it to Himmler. He was confident that through Himmler the Europa Plan could be accomplished.
>
> RUTH LICHTENSTEIN: What actually happened?
>
> ANDREJ STEINER: We couldn't get Jews outside of Nazi-occupied Europe to send us what we needed. I would say it was one of our group's biggest failures. Because the Europa Plan was for the Jews a very good plan.
>
> RUTH LICHTENSTEIN: Did Wisliceny say that the Europa Plan failed because of the lack of money?
>
> ANDREJ STEINER: Yes. Yes. He had the same feeling that we didn't live up to our promises, so they cannot live up to their promises. And basically, I really mean, if in this very critical position, the beginning of Europa Plan, we would have had the hundred thousand dollars, maybe...maybe we could have been helpful in other countries too.

RUTH LICHTENSTEIN: When Rabbi Weissmandl devised the Europa Plan, did you accept it?

ANDREJ STEINER: I immediately accepted it. I believed in it too.

RUTH LICHTENSTEIN: Do you believe that the bribe stopped the deportation?

ANDREJ STEINER: I believe that the working camps which I organized in Sereď, Nováky, and Výhne kept the thousands who worked there safe from being deported. So it wasn't only the bribery. I believe that the work camps and the bribe stopped deportations for those two years.

With the Partisans

Days before August 28, 1944, the Becks fled from the Záhorie region to the partisan territory of the High and Low Tatra and Fatra Mountains. The Slovak National Uprising surprised the Nazis, and Nathan, who was connected with the partisans in Myjava and Kúty, needed to arrive on time in Banská Bystrica, the partisan epicenter of the uprising. Mother's intellectual, political, and sexual awakening occurred precociously in this momentous historical period and marked her young-adult thinking. Mother never married the man she had met during the war. While she mentioned her first love in passing to me, she withheld his name, the time, and the role of this relationship in her life. I had a long way to go toward discovering how her silence led to then covered traces of this love. That late discovery finally would help me find peace regarding Mother's secrets and grasp their meaning for my own journey.

Nathan became the chief organizing force behind the partisan hospitals he directed in the entire rebel territory, while Mother worked as a mountain field nurse. She had no formal medical education at that time, so she must have learned the nursing skills from her father. The sixteen-year-old Magdalena living and working with the Slovak partisans is described in her various autobiographical résumés from the Communist era. I imagine an icon of Mother the partisan, Joan of Arc, a woman with a bandolier slung over her shoulders. Her hunger for justice reveals Shekinah's face. Mother writes about her time with the partisans as being one of her most joyous periods. Her youthful self-choice to be a Communist was molded by the partisan saviors in Myjava, matured by fire in her fighting the Nazis in the mountains, and solidified in the solidarity she discovered with her comrades in battle. Socialism inevitably signaled in her experience a more just future. Of that which could not be spoken, she kept silent. Whether it was because of the political regime or for personal reasons, her published bios skirt the period of Nazi persecution.

The end of the uprising was devastating, although those who spearheaded the active resistance had known the defeat was inevitable. Yet the very fact that a homegrown uprising had occurred wrote an alternative chapter for the Slovak historical present than the one already written by the homegrown Catholic-fascist Slovakia. Tiso and Hlinka's Slovak State betrayed the modern democratic Czechoslovakia founded by Tomáš Garigue Masaryk. This betrayal would haunt postwar Czechoslovakia. While the Communist takeover of 1948 was made possible in large part by the Czechs, the Soviet invasion of 1968 was legitimized by the official invitation from Slovak Communist Vasil Biľak. In 1968 Slovakia in turn got its federal arrangement within the Czechoslovak republic, prefiguring the formal grounds for its later separation. Slovak president Gustav Husák headed the postinvasion normalization period. After 1989 Slovakia began its nationalistic break from the Czechs. Political rhetoric and symbols echoed the clerical-fascist nationalism of the Slovak State. Today the young Slovak republic is still struggling to overcome its dark history, though many things are passed over in silence. The quadruple wounding—Tiso, Bilak, Husák, Mečiar— was laid to rest only on May 1, 2004, in the ironic remarriage of the Czech and Slovak peoples within the enlarged borders of the European Union.

Surviving Masada

In late 1944 the Germans pushed the Slovak partisans down from the mountain slopes, while gunners waited for them in the valley. The Becks almost died in a great battle under the mountains. In this desperate moment, Nathan decided on behalf of his family to opt for the Masada exit—the group suicide committed by ancient Judean rebels to avoid being captured by the Romans in the mountain fortress high above the Dead Sea.

28. Letter certifying that Nathan Beck worked in 1944 at the Slovak partisan hospital in Banská Bystrica

My young mother overheard her parents discuss their desperate suicide plan during the night. Nathan wanted to burn down their hiding place, a stall, as they slept in it that night. At first the two children and the wife were to swallow cyanide, and then Nathan would set the consuming fire as he took the last poisonous pill. My mother refused to taste the food of despair and convinced her strong-willed father to keep running. Life—her own and with her family—proved stronger than the forces of death in Auschwitz or death by suicide. As they managed to evade capture by the Nazis, Grandpa devised yet another plan in Zvolen. Nathan split up the family. Magda worked as a maid at the farm of a rich family, while her parents and little Ernest hid with another family near Zvolen. The Becks welcomed the arrival of Stalin's Red Army in Zvolen on March 14, 1945.

Ernest described the last days and the liberation in his remembrances. Intoning at the piano the song of the Red Army soldiers, he didn't realize that the Red Army's proverbial singing sent fear through German armies as the Hussite choral once did through German crusaders. By the time I had learned to sing about the Soviet artillery in my Russian language lessons, I no longer held it in awe but as a relic of our colonizers. Mother joined the mobile field-nursing station that traveled with the Red Army. The Becks returned with the advancing Soviets to Myjava later in that spring of 1945. The family survived against impossible odds.

Surviving Auschwitz

Ernest gives me the name of a distant relative, Blanka Löwingerová, from Komárno near the Slovak-Hungarian border. She's one of few relatives with whom he has kept in touch over the years. When we appear at the gate to her home, she welcomes Patricia and me as a "returning" family. In this early summer of 1997, it's my first encounter with her ever.

"I met my husband Matyáš during the war, and when we both survived Oswiencim," she says, referring to Auschwitz by its Polish name. She is setting the family record straight.

"You were in Auschwitz?" I blurt, astonished.

"I was taken there in my early twenties, but it was late, only in nineteen forty-four, when Jews were deported in greater numbers from Hungary." She has a strong, healthy appearance, a warm smile, and olive skin. She is six years older than my mother would have been. We search the map of Poland, but she's unable to locate Auschwitz on it.

"When the train arrived and we were pushed out of the carriages, we waited in a long line. I still remember a young, tall, light-haired, very handsome man. With his hand hanging in his coat, with his thumb he would point to the right, then left, then right again, and the line of deportees would split in two streams, left and right. He was gorgeous, but he was also cruel. This welcoming blond beast was Dr. Mengele, and he alone decided who went straight to gas and who to hard labor. I lived. Many more went to certain death. Of three thousand twins, only a few survived his biological experiments."

"How are you related to my family?" I ask, eager to find out.

"I met my husband, Matyáš Löwinger, in Auschwitz. He was a cousin of your Galanta grandma."

"You mean Ilonka Pressburgerová, later also called Helena?" I ask, not entirely sure.

"Yes." This already is getting quite heady. I know of another Löwinger—Lukács. György Lukács was a famous Hungarian philosopher who influenced the first generation of the Frankfurt School. Like Beck, or Bäck used by my family in the 1800s, Löwinger is a common surname. What if this critical theorist and I shared some distant Jewish ancestors? Blanka's family is fluent in Slovak and Hungarian.

"What was your great-grandmother's name?" I ask.

"Fani Löwingerová. She married Max Mordechai Pressburger. Fani died for sure in Auschwitz, though Max might have survived. He has an old tombstone in Galanta. Your grandma, Ilonka, and her sister Elisheva are daughters of Fani and Max; both were born in Galanta. And now you should know how you and I are related. I married Matyáš Löwinger, the cousin of your grandma, Ilonka, and of her sister, Elisheva. There was yet another Matyáš Löwinger. This one was Fani's cousin, and he died in Auschwitz. My husband, by the same name, died a few years ago."

Blanka has the genealogy figured out in detail, while I'm still struggling to connect the names and imagine the faces. More relatives were murdered in Auschwitz; choking on words, death had no taste.

Blanka speaks of her time in Auschwitz. She is my *speaking mother* to whom I figuratively speak, *Were words of cruel death overbearing life? And you want me to taste life? Is your silence stronger than death?*

"I stayed for some time in the camp, and I wouldn't have survived if I'd stayed much longer. In late nineteen forty-four, the camp population was increasing, with new transports every day, and the Germans couldn't gas prisoners fast enough. One night, my most horrific experience, I heard heart-wrenching cries from the nearby barracks. The Germans were burning down the entire gypsy camp, and men, women, and children were burned alive. The rest of them were gassed the next day." She is still shaken by the words. Roma and Sinti—the ethnic groups called "gypsy" (in the Slovak language, "to gypsy" means "to lie")—were targeted for extermination with

Jews, blacks, Slavs, homosexuals, Jehovah's Witnesses, the disabled, Communists, and any person caught in resistance.

"I was lucky," Blanca continues, "if one can say so, to be transferred a few months later to a munitions factory outside of Auschwitz. I could work hard, and the Germans needed all the help they could get to increase their military production. I lived and worked underground until the war's end. Then we marched west, escaping the advancing Russians. Many more died in the long marches, collapsing of starvation, cold, exhaustion, and disease. One morning I woke up, and the German guards were gone. Every one of them—the entire nightmare had vanished. I survived the camp with my sister Olga. We went to Prague. We were young, in our midtwenties; it was spring, a happy time. I married Matyáš when I returned home."

She sat down exhausted from her telling, as if she had lived through it all again.

"My sister emigrated to Israel in nineteen forty-six, married Cohen, and her daughter Gabi lives near Tel Aviv. When Gabi got involved with Stephen Spielberg's Visual History Foundation, she came to record my story for the Survivors of the Shoah Visual History Foundation. You can get the tape from Los Angeles. I'm sure it offers more details than I managed to tell you today."

I jot down the California address of the foundation. In January 2006 the Survivors of the Shoah Visual History Foundation became part of the Dana and David Dornsife College of Letters, Arts, and Sciences at the University of Southern California in Los Angeles.

"Gabi has been recording survivor stories around Slovakia; people are getting old and dying. In the coming decades, there will be no Holocaust survivors to tell the story," she says.

"Perhaps we should get Uncle Ernest record his? Could Gabi go to Karlovy Vary?"

"If she cannot, the foundation could send a team," Blanka suggests.

I never managed to get the Shoah Visual History Foundation to tape Ernest's story, as he died shortly after he finished his letters of remembrances for me.

"We should visit the Jewish cemetery in Galanta together," Blanka proposes.

It had been some time since she was able to make such a trip. With her at our side, we would be able to find out more about the family history. I'm thrilled. We take a group photo in their garden: Blanka, daughter Viera with husband and their two sons, Patricia, and me. I stand high above all of them, like a Gulliver, and though I'm of average height (neither short and stocky like Nathan or Ernest, nor tall and slim like my great-uncle Béla or my father Radislav), I rise up in life, the tallest in the group.

Stone Witnesses from the Past

The old Jewish cemetery in Galanta is better preserved than the one in Myjava. The names of all the Jews from Galanta who died in the Nazi camps are posted on the wall. It is there where I find the name of my maternal great-grandmother, Fani Löwingerová.

"Her tombstone is missing here"—Blanka points to the empty spot next to a tall headstone—"right next to her husband, Max Mordechai Pressburger." She places a stone on his tomb.

"Does that mean he made it back, but she did not?" I ask.

"Possibly, yes. Fani's other symbolic burial place could be over there." We walk back a few rows to a modern, low-profile gravestone. "Her ashes are most likely somewhere in Auschwitz," she says, and picks up another stone.

The kiddush cup, the Myjava furniture pieces, the old Bible inherited from Mother, Nathan's lost Beckov, and the turned-around Myjava headstones of my maternal grandparents—all are mute witnesses that supplanted Mother's silence for me, and they now surround me and speak to me. This Galanta memorial honors her grandmother and my great-grandmother in unequivocal words: THE HOLOCAUST MEMORIAL TO ALL GALANTA JEWS WHO WERE MURDERED IN THE NAZI CONCENTRATION CAMPS.

I am unprepared for this moment—and there are more to come—which claims me as a concrete witness, speaking to me about the unspeakable in my family. As Blanka places prayer rocks on the memorial, it's as if some heavy stone within me begins to lift off my entire body. If one could taste stones, they would taste of life like a parched desert after a rain.

"Others of her relatives died," she notes, "but came back home." We return to Max's grave. "Look at the several other gravestones belonging to the Löwingers. They were a widely known family in Galanta. And over there is the grave of the famous Galanta cantor."

I ask Patricia to take a photo of Blanka and me next to Max's gravestone. I shoot close-ups of the Hebrew text. Stones speak if they do not taste like food. Later, in Washington, DC, I have a language specialist translate the words. The dedication speaks of Max as a well-liked member of the Jewish community, a respected citizen in Galanta, a loving father, and a good provider for his family. He was the tall, stern owner of the tobacco and cigar store recalled earlier by Uncle Ernest. As we exit the cemetery, Blanka shows me how to ritually wash my hands after communing with our ancestors. We return to the city, and she makes me stop the car.

"I want to show you where Pressburgers lived before the war," she says excitedly.

"There's another house?" I'm astonished. I knew that Ernest had hired a lawyer after 1989 to recover some lost property in Galanta and that the attempt for restitution had failed here, just as it had in Myjava. Even though restitutions didn't cover Nazi confiscations and stopped in February 1948, Beckov is an immobile material witness whose story still grows, as once the Beck's Oak did.

"Here it is." Blanka touches the wall of a tall building as if she won a race.

"But this isn't—" I'm interrupted.

"No, it isn't their house." She has a knowledgeable look in her eyes. "The Pressburger house was razed to the ground, and the Communists built a supermarket here after the war. Ernest should have been able to claim the land on which the family house once stood, received some payment for its loss, and then either rent or sell the land on which the current business building stands today." She calculates that the restitution that either someone or the state (Germany?) would have to pay for the land wouldn't be a minuscule amount.

"But there was no record or deed that survived the deportations and the war. We couldn't prove the continuity of ownership because the books weren't in order. Who knows what the Communists did?" She's becoming visibly agitated and angry.

"So do you know whether the house was razed by the Nazis, the war, or the Communists?" I ask. "Would it have made some difference if the Communists did it after nineteen forty-eight?"

"All I know is that the entire Jewish district was destroyed. Over there"—she points behind me to the business building across the open space—"used to be a Jewish synagogue. It was the Communists who finished the dastardly deed after the Nazis were long gone. Do you see those Communist chicken-coop apartments? They are what replaced the synagogue and the Jewish houses. Why keep them once the Jews were gone?" she concludes her testimony, looking in disgust at the ugly Communist-era construction.

29. Martin Matuštík at the Jewish cemetery in Galanta, 1996

My Journey to Auschwitz

Patricia and I continue alone through the pristine beauty of the Slovak Paradise, the lower wooded mountain region where mist rises from the hills and time stops on Mondays because everyone is at the local pub. We cross over the Low and High Tatra Mountains to Crakow in Poland. Our destination is Oswiencim—Auschwitz. By car the road from Myjava or Galanta to Birkenau can be covered without a stop in a single day. If you're packed in a cattle car without food, water, air, or sanitary facilities, it is a cruel journey to hell. That most infamous extermination camp can be reached from beautiful Crakow in one and a half hours. Almost two million people, mostly Jews, died in the two adjoining camps of Auschwitz and Birkenau; the Nazis murdered four million more Jews in other extermination sites. Auschwitz One, the old camp, originally housed Polish and Russian military and political prisoners. The first rudimentary experiments in gas-chamber extermination were practiced there, though the Nazis began to perfect the ways for capital murder by car exhaust with specially adjusted vans some time before. After the secret plan for the Final Solution to the Jewish question (and what was that question anyway?), the second, newer camp, Auschwitz-Brzezinka (Birkenau), became the main center of human extermination.

Letter from Uncle Ernest to His Nephew Martin

Karlovy Vary

September 30, 2001

Dear Mato,

Several days ago [September 21, during the visit of Emil and Gerda Binetter from Sydney], I withdrew from the bankomat the September support gift from you, so that the food we could prepare for them would be really nice.

Now I want to write you briefly about my health and in connection with that about continuation of my writing of the "Remembrances of Life."....At this time I have only very special moments when I can sit down without to-tal fatigue and put on paper several new thoughts from my "Remembrances." There is one interesting fact. That first part, which you have received from me, I was writing only because you wanted it. With this second part, which I am creating now, it is a bit different. I suddenly found this engaging, and I am creating [it] not only for you but also for my own joy. I have written by now...fifty-five pages.

Remembrances of Life: 1944

Only much later did I learn how it was with our night convoy. In the middle of August 1944, those clever Slovak fascist guards who intuited the defeat and the end of the war began to gather various alibis suitable for the new era to come. For many of them, my father was a suitable focus who could provide them with such an alibi after the war. Father knew it, and he did not wait. He was among the few members of the Slovak resistance who knew the approximate date of the Slovak National Uprising and also its point of origin. He was to transport there a great amount of medical supplies that were prepared in secret for that occasion. What did he do? He made contact with the commander of the Hlinka Guard in Myjava, the teacher Štefan Čúvala, and he told him openly what task lay ahead of him, personally guaranteeing that if Čúvala secured the transfer of the medicines to Banská Bystrica (the originating city of the uprising), he would give him a perfect alibi after the war for immunity from prosecution. And so during the night, when our car took off from Kúty to Banská Bystrica (the distance of about 290 km), several meters ahead of us rode teacher Čúvala on a motorcycle and in Slovak fascist guard uniform,—with necessary permits for the road in hand. Early in the morning, we arrived at the agreed-upon place, Kalamárka, a mountain house above Banská Bystrica. On that same day at noon, a very well-known historical event took place: partisans stopped an international express train at Detva and shot dead several important generals who did not manage to escape. This signaled the start of the uprising.

Two days later we arrived at Banská Bystrica, and we were joined by father's brother, my uncle Ervin, now in the military colonel uniform. Father immediately began to work in the local hospital, which received its daily wounded. The fights with Germans took place across the entire uprising territory of Central and parts of Northern Slovakia, and Germans daily bombed the "free radio Banská Bystrica" but also the city, and Mother with Magda and me would run to hide four or five times daily from the fifth floor down to the cellar. Bombs exploded several times near our building, and at twelve thirty my severe fears resumed—similar to the panics I used to have as a child whenever a siren sounded. Magda, if I can recall, never suffered from fear. She had a different temperament, and her courage was based for the most part on her sense of wonder and desire for adventure.

The uprising was defeated in about two months, and by the end of October, Banská Bystrica too was overtaken by the Germans. Before the defeat, with no break in the bombing, the long lines of retreating soldiers and civilians stretched from the city to Bula, the Old Mountains, Low Tatras, and to Prašivá. It was an exhausting march in rain and fog, with heavy loads on our backs, into the unknown, into hopelessness.

In the mountains that mass of refugees fragmented into smaller groups, and each trekked in that damp fog and unknown mountain terrain to somewhere else. Our family was part of a mixed group of civilians, soldiers, and partisans—about fifty to sixty persons—that was guided by the Soviet captain Jegorov. He was celebrated after the war as a well-known partisan hero. In our group we had also two well-known Communists, Rudolf Slánský and Jiří Šverma. Both flew in from the Soviet Union to join the Slovak [National] Uprising. Šverma was very ill, and Father also took care of him in the mountains. In the end Šverma died and was left in the rain somewhere at Chabenec. (Slánský, who became a prominent Communist during President Klement Gottwald's years, built up the security apparatus in the 1950s and presided over the monster trials and executions only to perish the same death when his regime began to eat its own Jewish and Communist children.)

Mother caught an inflammation of the kidneys from the dampness, and she was unable to march. At the start of December 1944, exhausted and famished, wet and cold, we descended from the mountains and approached a small village called Nemecká. A few weeks later in that village, the Germans burned several hundred people whom they caught descending from the mountains. During the first night, we hid in a hay stack of the local farmer, and when Magda and I fell asleep, our parents decided that in this utterly hopeless situation we would not continue and that they would end it all with themselves and us. Father prepared cyanide that he always carried, and we were supposed to eat the tablets as a medicine against cold. But Magda did not sleep, and she overheard the entire parental conversation (she was by then sixteen), and with screaming, persuasion, as well as begging, she entirely reversed the parental decision, and so in the end, the group suicide did not take place.

Nathan's Chess Game with Death

The villages of Myjava and Kúty were prevalently Lutheran, and the Becks were warned, protected, and saved by Lutheran members of resistance. While Slovaks working against the Nazi regime infiltrated the Hlinka Guard, Nathan risked negotiating with several highly placed Slovak fascists. Uncle Ernest's letters to me, my father's letter before he died, and conversations with Brano and Ján during my visits in Myjava identified several Hlinka Guardists by name. I pieced together their fragmented, not always consistent memory:

The chief of police in Myjava, Michal Aujeský, warned the Beck family about the first wave of transports. From March 25 to October 20, 1942, the Becks were in at least two hiding places in Myjava until the transports from Slovakia ended.

After the break in transports until the Slovak National Uprising in August 1944, it was either one of the chiefs of the Hlinka Guard in Bratislava, Otomar (or Dr. Jozef) Kubala who had a sick mother, or the Guardist, Štefan Hačunda, who had a sick wife, or both, who provided a safe house for the Becks in Kúty.

My uncle Ernest also named his grammar-school teacher in Kúty, Štefan Granec, and his teen son, Edo Granec, as being part of his happy early puberty in 1943.

The chief of the Hlinka Guard in Myjava, Štefan Čúvala, was to escort the Becks from Kúty to Banská Bystrica before the Slovak National Uprising in 1944.

After the defeat of the uprising in fall 1944, a farmer, Fink, in Zvolen, protected the Becks until the arrival of the Soviet army in 1945.

Unlike the characters in Ingmar Bergman's *Seventh Seal*, Nathan and Fink played chess after the Soviet liberation from the threat of annihilation.[37]

12

"YOU WILL NEED IT IN LIFE MORE THAN TO REPAIR SHOES"

1776					**1978–1991**		Now

1776: US independence; 1789: the French Revolution.
1721–1917: the Russian Empire; 1804–1867: the Austrian Empire; 1867–1918: the Austro-Hungarian Empire.
1917: the birth of Soviet Communism; 1914–1918: World War I; 1938–1945: World War II.
1948–1989: Communist Eastern Europe; 1986: perestroika in Russia; 1988: glasnost in Russia.
1989: The Iron Curtain falls in East-Central Europe.

As a young adult in America, I begin a religious quest and in 1981 join the Jesuits. After suffering a crisis of faith, I arrive in Frankfurt in autumn 1989 as a Fulbright student of Jürgen Habermas; the Berlin Wall comes down; and the Velvet Revolution takes place in Czechoslovakia. After eleven years in exile, I return to Prague to witness Havel's ascent to the Prague Castle. I complete my PhD studies in philosophy in 1991.

My Spiritual Odyssey (1978–1991)

With my Czechoslovak police permit for India confiscated in Austria and with a new immigrant visa stamped on my stateless refugee passport, I discovered America in 1978. Still to taste native milk, I was separated from the matrix of my family's survivors by World War II, the relationships that were severed in 1946, my mother's Communist sojourn and her death, and my teenage Catholic conversion and exile from Prague. My exile amplified the loss of family, and this cumulative memory of breach fed my spiritual hunger and deepened my young-adult dreams of mending the world.

Pilgrim

It was Christmas 1980, and I made my pilgrimage to Israel. I flew to Tel Aviv and journeyed through sites of the Jewish, Christian, and Muslim Palestine. Arriving in Jerusalem, I was shaken by an uncanny sense of homecoming. I read these clues as confirmations that Prague and Jerusalem had a spiritual kinship. As Kafka I wasn't natively predisposed to Catholic forms of atonement, but this was the alias I knew. Rabbi Jesus didn't become a Christian. Three years after landing in the New World, I became a Jesuit novice.

I graduated from Loyola Marymount University in May 1981 with B.A. in philosophy. Unsure about the nature of my vocation to repair the world, I dated a girl I'd met while meditating on the beach. This California blonde competed with G-d for the passion of a celibacy-bound young man, which both challenged and delighted the girl. She lived in a big home, and we enjoyed nights there together when her parents were away. My spiritual life became livelier; instead of becoming a wandering celibate, I could have been a philosopher-rabbi. I was propelled by the ignorance of my origins on a Catholic Odyssey, and the female sex was a giant for me to tame. In the coed dorm, I partook in American slumber parties, learned more slang and colloquial English, and danced many nights with friends. My religious vocation reasserted itself by the end of my senior year. I wasn't ready for domesticity; I yearned for adventure, learning, and exploring the world. Because the Jesuits offered both, I chose greater love or what I imagined to be the most intense possibilities of loving. The religious passion had to be equal to or greater than loving all the girls one could embrace or could imagine embracing for eternity. Don Juan misunderstood his passion for the infinite, while I placed my eggs in one infinite basket of mending the world.

Scholar

In late August 1981, I collected my last paycheck from a store in North Hollywood, where I kept sales accounts of musical instruments; packed up my Los Angeles apartment; and engrossed my mind in philosophy, liberal arts, Spanish, medieval Latin, and the Jewish and Christian Bibles. Church history, philosophy, and theology mirrored in large letters my Kafkaesque shoes, and my tryst with the Society of Jesus illuminated my youth under Communism. I loved to learn about Arab scholars who had saved and translated the works of great Greek philosophers. I was moved by the story of the Jews in Spain and France who knew both Arabic and Latin and had translated texts long thought to be lost in the fire in the ancient Alexandria library. This feat influenced Jewish Talmudic scholars and Catholic thinkers, and then Aquinas heretically put it all together—Plato, Aristotle, and Saint Augustine. Aquinas did with Aristotle in the thirteenth century what liberation theologians managed to do in the twentieth century with Marx: Aristotle and Marx were married to Christianity. Just as Communism had its earnest believers, martyrs, heretics, inquisitors, reformers, and suppressed Prague Springs, so Catholicism suffered similar tensions.

Novice

In August 1981 I began what turned out to be a five-year sojourn with the Jesuits. Montecito's novitiate was situated between the sunrise over the Santa Barbara Mountains, with slopes of orange, citrus, and avocado groves, as well as sunsets over the Pacific Ocean. My neighbors were a Vedanta Center on the mountainside and millionaire estates all around. Never before had I lived in such privileged surroundings. The second novitiate location where I spent several months was in East Los Angeles in the poor, mostly Spanish-speaking, gang- and drug-infested urban territory. The novitiate program moved in regular intervals between extremes of setting and life circumstance—from wealth to poverty, seclusion to social immersion, contemplation to action, prayer to service. A Jesuit should discover a spiritual center within, not in the material contingencies of life. The novitiate time was composed of experiments with one's basic decision to live a religious life. It was to test one's desire, capacity, and constancy in sustaining one's inner center in motion and under duress.

November was devoted to a thirty-day silent retreat—the spiritual exercises of Saint Ignatius. The wanderer within me already lived in his mother's silence. During the Ignatian retreat, I spoke only twice a day for fifteen minutes with my spiritual director. I could utter prayers and chants during daily mass and listen to classical music at meals. For the rest of these thirty days, the wanderer kept a great silence. While one could consider this a form of solitary confinement or sensory deprivation, or some setup to mangle young men in one direction, I found it to be the most liberating, unencumbered, joyous month of my life. I used to hike up to the mountains after breakfast then walk down to the secluded beached in the afternoon. Silence, the surrounding beauty, and the spiritual food for thought were truly divine. The days became inwardly fuller, more intense, faster, and shorter.

For my first six-week world-immersion experiment after the long retreat, I was sent for a month to an oncology ward for the terminally ill in San Francisco. My mother had died of cancer, so this work offered an opportunity for me to heal. When one touches the pain of others, holds their hands, brings them food, reads them a book, and speaks openly about their death, there is nothing left for lies or even for one's own self-centered pain. If one transcends one's religious denomination, I thought as a young novice, one *can* dream of healing others.

In the second year, the Jesuits sent me with a group of novices to live among the poor in Mexico. We slept in a small house on bare cots, cooked on a simple stove, purified their water, watched out for scorpions, and ate tortillas with rice and beans as our main staple. The same life was reproduced during our stays at the second novitiate location in Los Angeles. Although north of the border, the urban setting was poor and volatile. During the day I visited downtown skid-row hotels where immigrant families from Mexico, Central America, or Cuba huddled in small, flea-infested rooms; at night I was kept awake by the gunfights and the search lights of police helicopters flying overhead. As a young Jesuit, I learned to live in the war zone of North America, studied more Spanish, and enjoyed unencumbered simplicity.

In Tijuana I worked with two Mexican nuns, Maru and Amanda, at Casa de Los Pobres. The Casa was a multiservice center serving the poor of Tijuana. These were some of the best-spent and intensely happy months of my twenties. In the morning I poured oatmeal from big pots to feed orphans who had gathered at the meal hall.

Then I'd open the bodega to help fulfill family requests for food, blankets, supplies, medicines, or weekend home visits. In the early afternoon, I drove a big red truck with a Casa sign painted on the front and embarked on long or short runs for food and supplies. The Casa had no financial resources of its own, so all its supplies were donated, and the nuns had to beg for them. I begged for food in open markets, in grocery stores, in restaurants; I visited rich Mexicans at their ranches or homes and made border runs to corporations and private donors in San Diego and surrounding Californian towns.

Tijuana's jail provided no food to its prisoners except potato peels thrown on the ground. The jail mixed men and women in a hellish three-floor cacophony and eyesore. There were no bathrooms or showers; prisoners were hosed down once a day. Occasionally a drunken American would end up there, in which case I would have to contact the US consulate. The prisoners were mostly poor people who were there for minor offenses and who were often forgotten. The third floor housed a slew of mentally ill individuals. A medieval jail or a gulag wouldn't have been much worse than this place. A Mexican priest came once a week to celebrate Mass, and on one occasion, I was allowed to speak to the prisoners about the readings.

On Saturday mornings I taught a religion class to small children, followed by a play or another activity we organized for them. On Sunday afternoons I'd make home visits in poor barrios.

Jesuit

I imagine the wandering Kafka as a Jesuit novice; he neither needed to inherit his parents' Communist aspirations nor acquire a Marxist reading of the Gospels or a Christian rendition of Marx. He found synergies between his struggle for human rights in Czechoslovakia and his care for the poor in the Western world. They were all part and parcel of his vocation to heal, teach, and repair the world. He would trace his growing concern for social justice to these months of social experimentation.

The novitiate culminated with my first vows to a Jesuit form of life. Taking my commitment to live in a family of celibates in earnest, in that late summer of 1983, I was a happy single man. After my teenage epiphany of the feminine face of G-d, I pursued significant father figures that began to populate my life as if the cosmos wanted to make up for their absence from my childhood. My Jesuit life was dominated by male friendships. I had grown up neither with a father nor for long with my brother, so the community healed what had been missing for me. In this life of repair and study, I didn't feel the lack of the presence of females as a persistent pain. As the midrash says, nights too are for the study of Torah.

Perestroika

In February and March 1986, ten years after I almost had wrecked my high-school final exams in Russian by recklessly praising Nikita Khrushchev for having destroyed Stalin's cult of personality in 1956, at the Twenty-Seventh Communist Party Congress, Mikhail Sergeyevich Gorbachev launched perestroika (reconstruction) in Russia, but I still was refused entry to Czechoslovakia. During my fifth summer with the Jesuits, I traveled to France to learn French and organized a secret meeting with my father in Hungary. In great haste a personal courier carried a message to Bratislava. Father and I met on several occasions in the Budapest cathedral. Like spies in a Cold War flick, we met on the fourth of our prearranged rendezvous. Ten years after we had drunk the bottle of gin in his Bratislava bachelor flat, the ex-Communist father embraced his Jesuit son under the secret canopy of the Budapest cathedral. The Communist father state rejected its citizen's homecoming; the earthly father returned to his once abandoned and now exiled son. We spent two weeks traveling around Hungary and discussed our lives more than ever before. We resumed our relationship as two adults. The prodigal father returned to a son who deliberately adopted him as his own and who clandestinely had sought him out.

My sojourn to France was to become the last test before the Jesuits would send me to study theology for priesthood ordination. Perhaps it was intended so by my superiors, who wanted me to face myself and my choice without any external oversight or controls. Echoing my growing up alone in Prague, I lived on my own for almost three months. A French family near Nice provided my first language immersion, and then for six weeks, I rented a flat while attending a language school and theater festival in Avignon. I recovered the sense of joy and solitude with which I had entered the novitiate.

In my language class in Avignon sat a strikingly beautiful eighteen-year-old girl from Germany. E. had dark hair that flowed down to her waist. She was a descendant of the French Bourbons who had fled to Germany, and she and I experienced a chemical explosion from the first day. Not long after we met, she moved from the home of her French host family and into my flat. She had a boyfriend in Germany, and I had a religious community in California, yet we felt drawn to each other. Not educated as a Catholic, and amused by the fact that I was a young Jesuit who seemed to her more mature both as an educated man and a lover than her German boyfriend, she made love passionately and without guilt. I had taught students her age in Los Angeles and became quite eager to act as her teacher in ways of the spirit as well as the body. We spent an intensely happy month together, learning French, going to the theater, cooking, and making love in our flat. I made love to her often and with abandon, as if to make up for five years of celibate life—indeed, as if to exorcise the form that surrounded my spiritual desire with a wounded intimacy. During this beautiful summer, we didn't care about the future. In a glorious city of antipopes, amid the theater carnival and the Russian thaw on the horizon, I crossed my Rubicon.

Divorce

Celibate nights were long and lonely. Various degrees of intimacy among the Jesuit peers grew out of the intensity of our shared life, close bonds, and the pains of maturation. This was not so unique for young men elsewhere, who also passed through periods of experimentation with religious and young-adult forms of life. My vocational desire was unripe, and it didn't click with the celibate kitchens. The austere menu wasn't native to Jewish life.

When I returned from my "hot" summer in France, I expressed my conscience to the Jesuit superior. I faced this "either/or": leave the order immediately or ask for a separation but not yet a divorce.

My superior asked only one question: "Did you get the woman pregnant?"

"No, Father. I received great Communist sex education in eighth grade; I practiced responsible, safe sex."

"You mean...you used birth control?"

"Father, is using a condom a greater sin than engaging in sex with a young unmarried woman while being married to the Church?"

"Are you planning to see her again?"

"She wants to visit me in the United States. If she does, I think I want to stay with her."

"Perhaps time and distance will strengthen your commitment to the religious life."

"Father, I want to ask for a yearlong leave of absence from the Jesuits."

In memories filled with warm moments and gratitude, this girl remains my messenger from Avignon with whom I traversed the manly period of father figures and entered my maturing adulthood.

Oedipus's Nightmare

From a practical standpoint, the Catholic Church always has been willing to take care of children and alimony while retaining its hold on the person who has chosen a religious vocation. No one seemed as concerned with my active sexual life as with the possible consequences of sex. Yet to me the institutional pragmatism bred cynicism behind these questions that could not but remind me of the long shadow I had left behind—that of the Communist Party. This is where the vow of obedience posed in itself as a vehicle for leading a double life. Obedience to the Church, leading a tolerated double life—how different is that from bending to the Communist state while believing otherwise?

Censorship: the "Catholic Index" was the name for the list of books or authors prohibited by the Church High Office for the Propagation of Faith. My parents were placed on the Communist index after 1968. Must one obey a duplicitous superior? The Czech heretic Jan Hus said no, and he was burned at the stake. The Communists wanted me to recant my association with Patočka and *Charta 77*. The structures of similarity between the Catholic Church and the single-party state blended for me. In horror I gazed at my life like the blind Oedipus who tried to flee the deadly prophecy only to find himself fulfilling it in flight and in total ignorance regarding himself. On my spiritual quest, experiencing an awakening self-knowledge about my path, I was moving ever closer to such a dreadful juncture.

Party discipline: Polish pope John Paul II not only suffered under Communism but also brought the administrative methods of his persecutors to bear upon making the Church more obedient, more conservative, more tight in rank and file, and more run by unquestioning bishops and cardinals. Discipline was a hallmark of Jesuit life, and much would be tolerated in the intimate sphere, while nothing would be tolerated in the sphere of disloyalty to the Church and the order.

Obedience: ever since my grammar-school troubles, I wasn't a very conforming young man. To bend my inquiring intelligence against genuine questions, including how happy and healthy can a celibate life lived in duplicity be or how honest is an intellectual life in which issues are silenced—all this reminded me too much of the first great institution, the Communist dragon or windmill I battled in my teens. When my superiors didn't ask me whether I was in love with the girl, whether she was in love with me, or whether I needed time to discern which love I truly desired—my religious life or this woman; when they sought containment and continued loyalty, I knew I was back in a lion's den. I no longer doubted where I stood or how I wanted to live.

Obedient duplicity under these circumstances would mean consenting to what I had refused to obey under the pressure from the Communists and the Czech secret service. When the Jesuit superiors didn't grant me a genuine yearlong leave of absence in my own apartment, I accelerated my decision to apply to Rome for "divorce" papers. To their credit the California Province remained materially magnanimous even at this point. I received a modest sum to procure an apartment in Los Angeles, and I was allowed to finish my second year of teaching at Loyola Marymount University university while retaining the full salary that before had gone directly to the community. My divorce was smooth and final. No one tried to persuade me to stay, and most of my Jesuit relationships turned distant and cold. Was I "excommunicated" from the brotherhood of friends? What were those friendships made of that died so quickly as if the leaving were more wounding than if I never had entered the order? I thought of my parents and their post-Communist years.

Fortunately the Church doesn't have the power of the Communist state to make its severance bite or prevent one's vocational flourishing, as the party did to its members who betrayed it. Yet I also never was considered as a PhD prospect for a post at Loyola Marymount University. Perhaps this would be too painful and close to the community I left. With five years of generous Jesuit training under my belt and even with my continued willingness to serve the order as a layperson, I was cut loose and never contacted by the Jesuits in any professional way.

A Little Onion

When onions are added to the Eastern European latke, *bramborák* becomes every villager's potato pancake filled with lard, pieces of pork, sausage, and even sauerkraut. To protect my family from the Krauts and ignorant Slovaks, Reverend Little Onion dipped the pancakes in the baptismal mikveh. Julius was no Caesar, but rather Reverend Julius Cibulka, a "Little Onion," a Protestant pastor. He baptized the Becks in Myjava in full public view during the first heat wave of the Jewish transports from Slovakia. The baptism was dangerous enough to call attention to the Jew-loving minister. I never heard about Reverend Little Onion from my mother, although he became a respected theologian who sparred with the Communist regime after the war. In Mother's Prague archive boxes, I recovered numerous notarized copies of her baptismal certificates from 1946 and 1947, along with her high-school and university transcripts. Mother stashed away the baptismal papers signed by Reverend Little Onion but never mentioned them after 1948. The evidence of baptism from 1942 posed as much danger to her during the Cold War under Communism as did her parents' 1937 kiddush cup, which she kept on her writing desk in Prague.

30. Lutheran baptismal record of the Beck family and their name change to Veselý in Myjava on July 28, 1942

My Second Emigration and Third Diaspora

I cherished a year of teaching philosophy to Loyola Marymount University sopho-mores. This "severance pay" and my job were the only ties to the order I retained for one more year. I never received a letter from any of my classmates or other Jesuits. It was as if I had died or emigrated anew. I returned to my birth. In five years with the order, I had built no credit, no savings, no pension, no insurance, no references, no home, no car, no furniture, and no other property. "Where did you exist for the past five years?" I would be asked. My philosophy colleagues gathered a collection of pots and pans for my first home after I left the Jesuits, and my undergraduate students helped me move to a Brentwood apartment and later to a rent-controlled flat in Santa Monica. In 1986 I paid $325 a month. I adjusted to my independence, in which my manhood sought its vital grounding, and I applied to PhD programs in philosophy around the country.

On my voyage to America and with the Jesuits, I wandered furthest and farthest from my Jewish origins. While entering the Jesuit Order could be classified as a radi-cal detour, I tend to view that emphatically fatherly and male-dominated period as a homebound journey. A grand religious form of male heroism, the Jesuits were in so many ways preferable to military service. Like a temporary Buddhist monk or Peace Corps volunteer, I had given myself over to service. This religious-quest period had started with the death of my mother; it was populated by mother figures, then father figures, and it culminated in a more integral sense of selfhood. Yet my Homeric imago of mature manhood had been shattered. There neither was a single home nor a simple return to it.

My Philosophical-Political Quest

During my philosophy studies (1987–1991), my adult crisis of faith blossomed to pro-duce its new architecture made of speculative flowers, and I stopped actively par-ticipating in Catholic life. For the next ten years as an ex-Jesuit, I would confuse my crisis of Catholic beliefs in the Church institution with unbelief. My inborn urgency to repair my broken worlds, still gestating in me only as my anonymous rabbi's desire, would become polarized through secular lenses. I was bound for a philosophical-political quest of liberation. I was returning to the world of my youth, embarking on my second exodus and third birth, after being ejected from a worn-out religious cocoon, just as my parents once had been broken by the failed Communist promise. A rabbi's wanderings through Platonic ideals and monastic family life fed the silent source of the trauma I'd inherited from Mother. Disenchanted dreams of mending the world gave birth to my second, self-chosen atheism.

Letter from Uncle Ernest to His Nephew Martin

Remembrances of Life: 1944-1945

After the hard journey, in the midst of the superiorly armed German military and the shooting Gestapo, Father brought us to the larger town of Zvolen. His intention was somehow to disappear here, start curing Mother, and await the arrival of the liberation front from the East. Everything happened according to this plan. In Zvolen Dr. Beck and family ceased to exist, and in their place appeared Pavel Veselý and the entire Veselý family. (All papers issued for the name Veselý—also for his brother Ervín—were prepared with help from his Slovak guard "friends" before our departure from Kúty.)

For our survival in Zvolen, Father chose similar tactics to those we used in Myjava and Kúty. After brief research he made the acquaintance of a rich farmer and elite member of the Hungarian minority, Mr. Fink. He learned that during the so-called Slovak State, Fink had kept close contact with the German occupying units, organized for them official as well unofficial drinking parties, and also financially supported various pro-German activities in Zvolen. Mainly, with the approaching front, Fink began to distance himself from the Germans and started to worry. I do not know how many times Father visited Fink in his residence, or what sort of conversations they used to have, but in a few days, we moved to a small shed (two rooms) in the distant corner of a larger yard at his farm, and Pavel Veselý, together with Helena and Magda Veselá, became employees at Fink's farm.

Father supervised various works carried out by the poorest workers in the yard. But he was "one of them" (he dressed as them; he grew a beard, and so on). Likewise he tended the horses, milked the cows, and gathered the manure. Anyone who saw him believed that for his entire life he had been a supervisor at the farm. Mother sewed an endless number of aprons, bedcovers, bags, and sheets for the farm. The highest-level position was occupied by Magda.

She was a dress maid (not a cleaning or servant maid!) for old Mrs. Fink, the mother of the lord. She fulfilled all her wishes and attended to all guests.

For me, Father found placement as a learner in a shoe trade with the forty-year-old bachelor Mr. Rajniak, but this was at the other side of Zvolen, far from Fink's farm. I learned to repair shoes as well as make various parts for the new shoes. I had to clean the workshop and the sidewalk twice a day. Almost every day, and sometimes more than once a day, I had another important chore. My boss had an insatiable erotic desire, and the ladies of Zvolen brought their shoes often only as an excuse or a cover. In reality they came to Mr. Rajniak for regular and most likely rather high-quality gifts of intercourse. Mr. Rajniak gave me an important job in this connection: when a lady arrived with shoes to repair, and he gave me a secret eye signal, I shut the doors to the workshop and hung on them the sign I AM AT THE CITY OFFICE, and I pulled down the shop cover on the door as well as the window.

And the master ordered me, "Then go to the keyhole and observe attentively how I do it. You will need it in life more than to repair shoes."

Master always approached his sexual encounters standing (the only help was the wide bench he had for this purpose in the workshop). Sometimes from the front, at other times from behind, but most often both ways.

My final task was to open the store covers, unlock, take down the sign, and politely bid her good-bye: "Thank you for your visit and come again!"

At the beginning of March of 1945, the Eastern front was about fifty km from Zvolen. The artillery fire was overwhelming, and the Soviet and Rumanian aircraft bombed Zvolen all day and night. I stopped working for Mr. Rajniak, and the selected elite to which Fink counted also our family moved to a huge bomb shelter underneath his residence. I was much scarred. My childhood fear that had begun with the fire sirens and then multiplied with the bombing of Banská Bystrica began in the last fourteen days to turn into sheer terror. The Germans were pushed out of Zvolen twice, but they again took over the eastern part of town, where Fink's estate and our shelter were. With each dropped bomb or explosive, we were covered by the crumbling walls and falling bricks.

I know that I asked my father, who suddenly appeared near me, "Do you think that we will survive this?" And I cried, gripped with fear.

"For sure we will survive! In only a day or two, we will be liberated. Why are you afraid all the time?" Father said.

Father went to a special room in the shelter, where he and Fink drank high-quality alcohol all day, played chess, and where Father, with all the greater detail, revealed to Fink who he was and how he had managed to protect himself and his entire family from the Germans for the duration of the war.

On March 14 (it was the anniversary of the declaration of the Slovak fascist state), Zvolen was finally liberated by the Soviet and Rumanian armies under the leadership of Major Malinovsky.

When we were in Banská Bystrica, I took a quick course in Russian with Magda. We learned to read and write and managed to sing a few Russian songs. This helped us later when the first group of soldiers arrived at Fink's house. They threw out most of the furniture in order to make space for the soldiers who needed to sleep. Among those things was also a piano that stood right at the entrance. When we woke up in the morning, the first group of soldiers left, and the second wave arrived. I probably wanted to gain praise for my loyalty, and so I sat at the piano and with one finger began to play and sing the Russian folk song "Katuša," which I had learned in Banská Bystrica. The Soviet army song tells about a girl, Catherine (Russian: "Katuša," "Катюша"), who is waiting for her boyfriend returning from the war. Suddenly a crowd of soldiers surrounded the piano, who, together with my one-finger playing, sang loudly, "Vychadila na bereg Kaťuša, na vysokyj, bereg na krutoj..." They sang in Russian.

"She was walking on the beach...Katuša...appeared on the bank of a steep..."

Reportedly our "brotherly" solidarity prevented these soldiers (most of them stayed at Fink's for several days) robbing and raping in Fink's house. It did happen elsewhere at that time.

It was clear that the end of the war was near, and we had no more reason to remain incognito in Zvolen. Father did not know where he wanted to settle with his family after the war—if in Myjava where he lived most of his life or somewhere else. Myjava was not liberated at that time, but the Germans were expelled from South Slovakia and so also from Nové Zamky, Komárno, Galanta, and Nitra. At that time we had a general belief that all who were deported to the camps would return home, and parents assumed that we could all meet in Nové Zámky, because the families of Béla Beck and Etelka Binetter lived nearby—and in Nitra, Komárno, and Galanta lived the rest of the family. And so, with our backpacks, we journeyed to Nové Zámky on foot because there was no transportation available yet.

Most of our family did not return from the concentration camp, and as our hope diminished with time, our parents reached the decision that they did not want to remain in Nové Zámky permanently. And so after about two months, we embarked on yet another long march—in the direction of Myjava. We arrived home on the day of the official end of the war, May 9, 1945. Myjava had already been liberated for several days.

"Observe attentively. You will need it in life more than to repair shoes."

Neither the homebound Ulysses nor the fleeing Oedipus walked in the shoes of a wandering Jew. Martha wrote several letters to Ernest, with whom she kept sporadic correspondence throughout the years, instructing him without any explanation that she and her family wanted to have no further contact with me. Uncle Ernest thought that his nephew must have done something terrible to deserve her severance. After her initial offer to sponsor my coming to the United States, Martha not only frustrated my attempts to learn about the whereabouts of other Jewish relatives but also actively erased all traces I might have found at that time. By the time I visited Israel at the end of my college years, then as a Christian pilgrim bound for the Jesuit novitiate in California, Martha's mother, my mother's aunt, Eržička, died. I used to ascribe Martha's breach with me to my Semitic enthusiasm for the Rabbi Jesus. I gave up that explanation when I realized how it turned my story into another childish myth. *Could my agency singlehandedly cause or heal such grand breaches?* I wondered.

In his Jerusalem speech, "Kafka and My Presidency," Václav Havel speaks this ironic truth to his new political power, and he mocks himself in order to ward off a kitsch version of himself: "I am a person who would not be at all surprised, if some-one, in the middle of my activities as president, would bring me before an obscure tribunal....if I would now hear the word "wake up!" and I would find myself in my prison cell." [38] Self-discovery may not be a silver lining. Yet my native urgency to re-pair leads me to this at once tragic and comic expectation and feeds my unformulated but pervasive motivation: *I have been coming to terms with irreparable dimensions of life. I must know more; I must approach the secret; I must come near this silence.*

But can I do anything to heal the irreparable? How can I be with this awareness that I cannot do anything on my own?

Karlovy Vary

October, 30, 2001

Dear Matenko,

I have finished that confession entitled "Remembrances of Life." I am going day after tomorrow to Prague to have a surgery with my heart. You did not say anything about the first part, and I do not even know if it served you in some way at all.

November 20, 2001

As you know, I had brain damage after the heart surgery in Prague. I will not be able to write as I did before. I wish you and Patricia all the best, happy holidays, and good New Year.

Ernest

Uncle Ernest's letter arrived with the last part of his "Remembrances." He died a few days later.

13

SURVIVOR'S SHAME

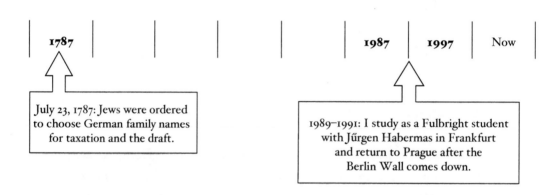

In dialogue with the heroes of my youth, Jürgen Habermas and Václav Havel, I witness my homecoming, welcome, and misrecognition. I must come to terms with the moral gray zones of my parents' generation. The secret to my life is encrypted in the family name that bears the scars of its silent memory.

The Sole and Soul Repairs (1787, 1987, 1997)

This handwritten note signed by E. is on a printed list of Sydney residents with the surname Vesely:

July 29, 1997

Unable to find Vesely or Beck with footwear or shoe. Good luck with your search! I have enclosed information about two Jewish magazines (one is in Sydney) and placing an ad may prove fruitful.

Cheers, E. (with the compliments of the Embassy of Australia Library, Washington, DC)

August 15, 1961

On Friday night, July 28, the Binetter Brothers, Erwin and Emil, founders of the Vogue Shoe Factory, Sydney, were hosts to a group of Goldberg executives....Looking back to earlier beginnings, the progress of this company has been rapid when it is realized that operations were commenced in 1951, in a small cottage located at Railway Parade, Sydenham, N.S.W. Production was then 250 pairs of shoes weekly....The total production space at the Vogue factory is now over 12,000 square feet...with 5,000 pairs weekly clearly in view!" (from "Progress of Vogue Shoe Factory," *Australian Leather Journal, Boot and Shoe Recorder,* pp. 104 and 108)

I didn't know challah as Jewish bread, but I had eaten challah in my first fourteen years whenever Mother had baked it at home for Christmas. Shame is the survivor's unacknowledged trauma. My mother's trauma has settled me with her generation's guilt and my own survivor's guilt. I have been suffering from her disrepair, even as I survive her traumatized silence. I wrestle with this double heritage of dis/repair.

Preheat oven to 180-200 degrees Celsius. Add the following ingredients to a large mixing bowl in the following order: 2 1/2 tbsp. yeast; 2 1/2 cups luke-warm water; 3/4 cups sugar; 3/4 cup oil; 2 eggs; 2 tsp. salt; 8 cups flour. Mix well (by hand about 30 turns). Sprinkle flour onto the dough and knead with a closed fist for about five minutes. Leave the dough to rise until it doubles in size. Then take the dough and roll it into six long tubes. Separate and braid three tubes together to make two loaves. Beat egg and baste the top of each loaf. Place in oven on a flat, nonstick pan for approx. 25 minutes until golden on top.

Two loaves for Friday, two for Saturday—I ate my braided bread, with the aroma and sweetness of the long hair running down the spines of beautiful Jewish girls, but I ate them on Christmas Eve and Christmas Day.

It is late summer 1997, and I'm a philosophy professor with a distinctly atheistic mind-set. My new-old atheism was driven by a survivor's shame about parts of the person I could not bring into a single room. Ten years ago I returned home from my religious wandering only to embark upon a new philosophical-political odyssey. This summer my anonymous Jewish wanderer's shoes have worn off again.

The recipes for Czech *vánočka* and Slovak *vianočka* are identical to the recipe for challah. Is the word *challah* derived from *vánoce* or *vianoce*, the words from Christmas? Or is *vánočka* or *vianočka* a Christian modification of Jewish bread? Czechs boast every year about the unique tradition of Czech Christmas, and the Czech dictionary incarnates my shame into its definition of *challah* as *židovská vánočka z vykynutého těsta*, Jewish Christmas bread from leavened dough. I celebrated the Friday and Saturday Sabbath meals with Rosh Hashana on Christmas when Mother served me rich, eggy, yeast challah. The word signifies bread, but challah is actually a small piece cut off from the rest of the dough before braiding. After the destruction of the Temple, rabbinical traditions mandated *Hafrashat Challah*, setting aside a portion of dough for the *kohanim*, the Jewish priests in the Temple. This requirement wasn't mandatory if the dough's owner wasn't Jewish. The Becks were *kohanim*; Mother was an ambivalent cook. Her silence brought up the male child cut off from native springs. She needed *this* severance of flesh for her survival. With no Temple rites or professional Jewish priesthood established in rabbinical times, no one could sustain ritual purity in traditional ways. I observed *Hafrashat Challah* in my diaspora. My tithe was paid to another priestly tribe when ambivalent cooks kneaded my body. Uncut, thrown into fire, dough rose to the sky as challah's burnt offering. My genealogy circumcised me by shame.

The child of a Shoah survivor suffers shame as a phantom limb. One misses aspects of taste, thirst, music, meanings, village feasts. One inhabits such absences as shame without knowing its origins. One never had the missing limb. Shame isn't about acts; shame is the person one does not know or cannot taste, speak to, love, or make love to. A survivor's guilt manifests as shame passed on in protective silence that triggers word gaps, hungers, cuts, bonds, failed cuts, impossible separations, hybrid loves, incomplete covenants, impure rites, thirsty communions, prayers to absent gods, alien sacraments. Inherited shame cuts generations into disrepair. It cuts both ways in holding together; it bonds both ways in shattering the whole. In the shame of the broken night, the covenanted shards break wedding glasses to shatter vows. Shame circumcises the heart's veins. As one eats Jewish Christmas bread and drinks *that* rabbi's unkosher bleeding heart, wine covenants the shame of unpure priestly tribes.

Patricia

I took a spring tour of the universities that had accepted me for doctoral studies for the fall term of 1987. I met Patricia, who was then a first-year graduate student at Fordham. On an early spring morning at eight o'clock, less than a month before my thirtieth birthday, we ran into each other in the hallway of Fordham's philosophy department. I was waiting to meet with professors and students. Thinking she was a faculty member, I extended my hand as she passed by me to fetch her mail.

"I'm Martin," I said. Naming myself never has been simple for me, and now it was supposed to be self-explanatory in this unscripted encounter. I shook her hand and met my witness and future life companion. Speaking my name without shame and fear of exposure has been a developing taste. My self-introduction stated the obvious, at least on the surface of decorum, yet failed strategically as a pickup line.

"I'm Patricia," she said plainly in response, leaving the question on my face unanswered.

"Are you a professor here?" I asked, bemused, bewildered, befuddled, and struggling for words.

"I'm a graduate student in the department; I'm supposed to do some work for a professor this morning."

When Dominic Balestra arrived, he took one look at her and one at me, then at both of us, and with words addressed to Patricia, he assigned her that morning's duty: "Talk to our visitor." And he shoved us into his office and left.

I've never stopped talking with Patricia since that March morning of 1987 when she was assigned her duty. With her I began to inhabit my vocation without flight from myself. I've been discovering the infinite country of mature love. For more than twenty years—sanctioned by neither a secular nor religious institution, with vows renewed daily—we've been companions and witnesses to each other.

Glasnost, Havel, Habermas

In 1988 Gorbachev brought glasnost (openness) to the Soviet people. At the end of our Brighton breakfast in 1988, Habermas invited me to come to Germany. In the spring of 1989, I defended my dissertation proposal, and with Habermas's letter in hand, I was awarded a Fulbright-Hays doctoral grant. Only weeks after I arrived in Frankfurt, East Germans began to climb fences into West German embassies in Budapest and Prague. After Gyula Horn opened the Hungarian borders to the West—honoring international agreements about refugees rather than maintaining the Soviet-bloc prohibition against letting citizens pass to the West without secret service permits—the refugee trains began to arrive en masse in the West. It took but a few more weeks; after demonstrations in Leipzig, Dresden, and Berlin, as well as Gorbachev's unwillingness to shore up Erich Honecker's East German regime with military force, the Berlin Wall came down on November 8, 1989.

My dialogue with Jürgen Habermas and Václav Havel transformed my epoch of the Church fathers as the two intellectual luminaries of my mature manhood and freedom. During my university studies, I discovered the Frankfurt School. Its secular Jewish yet strangely mystical purview prohibited any material utopia of justice. It was their negative, messianic hope against hope that brought me out of my desert and into the heart of Judaism. The death of the received images of G-d brought me unwittingly to the ancient Judaic prohibition of carved images of the holy. I encountered Habermas as the heir of the Frankfurt School thinkers. He oriented my thinking at the turn of the century with a theory of society that made intelligible my political experience on the two sides of the Atlantic. Havel, one of two sons of the expropriated founders of the Prague film studio Barrandov and of Prague's entertainment landmark Lucerna, became famous with his absurdist plays and as a Czech dissident. He had influenced me since my teens, when I had signed *Charta 77* with him as its first spokesperson. Once the Iron Curtain fell in 1989, he became the conscience of Czechoslovakia. Neither of my two intellectual fathers was Jewish or otherwise religiously identified. I gathered fragments of my Jewish body unawares. I began to reconnect with myself at deeper, spiritual level at the time when my philosophical-political quest ran out of soul food, just as I started to search for my prehistoric roots.

I submitted to Habermas's Monday seminar a paper titled, "Havel and Habermas: On Identity and Revolution." By that time the Velvet Revolution and Havel's first presidency in Prague changed the landscape for my writing, as if history had rushed ahead of me. I was the only Czech American in the seminar, and my writings were received by different sets of eyes. As Germans climbed both sides of the Berlin Wall, we sat with Habermas at the Greek German pub Dionysos. This was our Monday-night tradition. Karl-Otto Apel's seminar took place next door to Habermas's, and at the same time, we students had to decide to follow one or the other "father," although the two groups joined afterward in the Greek pub.

This was the scene: Habermas was sitting at a long table in a closed room reserved for us. He was a lively, vital, open person, always passionately engaged with the realities of his times. He often stayed with his class until closing hours, after midnight. The history we lived that fall was unlike any other since May 1945 and for me unlike anything I could have imagined since 1968 and after I had left home in 1977. As I was the only Eastern European in Habermas's seminar that fall, when many of us traveled to Berlin to cut out our piece of the crumbling wall, all eyes turned to me on November 17, 1989.

My first academic books had biographical elements embedded in philosophical arguments. This lived dimension moved to the foreground in my biography of Habermas.[39]

"I finally got to carefully read your biography on my Italian holiday," Habermas told me in the summer of 2003 as we drove to Purdue, where he would speak on new cosmopolitanism. "I was reluctant to read it for some time." He was afraid what I would say about the gray zones of his wartime upbringing. Habermas's father had been a member of the National Socialist German Workers' Party (NSDAP), and consequently Habermas had to be in the Hitler Youth. I had Communist parents and was required to join the Czech Pioneer and Socialist Union groups. My parents became pariahs and I a nonconformist youth. Habermas became a political conscience of postwar Germany and of the new European Union. When we parted, he thanked me for my earnestness; I thanked him for his ferocious honesty with himself and his generation.

31. At the Greek pub with Habermas at his Monday-night seminar, Frankfurt, fall 1989

The Velvet Revolution

Students of the philosophy faculty of Charles University in Prague were brutally beaten by special police squads on Národní Street during the march for Jan Opletal. They declared a general strike, and the Velvet Revolution began on November 17, 1989. This was the end of the Communist regime. That historical moment burst into my diaspora in ways I never could have choreographed. The personal had become the political; the political had been revealed in the personal; all was imbued with deep meanings. I left Prague too young to be able to enjoy a personal friendship with Havel, yet his writings had a formative influence on me from the early 1970s. That Velvet fall and winter I closely watched Havel's presidential inauguration in Prague.

Michael Tomasky, the American editor-at-large of the Guardian (UK) and executive editor of the *American Prospect* from 2003 to 2006, wrote on June 9, 2004, that it was Gyula Horn, the Hungarian foreign minister, and not Ronald Reagan, who ended the Cold War. For all the hagiography Reagan received upon his death in June 2004, Marx, ahead of his time, deserves some credit for grasping the nature of the momentous collapse of those modern evil empires. After Horn opened the Hungarian borders to the West in the summer of 1989, thousands of fleeing East German tourists overran the Western embassies in Budapest. The scene was repeated in every Eastern European capital. Gorbachev wasn't going to intervene as Brezhnev had in Czechoslovakia in 1968 or as his predecessors had in suppressing anti-Soviet revolts in East Berlin and Hungary.

Revolting students in Prague were joined by striking actors then by factory workers. This was the Marxist revolution in reverse motion! Theaters—analogically to the civil rights struggles carried from the heart of black churches in the North American South—opened their striking stages to debates and transitional political organizations: the Civic Forum in Bohemia as well as Public against Violence in Slovakia. Havel, the key dramatic protest voice of the Czech theater, played a role parallel to that of black church leaders in the American South. When he later held his presidential Sunday radio speeches from the Lány retreat, he supplied something like a pastoral conscience, giving sermons to this mostly secular nation. Echoing the nonviolent tenor of the mainstream African-American struggle, the Czechoslovak change was called the Velvet Revolution because figures of the hated power no were longer hung from streetlamps as they were in Hungary in 1956. There were no gulags for the Communists who had abused their forty-one-year tenure. Most were given good pensions or allowed to launder the money they had stolen into new, legitimate capitalist ventures.

The one ambiguous revolutionary outcome was the new law, *lustrace,* which prohibited politically compromised and secret-service characters from occupying key political posts for a number of years. The law, several times extended, was flawed, since it relied on the police files of the past regime. Yet what other records were there than those collected by the omnipresent StB (or Stasi in East Germany or KGB in the Soviet Union)? Perhaps other dossiers were "prepared" to discredit the prominent dissident figures? The hated files became pawns in the game. Vladimir Mečiar was accused of collaboration with the secret service but could not be prohibited from being elected as the first Slovak premier. Some continued to clamor for retribution; others were sorry that the transfer of power was even less violent than it was at the end of Nikolae Ceausescu's Romanian regime. For better or worse, Havel's "velvet" replaced the guillotine and the Jacobin and Stalinist terror.

The presidential elections were held in December after the interim regime took over in late November. It was the held-over parliament from the old regime that elected Havel by popular mandate as the first post-Communist president of the Czechoslovak Republic. Even though the presidential swearing in was a thoroughly secular affair, the moment was pregnant with deep symbolic meaning. The inauguration in Prague's majestic Saint Vitus Cathedral echoed previous centuries when luminaries of national life, such as King Svatý Václav (Saint Wenceslas), a patron of Bohemia, had been crowned. The ancient core of the cathedral lies in the chapel of Svatý Václav, built according to Saint John's apocalyptic description and with ornaments and precious stones of the heavenly Jerusalem. Havel was ushered by the people to the Hrad (Prague Castle) as their promise of deliverance, and history wrote the script in which he, albeit in a bit existentially absurdist and Kafkaesque manner, was assigned a role. Havel reminded his people of the fragility of freedom and the anxiety it can cause any newly released prisoner. On the last day of 1989, at midnight, Václavské Náměstí (Wenceslas Square) erupted in a great carnival. After Hitler and Soviet armies had marched there, after Palach had immolated his young body (and there is but an unobtrusive countermemorial marking the sidewalk spot of his human torch at the top of the square), after years of police beatings—my own too—as if to wipe clean the tears of deep sorrow, a champagne river flowed down the cobblestones, pouring over my head, soaking my winter coat with the joy of all who had survived so much.

Witness

Patricia and I worked on our PhD studies in Germany in our tiny room with its big bed, black-and-white TV, two small desk spaces, adjacent bathroom, and kitchen area shared with other scholars on our floor. Riding through Frankfurt's forested bike paths, we'd emerge from shared solitude and take outings at night and on the weekends. Happy in my element, I wrote my PhD dissertation in one intense stream in 1990.

A few years after the Velvet Revolution, Patricia and I visited with Dean Jan Sokol in Prague's Café Louvre. The café is a step from where students were beaten in 1989. It was frequented by young Kafka and Brentano, as well as Husserl and the Prague literary circles. Sokol and I started a Prague summer school for Purdue undergraduates, and for four summers, I brought them to Prague. Sokol taught art history by taking students to churches and museums. After the 2003 presidential contest with Václav Klaus, in which Sokol lost by one senate vote, people on the Prague streets would turn and watch our student group with great interest. Sokol would have been a fine follow-up to Havel. As we slurped our soup at Café Louvre, Klaus came for lunch with a young woman admirer and sat down two tables away from us. On our way out, Sokol and Klaus met—for the first time since the election—and exchanged polite greetings. Then Klaus immediately tooted his horn about the lectures he had given at the US Enterprise Institute.

In the year of glasnost, a year before the "velvet" change, Patricia accompanied me on my postexilic return to my homeland. We still lived on our Fordham stipends and accumulated loan debt to cover the summers. One advantage of not formally marrying is that we have enjoyed a honeymoon trip every year. Thanks to Gorbachev's perestroika and glasnost, and perhaps because it had been eleven years since I'd left Prague, I was granted my first Czechoslovak tourist visa in 1988. My three-year prison sentence for having illegally left the country, however, hadn't been lifted. Although dreams about being stuck behind the Iron Curtain had revisited me into my young adulthood, it was improbable that with a visa in my US passport I would be arrested. Having had Patricia with me made all the difference to a survivor. She has been my personal and historical witness, and she is now written and choreographed with me into these dramatic moments.

There were no signs of change in the air. If I had a gift of clairvoyance and told people of the Velvet Revolution and Havel at the castle, they would have taken me for a nut. This is how I imagine Socrates fared in Plato's *Republic* when he told prisoners in the Cave there was a better, sunnier life outside. The Czech and Slovak reality was as gray—and people even more sulking under the weight of their lives—as when I'd left eleven years ago. My first visit had to be circumspect, taking into account that the ever-present secret service might follow my moves. I took Patricia to the places where I was born, lived, and went to school and where great events of my youth had occurred. We placed fresh flowers on Mother's grave at Olšany. As mentioned, when I had sent my stepfather money from the United States to buy a marble tombstone for Mother's grave, I had this inscription placed on her headstone: SHE DIED WITH FAITH IN THE EXISTENCE OF GOD.

Would her multifaith end of life merit her rest at a Jewish or Christian cemetery? Did it merit a Communist mythology?

Misrecognition

Milan Kundera's *Ignorance* is a novel about an immigrant's shame upon returning from exile. Eleven years produced absences that either arrested me at the age of twenty or filled my identity with imaginary projections of lives that friends and family wished they had and hoped I was living for them. The gaps in turn manifested as disconnects between my existential reality and the imaginary me with whom I met. I had to befriend this ghost of my youth, talk to him, explain to him a bit of my travails, and hope I could cross the gap that separated us one day. In cases where this occurred, the thirty-one-year-old joined the twenty-year-old, and I was recognized as the person I have become. In other cases my flesh-and-blood presence occasioned some pain.

Catholic friends invested in my becoming Jesuit. They heard that I had left the order; now they saw me with Patricia at my side and witnessed my secular, world-savvy, intellectual, and free self. I grew up into an adult coming to terms with the trauma of uneven parental love, and I remained grateful for the Catholic circles that had helped me survive since my mother's death. Kafka fled the Communist state; Ulysses left the Catholic institution; and I had to confront my survivor's shame.

All this became apparent when I met with the Prague family whose mother was one of my godmothers and whose daughters I once loved with not so brotherly passion. The Catholic children had grown up and married, then had other children, and the oldest dated their future mates; all struggled to live out Christian lives behind the Iron Curtain. Having suffered the hazards of living on the inside of the religious profession, I could not but disappoint the expectation that I would return as a priest ministering to the family who once had received me as an orphan. Mine was paradoxically displayed shame, implicated yet unspoken just when I had returned as my own free man. The future would have to heal it.

There has been one constant: my grammar-school-teacher queen, Mrs. Alžběta Holá. She recognized me with her inner spirit when I appeared at her door after a gap of eleven years. We learned the full story of my dying mother's testament, in which she had asked my teacher to take care of me. Every time I returned to Prague, I went to see Alžběta, my teacher and a mother bequeathed to me by mother—Shekinah's love for orphans. We would meet over a strong cup of coffee and homemade pastry, free of shame.

My Father

Ever since the uncanny Hungarian rebirth of my dad and me as father and son, my visits with family in Bratislava and father's visits to America were punctuated by highs and lows before his physical demise and death took over. I was becoming the professor in the family, and Father lived through my success. We had a lot to talk about, and those intellectual conversations, from art to politics, were always captivating. He occasionally spoke to me about his Communist Party days and sometimes about his love for my mother. On two intimate occasions, he recited poetry and spoke of his many wives and of his death and finitude and of his folly as a thinker. As if anticipating his death, on one such night Father opened his art collections and gave Patricia and me a gift of several original graphics from his Slovak artist friends, Alex Mlynarčík, Vincent Hložník, Emil Fulla, and Albín Brunovský. In this moment of openness, Father genuinely gave these gifts.

He loved to accompany us to galleries and various places in Slovakia or Hungary, and teach us from the bottomless wealth of his learning of art history. While visiting with us for a week in our Bronx student haven, Father appeared to live his life dream touring Manhattan on foot. He introduced me to his intellectual friends with pride, and he warmed up to Patricia in a personal way. My brother was glad about this reconnection, though I am less sure how well our two Bratislava sisters from Father's other two marriages bore up under my new presence. Each struggled to find herself. Kyra, in her midforties, was still fighting to establish herself as an artist in Slovakia, but after our father's death, she chose to live in Scandinavia. Nina's mother—Father's fifth and last wife—died tragically several years after the Velvet Revolution, and Father became increasingly dependent upon Nina for physical and emotional care. He spent time separately with his sons and daughters, and he often complained to one about the others.

The Gray Zones of Our Parents

Mikuláš and Father were best friends for many years: Mikuláš, world famous as a Slovak musician dissident; Father, an ex-Communist art historian. In 1990 Father found Mikuláš's name on an unofficially published list of police informants. Theirs was the double shame of generational friends who had given birth to—then were slowly eaten by—the Communist regime. From the 1970s Mikuláš and Father organized underground dissident musical happenings in the realm of conceptual art. Patricia and I spent time with Mikuláš in his Slovak home in Trstená and at his mountain cottage. We stayed in the apartment he rented out to friends in Prague. Mikuláš visited with us in New York. He exuded charisma, warmth, and sharp intelligence. His work is respected in England, where he now lives part of the year.

On the medieval-like square of shame, after the fall of the Iron Curtain, Mikuláš was displayed on the list of spies as a high-ranking member of the Communist secret service. Were the secret service lists genuine or were they part of the defamation campapaign against the former enemies of the state? I do not possess a proof for or against the charge, but I was a witness of my father's broken heart over the demise of this friendship. Friends shunned Mikuláš as if he wore the scarlet letter of the regime from which so many benefited in the gray zone and in pedestrian ways. Father speculated that the police must have recruited Mikuláš when he was young, after 1948, as he was caught crossing the border to the West. Mikuláš's dissident identity provided him a great cover story and gave him entry into underground art circles. After 1968 Father's activities were chief among them. Best friends—the spy musician and the art-historian ex-Communist—each had their shame paraded in the public press. Father broke all contact with Mikuláš for some time. And Mikuláš never defended himself to Patricia and me or, as far as I know, to anyone among his friends and family.

Did Mikuláš inform on Patricia and me while we stayed in his Prague flat in 1988? He wrote my brother and me about how after 1989 he had defended Father against slander. Father was shamed on account of his own 1950s Communist art-history criticism. I think of my father's lost generation today when Heidegger's person is shamed due to his Nazi university politics from the 1930s. My ex-Communist Father and the ex-spy dissident friend reconciled when they no longer could bear the wages of shame.

Mikuláš compared my father's Communist Party era at Comenius University in Bratislava and in art-history circles with his own creative work. He and my father stand as Slovak luminaries, one in art history and the other in creative arts, sharing an untold story that allowed their ascent to prominence. Implied is Mikuláš's self-defense: he did not admit shame. For him there was no clear difference between his work with the police, which allowed him to remain creative and help others, and Father's Communist allegiance in the 1950s, which facilitated his writing and teaching.

Why was it easier for Father to reconcile his shame with a one-time-spy friend than any misunderstanding he migh have had with his sons? Does the son remind his father of his passionate youth when with his mother when they both believed in something real, whether love or socialism? I wished that some of that lost faith had quenched Father's rage in his remaining years and enriched the legacy he was leaving behind. My wish would soon be answered out of the silence of his dying, in a silent clue he left behind, in grace healing shame and grief alike.

The Secret Is Encrypted in the Name

It is midsummer of 1997, and I call myself "Martin Beck." Naming rises from deep wells out of which living ones draw hope. My mother's family received from their Myjava wartime rescuers a Czech Bible. *Kralická* Bible was one of the first printed vernacular translations of the sacred text during the Protestant Reformation. Cyril and Methodius translated the Bible and Christian liturgy into the old Slavonic some eight hundred years before. This gift, left in Mother's box of silent artifacts, signals the Becks' wartime Lutheran conversion and name change to "Veselý."

"Veselý" is an alias Nathan and Ilonka adopted on their baptismal certificates and false identity papers. The intent behind the Christian conversion of the Beck family was to survive. The Borsuk and Vrana families signed as Lutheran godparents and witnesses for the four Becks. All parties to the baptism knew what was at stake. Nathan became "Pavel," perhaps to honor his godfather Pavel Borsuk; Ilonka named herself "Elena"; Magda transformed into "Milica"; and Ernest emerged as "Ján," again most likely honoring the second godfather. The parish record lists Julius Cibulka as the pastor. The Vranas ran the village pub and worked as butchers, while the old Borsuk ran the wood and grain mills. One clue was left: my great-grandparents are listed in the parish records as Jewish. The name spelling "Beck" appears in the parish baptismal record:

Nathan's father, Jakub Beck, his mother, Cecilia Reiss, Jewish merchants in Myjava; Ilonka's father, Max Pressburger, her mother, Fanny Löwinger, Jewish merchants from Galanta. Children, Ernest (Ján) and Magda (Milica)—baptismal record shows that their parents, physician Pavel and wife Helena, are Lutheran.

Two notes are appended to the baptismal record from April 18, 1945, and October 8, 1946, indicating that the name change from the Jewish "Nathan Beck" to Lutheran "Pavel Veselý" was made permanent after the war. Another postwar document, called a residence record, issued on September 30 and notarized on October 22, 1946, by Myjava's district court, certifies the following origin of the Becks:

> Dr. Pavel Veselý, born 30 November 1899 in Myjava, has in this district residential rights from the day of birth in accord with the law from 1886. His genealogy follows his father, Jakub Beck, born on 22 November 1872 in Myjava, who had residential right in Myjava based on the law from 1871 and who follows his father, Nátan Adam Beck, born in 1841 in Vrbovce and who obtained residence in Myjava also on the basis of the law from 1871, as he resided in Myjava on 10 June 1871. This document is issued to prove residence in Myjava. His right to residence is shared by the above-named wife, Helena, née Pressburger, on 17 November 1904 in Galanta, and children, Magdalena, born 29 July 1928 and Ernest, born 30 December 1931 in Myjava.

My maternal grandparents' gravestones display their Christian names: Pavel Veselý and Helena Veselá—calling out to the Jewish cemetery across the road. For years Ján Vrana, the son of the Lutheran and partisan godfather, has been both the caretaker of Myjava's Jewish cemetery (his house sits right next to it) and of my grandparents' graves. Mother's legal surname remained "Veselá," as it reads on my birth certificate. In both Czech and Slovak "Veselá/ý" means "joyous" or "happy." I address my maternal cousins as "Ivo and Vlado Veselý," and their dad, my uncle and Mother's little brother, as "Ernest Veselý."

It is 1997, and nursemaids breathe tender-speaking milks into mute flesh. I complete my second philosophical monograph, *Specters of Liberation,* and display a chosen middle name, "Beck," on its cover. My birth at forty punctuates an academic rite of passage. Should an adult child of a survivor disown his baptismal middle name, "Joseph"? I chose "J" for my Catholic conversion at fifteen; that was during those intense Prague years of the Communist normalization. I utter, "J" unsounded, as if its silences echo the first letter of Hebrew. I read myself from right to left: "J. Beck." My full name, the given first and last name and two chosen middle names, mixes exotic spices of personal mythology and cosmology.

Should I be ashamed of bearing two middle names, each with its own spiritual significance? I wonder. *Must I disown the shamed me? Which periods of life should I own? The birthright of atheism? The years of Christian quest? My phantom limbs of Jewish life?*

Sometime in 2012 I discover a faded copy of my mother's petition for a name change. While I have a vague memory that she started to hyphenate her pen name, it is the petition that holds the missing key to her secret.

Prague, June 1, 1967

Petition

I hereby request a return to my original maiden name, "Bäck." These are the reasons: I was born in the family of the district physician Nathan Bäck, who was Jewish by birth. He came from Myjava, where he spent his entire life, except for the two years during the Slovak State. We were not deported only because the entire village vigilantly defended my father's family. During this period the entire family converted to the Protestant faith and became part of the partisan movement. We left for the partisan territory in August 1944 at the start of the uprising. Father directed partisan hospitals. After the defeat of the uprising, we fled to the mountains and lived until the liberation under an illegal name, "Veselý." After the war my father decided that the entire family would keep the new name. At that time I did not have a legal right to make my own decision. I had to change my name two more times, in 1950 when I first married...and then ten years later with my second marriage. I find it necessary to end this cycle with names and begin to use my original family name in my civil and artistic life. This has one essential reason: one can live with a full sense of freedom only when one feels wholly oneself. This is the name by which I am to this day known in the Myjava region because of the work of my father who is still remembered as doctor "Bek." I want to be in my life and work the person I really am, a daughter of my father.

Magda Matuštíková

Martha

Martha's last letter from July 1997 puts me straight about a fatal error passed on to me by Uncle Ernest, who also had introduced me to Martha in 1977 without any familial context. In her response to my retelling the family story as I had absorbed it from Ernest and understood it after our trip to Mother's native village, Martha revealed the name of my grandfather's firstborn survivor sister, whom Ernest had named among the Auschwitz victims. Martha wrote to me in outrage: "Etelka Beck lived through Auschwitz! Etelka brought her children—Olga, Erwin, and Emil—to Sydney and became the heart of a new life." The letter revealed a key survivor of the war, Nathan's firstborn sister, but Martha volunteered neither Etelka's married name nor her whereabouts in Australia.

USA

July 1997

Martin,

I got your letter. I found some of the stories you wrote me to be very amusing. But of course we both know they are not accurate. By the way, Etelka did not die in the concentration camp. I spoke with her and her three children after the war. They have a big shoe business and live in Australia. Also, no Jews were forced out of schools in Slovakia in 1939. Magduška was attending middle school during those years. Jews were thrown out of the schools in the middle of 1941. I could keep going on correcting all the mistakes in your letter, but I'm an extremely busy person, and my time is very limited. I don't have the time anymore, as I did in the past, to listen to inaccurate stories. My sons are grown up now. They are both very busy people. They do not have the time either. From my stepfather's side of the family, I have a few relatives spread around the world. By the way, those people that you mentioned in Israel—they are very distant relatives. I would not recommend that you bother them. From my late husband's side, they are all gone now. It's only luck that I got your letter here. Since I will no longer be able to receive your mail at this address, why waste your time and money writing to me and looking for my new address? As you very well know, I am not interested in meeting with you or ever having anything to do with you. You will no longer have anything to do with me. The best thing for you to do would be to forget that I ever existed. BYE. Martha

Forgiving, Forgetting, and the Gray Scales of Memory (1787–1997 and Now)

Women perform three good deeds: they light the Shabbat candles, keep family purity, and separate challah. Like the Zionist Gisi Fleischmann whom neither one of us knew, my mother observed all three mitzvoth. With light she saved the Becks from suicide's despair. As a Communist she worked for human flourishing. In silence she cut challah and spread Shekinah's shawl over her children.

The Holocaust marked the first earthquake in my maternal genealogy; the wartime alias couldn't stop the anti-Jewish persecution. The total collapse of Soviet moral authority in 1968 punctuated the second quake. Mother officially received her name change on July 27, 1967; she gave up her second married name, Smetanová (after the TV journalist, Miloš Smetana, whom she married and divorced during a period of psychic ups and downs and whose short-lived presence in our Prague abode I barely registered), and retrieved her prewar Jewish family name. Her chosen spelling, "Bäck," dates most likely to July 23, 1787, when Jews were ordered to choose German family names. Even with her mysterious impulse to change her name in

1967, Mother's Jewish genealogy remained hidden to me under its socialist-secular veneer. What this unnameable name signified, I would not grasp until the summer of 1997. Oswiencim, Auschwitz, Birkenau—Mother never connected these names to our family names.

"I want to be in my life and work the person I really am, a daughter of my father." Mother's name-changing letter was hidden in one of her shoeboxes with many typed carbon copies of important correspondence. I didn't have to rewrite my memoir on this name-giving day. The most cataclysmic discovery waited for me in just a few more weeks—on Independence Day.

Must not a postmemoir begin on a second page, as in the Talmud, in the middle of a story? Can one repair the irreparable if one cannot own the origins? These questions regarding turning, returning, repair, endings, and beginnings are also among my bookends.

I4

CHILDREN OF DIS/REPAIR

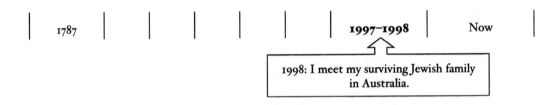

| 1787 | | | | | | 1997–1998 | Now | |

1998: I meet my surviving Jewish family
in Australia.

The year after this story began in the Chicago summer, I travel to Sydney. There I learn why Mother severed her ties with the survivors in her family and hid our Jewish origins. Only by the end of this story do I learn my mother's second secret: her personal reasons for hiding our Jewish heritage.

The Passover of the Firstborn (1997–1998, Now)

As a survivor's child, crying at my delayed birth, I learn to dine at tables free of what I have been in ignorance of and what I have failed to become. Even the best of choreographers could not stage my divine comedy. A child who wasn't stillborn out of silence slays dragons, and at adult deliveries, children agree to their being in the world by resisting hopelessness. I have yet to face the sirens of my birth that urged me on to mend the world. *And when I know the secrets of that urge, at which feasts shall I quench my thirst? To whom shall I go from my diasporas? How do I speak to the child of silence crouched within me?* I have realized for some time that the gray zones, even those not challenging my generation or personal integrity directly, aren't prone to easy repair and cheap resurrections.

It is a rainy late-fall Chicago day in 1997, and I write to Gary's father in Sydney. Emil Binetter is the youngest child of Etelka Beck. Great-Aunt Etelka was the stately elder who into her twilight in Australia exuded personal warmth and a survivor's strength. I miss her as if I always had known her; I shouldn't be angry with Mother for not telling me stories about her aunt. Etelka was Nathan's older sister, and Emil is my lost great-uncle.

Feasts of Return

In spring of 1998, I arrive in Sydney. I count thirty-two members of the Binetter family. They embrace me at their Friday family gathering. Sabbath candles are lit, prayers chanted; short and stocky brothers, my great-uncles Emil and Erwin, bless me first, then everyone. Recalling my group photo with Blanka, I am still quite tall. Who contributed to my extra inches, Jewish Great-Uncle Jakub or Grandpa's brother Béla or my Moravian father? Emil and Erwin preside over their two families. They are proud of their clan; they are proud to be the ones to have discovered me for the clan; they laugh; they hug me; I feel welcome; and I'm the center of everyone's attention. My coming to Sydney performs the Jewish story of the prodigal son. I wasn't so much prodigal, however, as sold into the slavery of my ignorance like Joseph to Egypt. A thanksgiving feast is thrown for my return. The best lamb is slaughtered, the finest Australian wine uncorked. When I think of it, I was truly lost to them, and now I return from my cradle as if Lazarus had been a newborn. With the Sabbath wine and food, I am embraced as if I always have been theirs. A dead man coming to life out of his living grave! Without shame, my cousin Gary relates to me in truth, I have lived as an assimilated Christian, and I must be taught how to walk, eat, drink, and speak anew. Yet I am the guest of honor, not a pillory of approbation. For several weeks I'm invited from home to home around Sydney. I'm the one to be taken out to dine. I'm at the center of each group photo. I'm at the heart of conversations with friends and coworkers I will meet during my stay. I'm taken to the club of Australian Jewish survivors, as if I myself have just returned from a death camp. Gary retells the story of our mutual discovery. The midrash grows and travels fast around the tightly knit Jewish community in Sydney, as if to provide solid proof against David Hume's "On Miracles," chapter ten of his *An Enquiry Concerning Human Understanding.* Philosophical atheism has nothing to say to the children of silence rising from the dead to life.

32. Etelka Beck and Michael Binetter with children Emil, Erwin, and Olga in Slovakia before 1942

My Slovak Village in Sydney

Three children accompanied Etelka to Sydney: Emil, Erwin, and Olga. They have their new families, and some of their children are married and have children. Although I stay with my cousin Gary in his townhouse, I spend most of my time with his dad, Emil. I am their discovery! Gary is a young-looking, lean, bright fellow. He graduated with a law degree to please his dad, but he works for Quantas as a flight attendant and happily travels the world. Gary's sisters, Debbie and Lisa, are jovial young Sydney women who run a successful travel agency. The entire family travels and vacations quite a bit. Three young siblings become my brother and sisters. They're still single and free to spend their time as they please, and we have some fun around town. Their parents are generationally my parents. What would Mother feel if she had lived to witness this day? Could she stay silent on a day when a feast breaks out for our return from the diaspora?

Emil married Gerda, a Holocaust survivor. Emil and Gerda, Erwin and Olga—fluent in English—speak with one another in Slovak or Hungarian. The children speak Australian English; it feels unreal to think of them as my cousins. I switch between Slovak and English; I don't speak Hungarian. My Slovak brings me one step closer to the migrant members of the family. I connect with them through our shared native language where their Australian children cannot.

The First Sydney Conversation:
At Home with Emil, Gerda, Gary, Lisa, and Debbie

We sit down in Emil's living room. The view opens to the Sydney Rose Bay. I promise my hosts that I will visit the zoo next time. Saving something for the future safeguards the present. I also promise to return with Patricia.

"In 1938 the Beck family tried to flee Myjava," Emil tells me on our first Friday.

His brother built a home on the same street block; they live in great proximity to each other. All the children do not live far away either. The entire Binetter family calls one another on cell phones several times a day. They assure themselves daily of their very existence. Each week is punctuated by a meal shared among children and parents, either at home or in a restaurant. I never knew a closely knit family structure; I never knew this closeness. Is this a different consequence of survival?

"The Becks were refused emigrant visas to enter the United States. They faced the long night of Nazi persecution." Emil switches to Slovak and turns to me. I am the only Slovak-American Beck in the room. He breaks into Hungarian with Gerda.

Then Gary asks him to switch to English. Emil nods and continues in English shaped by Australian diction and a Slovak-Hungarian accent.

"What happened to Etelka? I don't know anything about your mom?" I say.

"The eldest Beck sister, Etelka, married Michael Binetter in nineteen twenty-two. With her daughter and husband, Mother was deported to Auschwitz in nineteen forty-four." Emil paces his words with factual seriousness.

"I was told that Etelka died in the camp. How come Ernest had this so wrong about your mother?"

"Ernest kept in touch with his uncles, Béla and Ervín, who both lived at first in Tel Aviv—I believe in Ramantgan. After my mother died in nineteen sixty-four, they remained the main contact. That is all he would have had." This explains a lot of mysteries to me—how Ernest did and did not know.

"I did exchange a letter with your uncle Ernest's former wife and helped financially—you know, the one who left him and took their two children with her to Norway after the Soviet invasion of Czechoslovakia. What a shame! Ernest might have heard about us from her, but we haven't been in touch with him directly since the war. And you know, his ex-wife wasn't very cooperative with him." Emil is alert, but telling the story clearly isn't easy for him. He falls into silent stares out the window. His face is round but rather small, fitting his body build. He takes bites from chopped-up food on the kitchen counter. Gary enters the conversation while Gerda prepares dinner.

"Nové Zámky in Slovakia was annexed by Hungary in the fall of nineteen thirty-eight," Gary adds from his research. "Reunions with relatives in Myjava would have had to cross into the Slovak State, which became difficult. At most, those encounters could take place at the border until nineteen forty-two. Hungary came under German command in March nineteen forty-two. My aunt Olga, Omama Etelka, and grandpa, Michael, were taken from the city ghetto by train to Auschwitz-Birkenau in June nineteen forty-four."

"That only partially explains why their contacts were lost during the war," I say, unsatisfied.

"Our two families lost contact after nineteen thirty-eight because of the new Slovak-Hungarian border," Gary says.

"Was it more probable to get deported earlier from Slovakia than from Hungary?" I ask.

"The Slovak deportations took place in nineteen forty-two and then again late in nineteen forty-four," he replies, "which accounts for the early deportation of Etelka's sister Olga with her husband Hugo Benau and little boy, Peter. Olga Beck and her family lived in Nitra, which belonged to the Slovak State."

"That accounts for their early deportation and assured death?" I inquire.

"Eichmann accelerated Jewish deportations from Hungary at a time when the war was definitely lost." Gary is almost angry. "Even in those late Hungarian deportations in nineteen forty-four, all from the annexed Slovak territories, not only the elderly but also all families with children were sent straight to the gas chamber. The Beck sisters—Margit, with her husband Ernest Kemeny and little girl Klari, and Fridka with her husband Ladislav Klein and little girl Viera—were all murdered in Auschwitz." Gary makes a strong impression on me with this full account of names. He is moved by the freshness of the oral history he assembled.

"What about the Galanta family?" I say. "They must have belonged to the annexed territory."

"I know less about the fate of your grandmother, but for sure the Pressburgers were deported in nineteen forty-four. Your *omama* survived the Slovak deportations of nineteen forty-two and nineteen forty-four thanks to Nathan's ingenuity and some good luck. Her sister, Elisheva, was taken to the camps from Galanta in 1944 with her daughter Martha. But her husband Ernst Fuchs, just like my dad, perished there. This is somewhat similar to what happened with our family." He gets lost in thought; he appears sad; he never got to know his grandpa.

"The annexation explains why your family is fluent not only in Slovak but also Hungarian," I offer. "The same is true for another relative of ours, whom Patricia and I met in Komárno. Blanka was deported in nineteen forty-four and survived the camp. And she speaks Slovak and Hungarian."

"The fact that many were deported late in the war doesn't mean most survived. The contrary is true,—so many were immediately gassed," Gary says, eager to correct me. "Of the Becks taken to Auschwitz, only Omama and Olga came back. Others were gassed."

"Olga is alive?" I want to meet the woman who accompanied the surviving Beck sister to Auschwitz.

"Yes, and she's eager to meet you," Gary says.

I nod. "And of course Uncles Béla and Ervín survived."

"They were close to our families, and once they moved to Sydney, we spent a lot of time together. It was very sad when Omama died, and now they too are gone."

I realize that even his knowing them hasn't spared him. He is exposed, whereas I have been shielded by Mother's silence. My protective bubble has been breaking open with a vengeance. Gary fetches some old albums with family photos of Etelka, Béla, and Ervín all taken in Sydney.

It's time to light the Sabbath candles and eat. I again feel the stirrings of my inborn urgency to mend what has been broken; these urgings have been marking unspoken Sabbaths I never had with my mother and uncle. Tonight, tasting their silence, I eat my first Sabbath challah and drink my first kiddush cup of wine with family survivors and their children. I must resume the feast of words some other time.

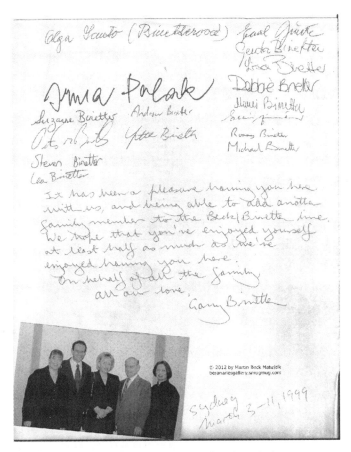

33. Martin Matuštík with the Binetter family in Sydney, 1999

The Second Sydney Conversation: Binetters' Vogue Shoes

The next day I join Emil on a trip to town; he's eager to show me the shoe factory.

"I sold this complex of buildings with all its equipment several years ago, but don't imagine that I started this big when we arrived in Sydney." Emil points to several warehouses of the former Vogue Shoe Factory. He wears a sport coat.

"Were you always into shoes?" I'm curious, gazing at his hands, marked by time and trade.

"I matriculated in Budapest in July nineteen forty-five," he replies. "My family stayed for some time in Nové Zámky, but everyone soon moved to Bratislava. I enrolled at the university, but I never really went. Instead I began to learn the shoe trade." That's the short part of the story. "Did you know that before the war my parents bought and developed a biscuit factory, and then my father started a shoe, handbag, and leather business? Mother always helped my dad. We saw our parents at night and on the weekends. Father didn't return from the camp. After the war, I had to learn shoemaking from scratch. I made several samples and sought commissions. The contracts were small at first, and earning a living was difficult. I didn't have enough money to buy materials; I could produce only on commission; and with each advance, I would purchase materials and more tools. Step by step I got breaks; the bigger commissions came later. I was eager to study new fashions, shoes that were attractive and in demand."

"So why did you leave Czechoslovakia?" I ask, searching in the dark.

"I was drafted into the army. The Communists took over in February of nineteen forty-eight. We knew there would be no future for free enterprise. I wasn't going to suffer the fate of my parents. We purchased a passage and let ourselves be sealed into a lorry train passing through Slovakia from Poland to Austria. It was on Christmas Eve nineteen forty-eight, almost too late."

This story reminds of the Israelites' flight from Egypt. Or was it like my refugee story in 1977? Given the liturgical time of the year, it could have been the flight of the holy family from the Stalinist Herod.

"I escaped to Austria almost thirty years after you—in nineteen seventy-seven—fleeing the decaying Communist regime you saw at its birth," I volunteer. Emil's face lights up as if I've taken him thirty years back in time.

"I was a healthy young man in nineteen forty-eight, and there were many women eager to date me. It was the most love-filled time of my youth. I had as many women at my side then as I could keep happy!" A bright smile lightens his face, as if he's still dating those eager maidens in postwar Vienna. He came unmistakably from Nathan's vital tribe. And there's no sexual shame in his telling.

"I continued to learn the shoe business in Vienna. I discovered a great deal more about shoes. Finally we purchased Australian visas for each member of the family, and one even for Olga's former husband. We arrived in Sydney in early nineteen fifty."

"That's much later than I thought. That means you waited two years in Vienna for the passage?" I had thought my eight months in the refugee camp was a long time.

"As I said, it wasn't lost time. I was very happy. My brother so enjoyed a good life—you know what I mean—that he postponed his departure to Australia for another year."

I don't find parallels in my refugee camp to compare with their Eden. Jews in our family seem to be so alive, healthy, unrepressed.

"So you had to start from the beginning again," I prompt him.

"I worked hard after our arrival. I had three jobs. I slept two hours a night for seven years. I married Gerda in nineteen fifty-seven." Emil looks tired, as if all three jobs are still his daily order.

"I was born that year," I interject.

"I could be your father," Emil says. "Erwin and I opened a shoe factory. First we were in a small rented house. Later we grew into a full workshop with several hundred workers. How did you hear about the factory?"

"That knowledge was the fragment of the family history that I had, but I knew nothing else." Were it not for Martha fated and Gary's miraculous letters, I never would have found Emil and his family.

"The factory operated for six years," Emil continues, "but then I developed asthma. It was most likely a reaction to glues used in the factory. I continued to work in the shop even as an employer. I was developing new models and remained involved in the full operation. Erwin took care of the economic side of our business. He had little practical knowledge about making shoes, but he kept the books. Eventually we switched from making shoes to importing them and bought a footwear-importing business. I traveled to India and taught workers how to make shoes using our models and craft. We sold the products in Australia. The entire shoe business I developed from scratch was sold in nineteen ninety-one."

Had I known my Sydney family in 1977, would I be in the family shoe trade instead of becoming a Jesuit novice in 1981 and then a philosophy professor in 1991? I wonder.

The Third Sydney Conversation: With Emil at Bondi Beach

Emil is happy, and he has been enjoying his time with me. We stroll and talk as nephew and uncle, and he exudes the keen presence of his father and mother. I find myself walking with Nathan in Myjava.

"Let us have lunch at Bondi Beach," Emil suggests.

"I have yet to see those proverbial Australian beaches!"

We resume conversation after lunch at the beach. "It's nice that you can enjoy your retirement with your children living so close," I say, as we start our promenade on the Bondi Beach boardwalk.

Emil places his right hand around my right shoulder. "Indeed!" he exclaims. "We have everything here—the ocean, mountains, beach, and as you can see for yourself, many beautiful girls!" Still images, photos I received from Sydney, become alive, vibrating even more with Emil at my side; they're almost visceral, archetypal. I'm eating something long forgotten, perhaps forbidden at birth. It tastes so delicious; it smells of the vital blood rushing through me. I'm aroused in spirit, sublimely renewed, experiencing a sensation unlike that of any known pleasures. Intimacy with my deeper self doesn't rush to leave. Undying, a meditative repose of the living body, serene beauty without purpose, inward peace—these new gifts of bread and wine remain. My self, once cut off, rises and feels itself out to the surfaces of its matter. The formerly mute taste claims me into an even deeper intimacy out of its shamed, thirsty, hungry, mutilated, choked, uncrying, sternly laughing, stillborn silence.

"Do you mind returning to those painful days of the persecution?" The pain in me wins over pleasure, and it wants to speak out and be responded to. I address Emil out of the tension I just managed to shed. "Your ordeal was so different from the Myjava family's! Was it all because of the Hungarian annexation of Slovakian regions of Galanta and Nové Zámky, where the rest of the Beck family lived?" I return his thoughts to his past, and this particular dimension of his past influences my postmemory: the past that hasn't formed my lived experience yet has been living in me through Mother's silence.

"We used to visit with the Becks in Myjava before the war. Nathan built a nice house. There was a swimming pool and a garden, and we children were eager to spend time in Myjava. We were between ten and sixteen, and I was the youngest of the three, with Erwin in the middle and Olga the firstborn."

The Becks and Binetters in Myjava

My great-aunt Etelka married Michael Binetter in 1922, the year their daughter Olga was born. My grandpa Nathan was born in 1899, a year after Etelka. I imagine my mother, little Magda, in a cradle held by her parents: it is a year after the wedding—1928—two years after Etelka's youngest child, Emil, was born. Gary is one year younger than I am; we're generational mirror images, contemporaries. I've been speaking with Emil, Erwin, and Olga about the war, and I question my silent mother. In 1938 Magda was ten; her brother Ernest was seven. If the joint Beck and Binetter photo was taken in Myjava in 1937 or early 1938, then everyone present today would have been old enough then to retain fond memories now. The war shattered ties, traditions, and lives. Bodies remember inherited abysmal silence from before birth; they drink silence's first milk.

"I know more or less exactly what happened to Nathan," I say, breaking the pause. "But I haven't yet learned about the ordeal suffered by the rest of your family. Your mother and Nathan both seemed to be formidable survivors. What about you?" I urge him on as we make a U-turn back to where a large lap pool contains the seawater and makes swimming easier, since it's free of ocean waves. Young people cover the beach, worshiping the sun and one another, playing, laughing, their naked skin glowing with various shades of tan. Time stops by the decree of divine beauty. Unlike on other days, however, I couldn't care less for people watching, as if I'm famished by unknown hungers; famished and malnourished by my lack of voice, I digest his story.

"I avoided the transports by working first in a labor camp in Hungary. I was eighteen, my brother Erwin twenty, and my sister Olga twenty-two. We were taken in different directions. My initial task was to move the Jews into a ghetto in Komárno." Emil appears very sad as he recalls that among the Jews were two of his aunties. Today's Slovak Komárno was annexed during the war by Hungary. Was Blanka among the Jews Emil gathered in the ghetto for future transports? I don't dare to reawaken his pain by asking.

"Then I was taken to work the fields in Hungary," he continues. "To make rope we had to pull flax by hand, pull it out of the ground. That was very hard." My mind wanders off to the cotton plantations, imagining Slovak Jews as African slaves. The American South was built by slave labor, just as Nazi Germany had been.

"When the Russians and American Allies started to bomb Hungary, I was taken back to Komárno and assigned a job in the petrol refinery. To escape constant beatings and cruelty, I volunteered for an easier job—to dig up live bombs." Emil smiles ironically as he says "easier." "I must have had a lucky star because when an unexploded bombshell went off near me, twenty-six Jews died." Emil's irony is deadly serious. "I survived." He believes in his survival just as strongly as Nathan and Etelka did, and I realize how much I share the strength that comes from my Jewish matrilineage.

"I was moved in the last year of the war. The transports in Hungary intensified. And then I worked building a railway line in western Hungary. The situation became too dangerous for all Jews. In late nineteen forty-four, deportations also began to swallow the hardworking Jewish labor force. It was then that I finally managed to escape from the labor camp," he continues with a visible sigh of relief, as if he has just now made it out.

"You survived this long because you were skilled and young," I say, "something your aunties and children were not."

"Yes, but had I stayed in the labor camp through nineteen forty-four, I wouldn't have been able to avoid deportation. I was getting exhausted. I would have died during the long marches prior to liberation. If my brother Erwin hadn't escaped earlier to Budapest and survived until then—" He interrupts himself, and his mind wanders off. "Where was I? If Erwin hadn't helped me, I don't know whether I would have avoided capture."

I picture the Holocaust fever of nineteen forty-four and the first months of nineteen forty-five when the Nazis intensified the killings even as they had accepted their defeat. Killing Jews became the sole purpose and legacy bequeathed to Europe by that greater Germany.

"My brother sent me Aryan papers," Emil discloses as the final drama of his wartime flight.

"How did he manage to protect himself and you?"

"Erwin hid in Budapest sometime before I escaped and—"

"You mean Erwin, your bother, not Uncle Ervín Veselý?" I interrupt.

"I know it's confusing with names, the way Jewish families often give their kids the same names. So there is Etelka and Béla, daughter and son of Marcus Bäck and Bertha Reiss; then there is our mother Etelka and our uncle Béla. Theses two were children of Jakub Beck and Cecilia Reiss, parents of your grandfather Nathan. There are two Erwins, the brother of my mother and also her son."

"Uncles Ervín, the lawyer, and Béla Beck, the dentist, were hiding with the partisans. Béla—we called him 'Vojtech'—spent the greater part of the war at the Russian front." I imagine Béla, who liked to pick fights in Myjava, and Ervín. Russian rifles and bandoliers over their shoulders, looking like Zapata's or Zapatista *guerrilleros*, men made tough—their faces worn out by war, showing signs of strife, fatigue from fighting.

"Brother was able to obtain for me new papers from the Swedish diplomat in Budapest, you know, the famous Raul Wallenberg. Erwin was in hiding in the Swedish-protected houses. He worked as a manager for one of them. Wallenberg's protection allowed us to survive in Budapest. The insane end of the war was raging in the city. Death was everywhere. In Budapest I became a baker." I picture the bakers baking challah for my feast. "I had many close calls, and my appointment with death seemed unavoidable."

Cyanide was the last medicated food that Nathan prepared for his family in Zvolen. *Did my mother stop him because she wanted to bake challah for her children?* I wonder. *Did she cook silence into the margins of her writing? On which strange, inaudible words were the children of silence nurtured?*

"Jews were hunted down, murdered daily in Budapest, often shot by a squad, their bodies pushed from the banks of the River Danube." Emil and Erwin survived thanks to Wallenberg. "I ended up driving for a Russian Red Army captain. He was Jewish." Emil is coming to the end of his story. "I returned with my brother Erwin to Nové Zámky. Uncles Béla and Ervín arrived from the East, first with the Red Army liberating Budapest, then home. Béla had nothing." Emil points to his body's imagined nakedness. "I had to give him clothes to wear." We sit on a bench so he can rest.

"What happened to your mother and sister?" I remind him about the women, who have been absent from his story.

"Etelka and Olga arrived home three months later. Until the day of their return from Auschwitz, we didn't know who had survived," Emil answers dryly.

"You didn't say anything about your father," I risk.

"Ask my sister to tell you about Father. You're having lunch with her tomorrow, right?"

Emil, visibly fatigued by words, isn't taking more questions. My stomach growls; I'm hungry.

The Fourth Sydney Conversation: With Gary and the Ancestor Becks

Gary takes me to Sydney's Jewish cemetery. I want to pay my respects to Nathan's three siblings with whom Mother didn't speak after the war. In the quite modern Jewish cemetery, many of the newer graves house war survivors.

How many children come back from the dead to speak to their dead?

"Our uncle Ervín Veselý arrived in Sydney from Israel in nineteen sixty-three," Gary says. It tastes strangely familiar, has the aroma of a dish I ate a long time ago, his saying "our uncle." "He came with his wife Ilonka Stiglitz. Their daughter, Eva, joined us earlier," he adds. We walk between stones and lay small rocks on the tombstones.

"Did he resume his legal practice in Israel?" I ask.

"Yes, but life wasn't easy."

"Is his wife still alive?" I continue.

"Ervín's wife died in nineteen ninety-two. Their Eva was born in Bratislava in nineteen forty-six, the year of her parents' marriage. All three left Czechoslovakia in nineteen forty-seven, before my mother did. Eva married a lawyer, and their two children were born in Sydney."

"A thoroughly bilingual family!" I exclaim.

"Uncle Ervín didn't resume his law practice. He worked in my dad's shoe factory once he made it to Sydney." Ervín Beck was the trailblazer, but Emil had built the foundations. "It was well known in the family that Eva had a gambling problem. She tried a number of times to 'borrow' money from my dad, uncle, anyone she thought would be stupid to gamble on her. She approached friends of my parents whilst they were overseas. She told everyone that my father had urged her to go to them if she needed anything."

"I guess every family has at least one Dostoyevsky-like underground character," I offer.

"Gambling is an addiction, just like alcoholism. It can ruin yours and everyone's life." Gary speaks with compassion for Eva; he's realistic about the extent of family obligations he should accept.

"The gambling addiction could have been one of the side effects of surviving her dad."

"Eva needs help. Right now she's completing a jail term for defrauding an elderly lady. I'm just glad her father didn't live to know what happened to the apple of his eye."

"Shouldn't one consider whether these problems visit some children of survivors, the persecution passed on to the next generation?" I venture. "My mother couldn't cope; she cut off the family ties; she suffered psychologically; and I'm trying to come to terms with her silence only now. I could have gambled or taken drugs or become a criminal." I speak obliquely about my inherited gray zones.

"But you didn't. Eva's Karen and Alan live in Sydney. I haven't seen them since their grandmother Ilonka's funeral." Gary doesn't answer my question. Some ties break with proximity; silences invade the conversations of the adult children of survivors. The ripples reach far, all around, late, and last long.

"What about Uncle Béla?" I turn to the next gravestone for the tallest Beck.

"He arrived in Sydney with Lilly from Israel in nineteen sixty-five. Like his brother Ervin, he also practiced his profession in Tel Aviv, but once in Sydney, he retired from dentistry. He was ten years older than Ervín. Lilly was his second wife. They gave birth to Tom Beck. He was born in Australia and lives in Melbourne," Gary explains. "All my information was passed on by Béla and Ervín." And now he is passing it on to me. "My cousin, Michael Binetter, recorded it all for the family. He's one of Erwin Binetter's four sons born in Sydney."

My hunger doesn't seem to subside. "Did Béla and Lilly meet after the war or later in Israel?"

"I'm not certain of the year. While Béla was fighting on the Russian front, his first wife, Gisela Adler, was taken to Auschwitz. It must have been in nineteen forty-four, and she didn't return. Most tragically their little Viera was murdered in the camp along with her mother." Gary must have learned this from Béla.

"Viera must have been the same age as your father," I start. "My mother..." Some children go straight into a great silence. *What does my silence share with theirs?* I think. *Can my resurrection bring food to the dead?*

"Yes, she was born the same year as your mother, nineteen twenty-eight," he says solemnly. "We are children of survivors. One young child died in Auschwitz with each of the Beck great-aunts, and with their husbands—the Kemeny, Klein, and Benau families. Etelka is the only Beck sister who made it out with her daughter." Gary leads me to her gravestone last. I finally make it to my roots.

"She died still quite young!" I exclaim.

"It was hard for us when Omama died. Great-Uncle Ervín had just arrived, and Béla didn't come to Sydney while she was still with us," Gary recounts. "My aunt Olga is the last survivor who can tell you about Omama. Olga married in Sydney. Her daughter Francesca lives here. But her son Michael works as an investment banker in New York." He goes on to tell me that Olga didn't like being separated from her son.

We eat lunch with Gary's sisters. He muses about having given up law for travel. He gets to stay in Europe and Asia several times a year. Gary shares my urgency, and we meet to eat and drink to quell its pangs.

"I've been tracking the Binetter side of the family. I was in Auckland last weekend and found a book called *Jewish Heritage Travel*," Gary says excitedly.

"He's always digging up family genealogy. It's almost an obsession," Lisa says, laughing.

"But without Gary, we never would have found you." Debbie turns to me and nods to her brother.

"The book," Gary continues, "mentions a couple of things that are of interest to me. Father told me that one of the Binetters had been given a title and a grant of land by the kaiser, under the Austro-Hungarian Empire. Another Binetter I discovered in Israel in July confirmed this. The emperor was most likely Josef the Second," he finishes proudly.

It's as if someone jolted you and me last July, and we started to dig, I say silently.

"In the bibliography of the book I found in Auckland"—he won't be deterred from driving home the point—"two other books are noted. And I need to locate those books and see whether there's any mention of Binetter, Binet, or Benet in them. If you could help me, I'd be very grateful." With that Gary finishes but not without writing down the names of the two books on a slip of paper:

William O. McCagg Jr., *A History of the Hapsburg Jews 1670–98*. Indiana UP, 1989.
_____. *Jewish Nobles and Geniuses in Modern Hungary*. Columbia UP, 1972.

The Fifth Sydney Conversation: Olga's Survival in Auschwitz

In Sydney I'm pampered in the way Father never tried to treat me and Mother never could. Life showers me with tender care as if to soothe me after a long journey. The next day I eat lunch with Olga. She takes me to Sydney's Jewish club, where she shows me off to her friends. There's a full dining room of camp survivors among them. After the meal we visit at her apartment and talk for some time.

34. Martin Matuštík and Olga Binetter in Sydney, 1999

"Did you know I survived the war with my mother?" Olga's youthful dark hair has faded. She's a delicate lady of medium height, well-mannered, evenly spoken. She grabs my hand at times, especially when she wants to stress something. She's vitally outspoken and refreshingly bold.

"It still doesn't cease to amaze me that I'm learning your story only now," I reply. Listening to Olga recalling Etelka is like hearing Mother portray Nathan, a conversation we never had. I'm figuratively sitting by the Beck's Oak of my matrilineage. Olga is nine years older than my uncle and six years older than my mother. I learn the painful truth of the Auschwitz death of Etelka's husband.

"I recorded everything a few years ago for Steven Spielberg's Survivors of the Shoah Visual History Foundation," she continues. Olga serves me a piece of homemade strudel—both a Slovak and an Austro-Hungarian specialty—and a strong cup of coffee.

"If I'm not coherent today, just watch the video!" she says. "Here, I made a special copy for you to take with you when you return home." She hands me her recorded testimony. Erica Turek interviewed Olga on February 23, 1996, when the story line was freshly accessible to her memory. "They don't give out copies, except one for the immediate family. Brother Erwin recorded his testimony a month after me; you should ask him for a copy before you leave Sydney. But Emil didn't want to record anything for Spielberg's archives," she regrets.

"I've spoken with Emil a great deal since my arrival, and I made my own tape recording, with his permission, so we do have something now," I say, and go on to tell Olga of our day at Bondi Beach.

"Emil and I haven't spoken for some time. It has to do with shoes," she complains.

Olga suffered a heart attack a few years after my visit. She reconciled her differences with Emil, and he took her home and cared for her in his house. I realized how often Slovak families decide for intractable reasons—but often in hardness of heart—to impose silence on each other. They do so for long periods of time. So many silent treatments and rejections practiced in different times and contexts by Slovak families and their friends...Was my mother's silence one of these? Who rejected whom?

Olga survived Auschwitz with her mother. Emil and Erwin stayed alive in forced labor. Nathan's family outran their death. They all lived, yet their survival didn't erase those Old World traits.

"I was taken with my mother first to the city ghetto," Olga says. "It was in March nineteen forty-four. We were held for two months. I lost all contact with my brothers there. From the ghetto the Nazis took us to the brick factory in May. On June second they shipped us by train to Auschwitz. The ride from our region took twenty hours, and we arrived on June third." She recalls the specific dates with definitive sharpness.

"I learned from Gary and Emil that your family lived in Nové Zámky," I interject. "This part of Slovensko was now part of Hungary." We speak in Slovak all along. I recite the date: the German takeover of Hungary occurred on March 19, 1944. Eichmann's Final Solution for Hungary affected Olga, Etelka, and Michael.

"Our relatives, except for Nathan in Myjava and Benaus in Nitra, were all taken in nineteen forty-four," says Olga.

"You knew my family in Myjava?" I ask. By now I know; my question prompts her to continue.

"I speak in the video about Nathan and Magda and Ernest and our prewar visits in your Myjava house. I explain there what I knew of their flight during the war." She astonishes me; after Ernest's account, this is the first survivor's record of my own family's travails. Mother's silence has been broken for posterity.

"We were taken by cattle cars directly to Auschwitz-Birkenau. It was a short but horrible journey. People dumped their shit and piss where they stood; they slept in their decay; and they collapsed on the same spot of exhaustion." Olga speaks with expression—vividly, visually, viscerally—just as in Max Beckmann's art.

"Was there any way to avoid the transport...you know, like Nathan and his family did?"

"I was offered a place to hide before we were taken to the ghetto," she replies. "It was in the neighboring village on a Slovak farm. Father turned this down; we had to stay together, hoping to survive that way. Who knows? I might have made it, hiding during the war; they looked sincere. Or perhaps they were going to use me for one thing only—I was young and pretty—and then what? Who had any idea at that time about what the best thing was to do?"

"Your father, Michael Binetter, died in the camp." I state the brutal fact; I want to hear it.

"When we arrived we were literally run out of the train carriages under the barking dogs and Nazi shouts, then began division into lines. Women went to the right, men to the left. This was the last time I saw my father; he turned and waved at us," Olga says, crying. It was only after the war that a shopkeeper told Olga's brother, Erwin, their father's full story. This silence wasn't willed by survivors.

"Each line was divided into two branches," Olga continues, "those who were old or women with children went straight to the gas. Mother lied about her age; she was forty-six, she looked forty and was well built, so they selected both of us to live and work."

On my Slovak trip, Blanka described Dr. Josef Mengele, who often stood at the ramp and decided who went to death and who to work. Though he didn't welcome her arrival, Olga recalls that he was in the camp every day. "A good-looking and cruel sadist. Mengele was worshiped by Germans in the camp as a half god." She sketches her impression of the man who fled Germany but was captured in Latin America.

"No one had any clue which line would be better. We all just tried to stay together as families, and when families were being separated by sex, men and women at least tried to remain close to their friends and women to their children. We fell behind Father early on. Later we learned his tragic end from Mr. Fleischer who was with him in the line: 'I was in the row with your father.'" Fleischer told the story to Erwin, and Olga reproduces it to me. "'I never thought I would ever live to tell you,'" she says, imitating Fleischer's voice. "His older good friends stood on the other side of the road and yelled over to him, 'Michael, come over to us oldies; the young ones will get harder work than us,' and your father crossed over to the other side. The next day they all went to the gas chamber." Olga cries again and says, "The guards didn't care that he changed lines, thinking he deserved what was coming to him."

"We arrived at Birkenau, B-3 camp. We were shaved and could not recognize each other. There were four hundred women on the block. To sleep, body upon body was piled at night; to eat, pigs were given better food. I started to eat only after a week, when hunger prevailed over disgust." Her dramatic recollections smell and taste of the memory on her face.

Two months after their arrival in Birkenau, there was yet another major selection. The camp's purpose was extermination, and as loads of new prisoners arrived, room had to be made by killing earlier arrivals. While a minority of prisoners was selected for labor, it was only a matter of time before they too would be used up and sent to death. All were stripped naked in the selection lines.

Olga describes the horrific chaos. "I could not see Mother in line with me, and I cried as I was selected into a line to work. Mother didn't come for thirty minutes, and I asked her what happened. I thought for sure they took her away, and I wouldn't make it without her. My mother listened to the German commands. As she went close to the front of her cellblock, a young woman prisoner pleaded with the selecting officer to let her own mother pass with her. When the selecting officer said to let the next five through, Etelka made sure to be the third in line. She maneuvered her selection with the next five who lived. This is how we survived, thanks to Mother's intuitive intelligence." Olga cries yet a third time as she revisits this scene with me.

"But how did you stay alive until the liberation in nineteen forty-five?"

"We were moved and assigned to a work detail in an aircraft factory, making parts. From here we were later taken to Ravensbrucken, where we continued in similar labors. Germans were desperately in need of military hardware, munitions, repairs," Olga explains. "While we could work, we wouldn't be destined for the gas chambers, though eventually they were to be the final stop for all of us."

Olga remembers how the gypsy camp was burned down and tells me the story as I also heard it from Blanka. More than a thousand Roma and Sinti were burned alive in a large open fire set by the Nazis. Gypsies were pushed into the flames alive. Etelka's dark hair turned gray on that night of desperate screams.

"Our last assignment was in Berlin. We dug trenches. We left for Oranienburg on April twentieth, nineteen forty-five. We were forced to march—two thousand women—for about two weeks, thirty to forty kilometers a day. We had no water and little food. The road was littered with the corpses of those who were shot dead for being weak or who simply collapsed. At one point, on May fourth, we were all herded and pushed deep into the dark forest, thinking our end was imminent. Suddenly we were left alone, and our guards vanished, and the Russian front arrived." She sighs; the survivors in my family wrestled to live to the end.

"We moved to a large vacated house. I slept in a bed for the first time since I had left our home. The next morning a middle-aged guy entered and said in Yiddish, 'Don't worry, children. I am Jewish too,' and he promised to take care of us. We were finally safe."

There would be no rapes. Women who weren't lucky enough to be found by Russian Jews were violated by their liberators. Olga was twenty-three and her mother forty-seven when the war ended. Olga and Etelka were repatriated to Nové Zámky. They waited for their father, but he didn't return.

Mother's First Secret (1997–1998)

I muster the courage to ask the Binetters about my mother. At our last supper, we gather in an elegant Hungarian restaurant, the favorite of their family and friends. Emil sits at the head of the table; I lean against his shoulder.

"There's something I need to know before I leave Sydney," I tell the group in all earnestness, turning to Emil as if to seek permission and strength from him. "You know there has to be a reason why I didn't have any contact with any of you. There must be an explanation as to why I didn't even hear that my grandfather had a sister, who, like Moses out of Egyptian slavery, brought you here. My mother never told me about you. She never even mentioned your names. I can't fathom her reasons for this. I must know."

They look at one another as if this were the most obvious thing.

Erwin speaks first. "Your mother bumped into Béla, our family, and several other relatives while I was on my way to the university. It was in Bratislava after the liberation...I think early in nineteen forty-six. We instinctively crossed the street to greet Magda. It was the very first time we had seen each other after the war. We lost all contact after deportations began in Slovakia in nineteen forty-two. We were the only survivors."

The fog lifts, and I recognize how the diaspora, deportations, and exterminations—that constant flight of Nathan's family—shattered the kin structure.

"Your mother told us on the street, 'I do not want to be seen with Jews.'" Erwin glances at the others, as if to confirm his account of the events.

"She obviously wanted to sever all Jewish links, but perhaps her exact, though only implied, words were, *I cannot be seen with Jews anymore,*" Emil rejoins, placing emphasis on the "cannot," as if to stress some mysterious constraint laid upon Mother's denial.

"It was the first and only meeting between the surviving Binetters and your mother after the Holocaust. After saying that, your mother crossed the street again, and we had no contact ever since," Erwin says. "Your mother broke all family relationships with everyone who left Czechoslovakia in nineteen forty-six and nineteen forty-seven for Vienna and then either for Israel or Australia," he concludes. More than Simon Peter's fearful denial of Jesus as he was taken by the Romans to be executed, after the war, hers was a betrayal after executions and survivals.

Mother's "do not want to" or "cannot be"—how did those active modal verbs make a difference to her silence? Silence had a name and price. She rejected her own origins and those of her children. If Martha and Elisheva heard or learned Mother's words, it would explain Martha's rejection of me. And my desire to become a rabbi for Jesus must have multiplied Martha's sense of Mother's betrayal.

"Everyone dealt with that war differently," Gary interjects. "Many people turned away from their heritage in hopes that if there were another war, they would be safer that way."

"This anticipatory anxiety must have been one key motive," I say, groping for some answers, "a fear of some new persecution. But Mother didn't opt for emigration; she became a Communist instead. At least until the nineteen sixties, there was no room for combining religion, even the secular observance of Judaism that your families enjoy in Sydney with a materialist world view."

"We are not particularly religious," Emil clarifies, "but we are not Communists either."

"You all stayed identified with Jewish traditions. You stay close to each other and to the Sydney Jewish community," I say, "and you keep trying to repair the fragments of lost family life. You found some form of solidarity among you. My mother deepened the family catastrophe inflicted by the Shoah. She was enacting the breach and destruction she suffered." Partly angry, partly horrified, I protest her silence.

"In any case," Gary comes back again, "under the Jewish law, *you are a Jew!* Under Hitler's rules even your grandchildren would be Jewish!"

Although Mother had severed my body from the Jewish food, prayer, and the covenant, her actions wouldn't have saved me from Hitler's henchman, had I been captured.

"I'm glad that you see me as part of your life, that you've received me back," I say, visibly moved. This homecoming has transformed our last supper into forgiveness, food offered for Mother—and me. Eating and drinking forgiveness tastes of self-transformation, *teshuva*; this metamorphosis of me yields to a mending of worlds, *tikkun olam*; what was held back in horror of emptiness speaks in soundings of silence, *chasmal*. Communion's gifts are blessings of unconditional love, *berakhah*.

"And we're glad you have found us. By looking for us from across time and distance, you have atoned for your mother's breach with us. Nothing stands between us now. Her, your, our story belongs in the same Book of Life." Emil speaks as a wise rabbi at Yom Kippur, inscribing Mother and me into the Book of Life, calling all the living and dead to one table to break challah and bless the kiddush cup of wine. This repair is not something I could have accomplished by myself.

"When I first saw you, I thought as if young Nathan had come back to visit me—your apparition before me was so striking." Olga's first words shift everyone's attention.

She could have cited from my mother's letter to my father after my birth: "Baby Martin looks every bit like Nathan."

Ezekiel fulfilled his promise that the dry bones will have risen. Yet I have been learning for some time that Ezekiel's promise, Solomon's prayer, and the costs of resurrection aren't settled cheaply. Olga died in Sydney in 2012 around my birthday. She was the last living survivor of Auschwitz in our immediate family; I discovered Mother's second secret in the early summer of 2012.

35. Magda Beck in fourth grade in Myjava, 1937–38

I *Did Not Want to Be a Jew,* but "She Was Too Jewish"

In the 1940s Gisi, Andrej, and Reb Dov, the leaders of the Slovak Working Group, were bribing the Nazis in order to save the Slovak Jews. Although they didn't manage to save all European Jews, their bribes most likely stopped deportations from Slovakia for two years. Without this lull in deportations, my family might not have survived in Kúty from the end of 1942 until the partisan uprising in late 1944. On a late-September night in 1944, the Germans raided the Bratislava Jews. About 1,800 Jews, including most of the Working Group, were captured and deported. My Galanta relatives who were deported in that last wave of transports to Auschwitz still kept kosher in the death camp. Reb Dov died in Switzerland in 1956, a year before I was born. Andrej died in Atlanta in 2009, a year after I moved from Chicago to Phoenix.[40]

In May 2012 I still need to assure myself that Pavel and I shared ignorance of our origins.

"I want to look for your friend," I tell him.

"Neither of us knew we were Jewish when we were boyhood friends in Bratislava," Pavel says.

Pavel finally spells out the full names of his childhood friends as we are passing through the winter solstice that marks the end of the Mayan calendar. Soon I discover someone called Breuer, who in 2008 translated some Hebrew literature into Slovak. Peter Baruch Breuer is my brother's childhood friend. Born in the same year and town, they knew as little about their Jewish origins as their younger brothers, Vlado and me. Peter Baruch and I make a Skype appointment for a week after the New Year in 2013. I'm sitting in my Phoenix home office. On my monitor a warm face with deep Slovak diction appears. An Orthodox Jewish man in Jerusalem, he remembers me from Prague when I was a boy. His father, Ernest, was deported to one of Andrej Steiner's Slovak work camps in Nováky. Peter Baruch's dad was a partisan and Zionist.

The Breuers and Becks knew one another, perhaps from wartime or the Slovak partisan uprising or postwar Slovak intellectual circles. Peter Baruch's dad wanted to study the humanities after the war, but his wife advised him that Jews could not advance in those fields, so he became a physician. Our mother took two semesters of medicine in Bratislava, most likely to please her father, but she couldn't stomach the sight of blood and switched to dramaturgy.

The two families kept their silence at home and work, and most likely they met with others like them on Sunday walks in the Koliba hills overlooking Bratislava. The Jewish intellectuals talked freely on those walks without fear of postwar surveillance. Peter Baruch's dad was expelled from his hospital post in 1959. Jews were kicked out from the Communist Party during those years, and some purges ended in executions. When the Breuers fled Czechoslovakia in the late 1960s, Pavel lost contact with them. Peter Baruch remembers spending one summer with us in Prague when his parents were in Russia. A great many individuals in the postwar Jewish generation who remained in Eastern Europe chose the Communist path; they kept silent about their Jewishness, and then the entire generation was betrayed.

Peter Baruch tells me how one day, when he was eleven, he observed in Bratislava a man in a long coat with a big black hat. After the war they lived on the same Palisádová street in Bratislava where Gisi Fleischmann had lived before the war—she at number fifty-two and they at number twenty-five. His friends told him the man was a Jew. When he went home, he asked what a Jew was. "Jews no longer exist," his parents told him. He then discovered a photo album at home with family pictures of people in long coats and hats.

Two years later, around 1964, a Bratislava tragedy occurred in a Metodová high school. The event involved the family of a well-known Slovak playwright, Peter Karvaš (1920–1999). A nationally distinguished artist, he passed as non-Jewish in the same way my mother did, as Peter Baruch's parents then did—by not talking about it, by hiding it. Our parents' generation knew; they didn't speak of this across the generation to their children; they were silent at home; they met in secret above Bratislava and occasionally in the Tatra Mountains. The playwright's son, Vlado Karvaš, didn't know that his father was Jewish. This was a period of heated Arab-Israeli conflict, and Vlado was writing zealous anti-Israeli articles in a student paper: good Arabs are oppressed by bad Jews. The essay was overtly anti-Semitic. A discussion took place at school and someone shouted at Vlado, asking him why he was writing such heated stories when he too was a Jew. Vlado ran away from his teenage cohort and in despair jumped under a train. He was a high-school senior. Jewish families in Bratislava were shaken up. Peter Baruch and his younger brother were taken aside at home. "We too are a Jewish family," his parents divulged.

"I've known for two years now that we were Jewish," Peter Baruch told his mother, "from the family photo albums." Our mother didn't tell Pavel and me anything, and we didn't know we were Jewish.[41]

Peter Baruch recalls that another famous Prague Jewish survivor, writer Arnošt Lustig, knew the Breuers. Lusting and Peter Baruch's father used to ski in the Tatra

Mountains together. Their group of friends would walk and talk freely. Lustig, unlike others in his generation, decided to write only about the Holocaust. He knew my mother, who wrote about everything but that. I too stayed with Mother in the Tatra Mountains: Kafka tried to cure his TB there; my mother took me there to cure my bronchitis. *My mother also was Jewish!* I think. *Did she never disclose anything about herself when she could walk and talk with her friends freely?*

In 1994 Slovak journalist and writer Juraj Špitzer published an autobiographical book, *I Did Not Want to Be a Jew*, in which he came to terms with his generation in postwar Czechoslovakia. In 1942 Špitzer was interned in the Slovak work camp in Nováky with Peter Baruch's father and some 250 young Jews who formed a partisan group. Peter Baruch's dad served in 1944 in Špitzer's partisan unit. After the war they relied on their partisan credentials to advance to the university and professional appointments. In 1946 this young, Jewish, partisan group of intellectuals met regularly at Comenius University in Bratislava, where my Jewish mother dated my Goyim father. From 1956 to 1967, Špitzer wrote critically against the aberrations of the Stalinist era. Then the Fourteenth Congress of the Union of Czechoslovak Writers paved the way for reformed Communists to usher in the era of the Prague Spring. At the congress many writers like Špitzer, Milan Kundera, Ludvík Vaculík, and others unmasked the practices of the Communist Party. After the Soviet occupation in August 1968 and until the Velvet Revolution in 1989, Špitzer could not publish his writings. His analyses of Eastern European Jewish culture during the Holocaust and under Communism appeared in the wider public only after the fall of Iron Curtain.

In December 2012 a new documentary about Gisi Fleischmann opened in Bratislava. A dramatic version of the story was produced at the same time on the stage of the Slovak National Theatre, where once my mother's first play had its premiere.

"She was too Jewish." In our Skype conversation, Peter Baruch recalls what his mother told him about my mother's postwar attitudes. My grandfather and my mother also relied on their partisan credentials after the war.

"She did not want to be a Jew," I tell him, using Špitzer's book title to interpret what my Sydney kin told me about my mother's reasons for her break with them. Mother did not or could not be seen with the Jews anymore. After the war she impressed her Zionist friends as being "too Jewish" because she yearned and worked for universal justice. Gisi was "too Jewish" because she was a Slovak Zionist who refused to save herself by fleeing the site of annihilation and rescue. Gisi was thirty-six when my mother was born. Had she lived, she would have been seventy-nine when my mother died of cancer. When Zionist Gisi went to her death, my Communist mother suffered the partisan defeat; Gisi was then nine years older than my mother was when she was dying. Mother never spoke to me about Zionist kosher cooking. Her break with the "capitalist" wing of my surviving Jewish family dramatizes a major rift of the twentieth century. Some survivors left for Palestine as Zionists; others followed their secular messianic star from the Communist East; and still others pursued free markets in the West.

Jewish Survivors in Myjava

One of my maternal grandpa's sisters was taken with her husband and small son to Birkenau in 1942. His other two Slovak sisters—as well as my maternal grandmother's parents and their relatives living in the territory annexed by Hungary—were taken with the last Hungarian deportations of 1944. None of them returned.

When two Slovakian Jews escaped from Auschwitz, the Working Group helped send the escapees' report, "The Auschwitz Protocols," to the free world. This was the first eye-witness confirmation that the Nazis were gassing Jews in Auschwitz, a truth the Nazis had worked assiduously to hide from the world through every means of deception. The group also attempted to alert Hungarian Jews to the true meaning of the euphemism "de-portation." And although they called for the bombing of Auschwitz—or at the very least, the railroad lines that led into that extermination camp—the Allies ignored both pleas.

Until 1944, neighboring Hungary, itself a Nazi satellite, hadn't collaborated with Germany in the mass deportation and extermination of Hungarian Jews, though the Jews there were stripped of basic civic and economic rights, including the right to own and run businesses. By 1941, 17,000 Jews had left Hungary. While their daily lives were similar on both sides of the post-1938 Slovak-Hungarian border, from 1941 to 1943 some Jews fled from Slovakia to Ruthenia and Subcarpathia to avoid deportation. By 1943 Hitler had grown angry about Hungary's failure to eliminate its Jews. On March 10, 1944, Eichmann presided in Mauthausen over the plan to deport 750,000 Hungarian Jews. On March 19, 1944, Hitler installed in Budapest SS Edmund Veesenmeyer to carry out the project. From May 15 until July 7, all Jewish communities except those in Budapest were concentrated in ghettos or factories. Starting with the Ruthenian and Subcarpathian Jews—about 17,500 per day—by June 7, 290,000 were taken from the Slovak and Transylvanian territories annexed by Hungary in 1938. By the start of July 1944, 438,000 Jews were deported to Auschwitz-Birkenau. On July 7 the regent of Hungary, Admiral Miklos Horthy, ordered the end of deportations, but he was deposed in October and replaced by the Hungarian Nazi Ferenc Szalasi. About thirty thousand Jews were then con-scripted for forced labor and brought to Germany.

With Budapest remaining the only Hungarian Jewish community after July 1944, many Jews tried to flee from forced labor into the city. The Swedish diplomat and agent of the newly established American War Refugee Board, Raoul Wallenberg, arrived in Budapest in July 1944. With blank Swedish government passports issued for 250,000 Jews in hand, in the last raging months of the war, Wallenberg was able to protect twenty thousand Jews by arranging for their emigration to Sweden, while saving about seventy thousand other Jews from outright murder by the Nazis. He purchased or rented thirty-two buildings in Budapest and converted them into diplo-matically protected houses. In 1945, four to five thousand Slovak Jews were in hiding or living with forged Aryan identities. Some 25,000 to 28,000 Slovak Jews survived the Shoah; most of these individuals left the country, and many settled in Israel.

After the Velvet Revolution in 1989, the Slovaks issued an official state apology for Jewish deportations, though no reparations were offered to its former victims by the succeeding Slovak Republic, which was established in 1992.[42]

From the trial of Eichmann in Jerusalem on May 23, 1961:

WITNESS DR. BEDRICH STEINER, lawyer from Prague: In 1942 a total of 57,837 Jews were deported, by fifty-seven transports, divid-ed as follows: to Auschwitz, nineteen transports with 18,746 Jews; to Lublin, four transports with 4,501 Jews; and to the Opole area, thir-ty-four transports with 34,590 Jews. Each transport contained about one thousand people. Of those deported in 1942, 284 came back.

In 1944 and 1945, it began in September and ended by the end of March. In 1944, or rather in 1944-45, 12,306 Jews were deported, in eleven transports, the first five of which with 7,936, and the other six to Sachsenhausen and Terezin—2,732 to Sachsenhausen and 1,638 to Terezin. The transports were divided up on the way; they includ-ed women and men. The women and children were sent to Terezin and the men to Sachsenhausen. That, at any rate, was the case with my transport....After the war about 150 mass graves were found in Slovakia. It was determined that 12,000-15,000 persons were interred in those graves, amongst them women and children.

Of the first deportations about three hundred came back; 57,500 perished; 3,500 are estimated to have been killed in Slovakia; of the 12,000 who were deported in 1944–45 about eight thousand perished....In 1942...seven thousand to eight thousand Jews from Slovakia fled to Hungary; some of these came back and were deported in 1944–45 (also from Hungary). Of these seven thousand to eight thousand, it is estimated that two thousand did not come back. The total losses, therefore, add up to about 71,000 from the 89,000.

In 1940 a census was carried out by the Government Bureau of Statistics, according to which the total assets owned by the Jews in Slovakia amounted to 4,300 million kronen [one US dollar = thirty kronen].

My Jewish Odyssey

It is early summer of 1997. I have no deeds to the lost family houses; I have no Red Cross record about my family; and I have no direct proofs that heaps of Auschwitz ashes hide atoms of my genealogy. I read the witness records and saw the secretly made photos of the naked women marching to the gas chamber. I saw photos made by prisoners at their own peril. Those who administered the crematoria still held hope—they buried hope or smuggled it out in still lives of the camp and gassing.

Mother's silence was pregnant with the family names of those who went before me down the train ramp—they passed Mengele's thumb sending them right to live, left to one of the large crematoria—and those who rest nameless in the lake of ashes. The fleeing Germans dynamited the crematoria, but cement steps leading down to the gathering spaces of death still point into an abyss where murder awaited the innocent. I was used to living for years surrounded by silent witnesses.

Did such silence nurture in me a capacity to hear it one day? Was this one of the hidden purposes of my upbringing? I didn't consider myself particularly prone to personal mysticism, and during this summer I was a disillusioned, lapsed Catholic. I was a philosophical atheist to boot, and I couldn't assign to my Communist mother such a stunning purpose. In Chaim Potok's novel *The Chosen*, a Hasidic father/rabbi brings up his son in silence in order to cultivate in him a capacity to hear the divine presence. Mother was neither a rabbi nor a Hasidic sage, yet—even though unlike the father in Potok's novel, she took her secret to her grave—her silence produced in me echoes whose sound I heard at forty.

Silent witnesses spoke clear words. Inaudible words, they came as if from within me. The stone began to lift off me at Galanta's cemetery. Spoken silence lifted the weight that force or words could not lift. The stone was a phantom inscribed with family names, each revealing and gone at the same moment. With silence audibly coming to life from within the body, constrained by its ghostly weight—as if blood never could flow under such heaviness—I trembled with what I tasted in the intervals between unsounded syllables and unsung tones.

By the end of my visit in Sydney, the silence of my mother, like Jonah's abode within the whale, gave up its first guarded, dark secrets. The Cyclops of Communism and the sirens of the Church and the windmills of the academy couldn't occasion so much strife and sorrow. Catholicism and Communism would both seem wrong religions for an Orthodox Jew, and each would signify a betrayal of the Holocaust survivors. My post-Jesuit atheism seemed to offer no cleansing or improvement either. Even though many Jews today are secular, I was a doubly tainted offspring: Communist and Catholic. I came no closer to being recognizable as a bona fide Jew by those who should know my origins. Enveloped by silence, orphaned early, classless in Communism, rootless by upbringing, refugee by necessity, I had no traditions or home but those I chose. Deeply frightened by the memory of Nazis hunting down and stripping Jewish boys to their shame and certain death, Mother had severed my flesh from the covenant, wanting to preserve my life not only from her ambivalent husband but also from any future pogrom. I have yet to cry the tears that visit the lost children of silence. Ripples that travel on an immense lake one can hardly drink up, *a Jewish odyssey*—they have not come to a standstill among the generations of other survivors.

Is there a category of unchurched, anonymous Jew—a Jew by choice? This question as well as such a desire would be tragic in Nazi times but perhaps equally comic among assimilated, secularized Jews. I was looking for a community that would accept me as the hybrid I had come to know and befriend.

Mother's Second Secret (1969?, 2012–Now)

In the gray zones of theodicy, G-d may be wrestling by our side for love. But where or to whom do we go when our G-d betrays us? Nothing prepared me for Mother's gray-zone archive, where I found her story in late summer 2012. It was hidden deeper than her silence. I never had heard it told before. If life is like a dramaturgical composition, her secret had to wait for the right moment to punctuate my story.

The historical references of my mother's undated, untitled six-page autobiography fall between Palach's death and Mother's death (January 1969–January 1972). She recalls her tweens (1938–1940) and teens (1941–1949). She wrestles with her life journey as she understood it after the 1968 Soviet invasion of Czechoslovakia and the attempt of her generation to forge socialism with a human face.

> *When I was ten [in 1938], fascism gradually took over Slovakia. Father was Jewish, later baptized as Lutheran....I was not allowed to attend gymnasium....In 1939 I could not attend any public school, and my father lost his medical practice....Then [in 1940] I discovered that there was a school I could attend—a Jewish school. I did not know anything about that world, but I insisted that I would be driven to the neighboring village to attend this school. I was fleeing loneliness and my father. It was difficult: thoroughly different customs, a different atmosphere, songs and poetry in Hebrew, unknown myths and holidays. But I found there incredible friendships [and] a magnificent teacher.*

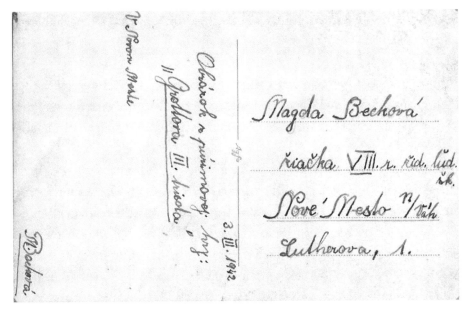

36. Magda Beck's unsent postcard from the Purim play in Nové Mesto nad Váhom; March 3, 1942

"And the wounds from home were gradually healing," Mother wrote. *What else can a good mother tell her teenage son about wounding as she is dying and leaving him behind? What else can she tell except telling by her silence?* It is the same silence with which I want to prevent my words from spelling out the possibility that my mother was sexually violated. She spelled out "the wounds from home" without naming the poison. Whatever name I can now assign to her cloaked telling of intimate boundary violations, *her* story breathes new words into *my* story. My painful discovery repairs me across generations in ways I never thought I could have imagined or mastered.

> *When I was twelve, father wounded me so that it deeply marked my youth almost until the age of twenty. And the wounding expelled me from the bliss of my relations with father forever.*

Shame bleeds words over the proper margins of this story. Yet now I hear how Mother's silence drips not with Jewish self-hatred but with familial shame! Mother didn't run away from her *Jewish* home but rather from her father's home to an uncertain Slovak Jewish world. She fled in order to repair her life. She preserved her parents' wedding-anniversary kiddush cup against the risk of persecution from Nazis and Communists alike. That cup suffered other wounds of public violence; it carried a promise of repair across the generations. I wanted to repair, but foods, grammars, and creations remained unmastered by me. Other milks have been repairing my native urgency to repair.

"There would be no rapes of women who were lucky to be liberated by the Russian Jews," my great-aunt Olga told me during my visiot in Sydney. With Etelka, my granfather's firstborn sister, they survived the wounds of living through Auschwitz.

Sexual violence against Jewish women during the Holocaust has been relegated to the margins by the survivors and tabooed by serious Holocaust scholars. As if it were an entirely new fact, discussions exploded in mainstream media with the 2010 publication of the book *Sexual Violence against Jewish Women during the Holocaust*. For decades this topic has been sidelined by interviewers or covered over by the shame of survivors. Sexual violence against women apparently distracted scholars from the master narrative of the Shoah.[43]

Eva Fogelman, a well-known clinician who works with survivors and their children, admits, "It didn't even occur to me to ask about sexual assault....These people had lost so much of their dignity and privacy. I didn't want to take that last bit of privacy away from them."[44]

When I told Eva about my late discovery of my mother's letter, she encouraged me to speak out so that other women might get the courage to heal. *Sexual Violence against Jewish Women during the Holocaust* is dedicated to "the victims of sexual violence during the Holocaust—those who were silenced, those who have spoken out, and those who have chosen to remain silent." My mother's wounding—I do not know its precise character—echoes the secrets of these survivors. Mother's story held deeply private reasons for her hiding our Jewish origins. I know now with my heart that she broke away from a more complex trauma of familial relations compounded with the public trauma of the Shoah. I know now in my gut and soul how deeply Mother has remained part of many Jewish worlds.

"I loved my father as God. I admired him and feared him as God," Mother wrote in the paragraph leading up to her disclosure of the wounds inflicted by her father. In all her public résumés from the Cold War era, she emphasized that Nathan was a partisan doctor who had brought her up as a Communist. Mother didn't let him commit a joint hara-kiri, the brave death of a Jewish samurai in the partisan defeat of late 1944. *Her love was stronger than wounds from her home*, I think.

"I have been marked by the uprising for a lifetime. Perhaps I will never cease to feel this pain of its futility, betrayal, and dirt that came from without. I realized these connections only in 1967," she wrote about coming to terms with this transgenerational collapse of universal justice. Admiring her father as a god, she was wounded by the Communist gods for the second time.

"[He] rolled his stone...like Sisyphus." So Mother describes her father in nonreligious terms depicted by Albert Camus. He was a skeptical, proud materialist who didn't believe in any of the usual meanings of life. Daughter made Father happy, and he opened the world of learning and imagination to her. Her father's wounding combusted on the eve of a double trauma: her puberty and the Shoah.

"I was fourteen and he was sixteen....The concentration camp separated us. I waited for him two years after the war until I turned eighteen." In 1942 Mother met her first love in the Hebrew school to which she fled from the wounds she had suffered at home. She also fled there from the growing anti-Semitic tsunami that would wash away her native country. Before she turned twenty, in February 1948, the Communists took over Czechoslovakia. Liberating herself from her family and her past, Mother fled to Prague after the war.

"What essentially formed me was the uprising. I experienced the pathos and the movement of a mass human revolution. I have never met such greatness in such a crystallized form—with the exception of Jan Palach." She wrote these words not after the Slovak National Uprising but after the crushing of the Prague Spring. Mother hooked the summer uprising of 1944 to the spring of 1968. Gisi Fleischmann was sent to death from my native Bratislava in 1944; a boy in me woke up in 1968 from his childhood as the Soviet hardware rolled over the Prague cobblestones; and a grown-up survivor in me is waking up out of his mother's silence in 2012. I muse, *I meet another greatness crystallized in this transgenerational story: repairs are as strong as betrayals.*

Did Mother realize all these connections in her earlier request for her name change, when she wrote in 1967, "I want to be in my life and work the person I really am, a daughter of my father"? The keys to her survival and life weren't necessarily reducible to Jewish or non-Jewish shame marking the trauma and secrets of the first order. Her disclosure unlocked the iron box packed with a survivor's gray matter. These zones are made of that second-order trauma in which I find universal human struggles. I taste this bittersweet fulfillment of Ezekiel's promise: ashes rise with Ezekiel's dry bones. I am true to love's wrestling with death. But my mother's Jewishness must no longer be distinguished, unique, or chosen, whether for a final extermination of the human condition or for healing and mending human shame. I rest here at the end of anti-Semitism. Here, genocide doesn't punish imagined sins of parents, and no one and nothing can require survivors to justify their living by moral and spiritual impeccability.

My grandfather, Nathan Beck, a charismatic personage and caring physician, was an incredibly cunning and vital man who wrestled gods and demons for the survival of our family. I'm not ashamed to say that he was a great man, a legend, a miracle worker who bequeathed to others life and lust for living. I shall never find out the facts of Mother's disclosure, nor do I need to find that archival footage to grasp the meaning of what mattered to her and what matters to me and my generation. Mother's survival has been distorted by my grandfather's human (all-too-human) shame. She had to negotiate her will to live, her courage to love, her pride to name herself by her origins, and her honesty to tell and not tell me and the world about these wounded truths. She masked her familial secret with public reasons for hiding her Jewishness.

I feel a huge relief. I know why Mother didn't want to be a Jew and couldn't be seen with Jews and also why she was *too Jewish*. She couldn't be otherwise. In that costly resurrection of a truer memory of her, I imagine Mother as Jewish *and* human unto death. I imagine her moral and spiritual possibility for a wholesome self and loving community in that infinitesimal moment of teens: Jewish schooling and fractures of the first love. In her Communist yearning for universal Zion, she never betrayed those sparks of hope. This isn't what I imagined I would find in the archives and afterlives of memory. Mother's transmission of shame and suffering to me and her partial liberation from shame and suffering come at the cost of my admitting a sharper, more honest picture of betrayals. Even the motivation to change her name in 1967—and become known as the daughter of her father—screened this deeper disrepair. She waited for her first Jewish lover until 1947, the year when other survivors in my family had left for Vienna. It was too early then to be afraid of new Communist anti-Semitism. It wasn't too early, however, to be marked by a survivor's multiple shames, which redoubled the suffering brought about by trauma inflicted once, many times recalled, and was transmitted without an apparent terminus to multiple lives.

Are we all still waiting for our first love to return? The survivor's shame explains why Jews and non-Jews cut off their memory and kin. My mother's reasons were neither Jewish nor non-Jewish but human. Children of survivors live in and through the gray scales of memory. *How can we repair this brokenness transmitted across generations?* I may become free of inherited survivor's shame and my own survivor's shame if I resurrect and then observe with an open and quiet mind my broken human worlds in both their greatness and failure. Here my traumatic silence gives way to meditative silence; my urgency to repair grows seeds of aware compassion for all that is mended and broken: the evil of annihilation and the will to survive against its impossible odds never will be diminished by the moral and spiritual failures of those who must live through such dark passages. Nor must anti-Semitic or other group hatreds find justifications in the gray zones of those who failed to love better or govern their societies with greater justice.

Survivors do not necessarily need to be better human beings—unique, chosen, other than human—to merit love over unjust death, compassion over shame. Their religion and politics must not be judged by higher standards than those with which we evaluate all human history. One must not interpret G-d's covenant, Ezekiel's promise of the resurrection, and Solomon's prayer that love should be as strong as death in a theodicy that never would survive in the spiritual and moral gray zones of violence with which so many groups constitute their origins. The question of whether G-d exists dies of its abstraction from living; even the best answer to this speculation fails to console the living who await healing in our compassion. Even if we imagine a midrash about G-d creating everything anew by surviving the shame of creation, we must not waste time judging such a midrashic G-d. This story would be about us, who must console our G-d in order to be consoled.

Mother concluded her incredible autobiographical narrative without revealing to whom or for what purpose it was written.

In 1944, when children Brano and Jan visited the Becks in their hiding place in Kúty, they spoke with young Ernest near the stream that ran along the edge of the house's garden. As adults Brano and Jan recalled the conversation they had with my uncle Ernest.

"If you let a boat down the river in Myjava, it will come here," young Ernest told them.

I accept Mother's iron-locked letter as her testament and message in a bottle. When her story intersected with mine in this book, the key with which I unlocked her shoeboxes was returned to me. I know myself apart from the compounded impact of her family trauma and the Shoah on her stability. "The wounds from home were gradually healing," Mother wrote in the 1970s! Her familial secret draws pieces of *my* puzzle together because it smiths *the* key that unlocks *my* iron box. I discover the complexities of a survivor's shame and the loss of innocence. The secret of my mother's Jewish origins is decisive only within this larger repair. The reasons why anyone may lose or survive innocence, why Jews and non-Jews may betray their heritage, are not necessarily Jewish or non-Jewish but human fears. These fears point to the sources of all self-hatred and hate crimes. One doesn't need sacrificial scapegoats, whether animal or human or divine lambs, to redeem human innocence and justice

"I am at peace with my aloneness, and I want to walk on the road I began," Mother wrote, concluding her devastatingly direct and uncomplicated six-page autobiography. This too is one of my bookends. I know now that I can walk on the road upon which I have begun to travel.

Shabbos in Sydney

During my second Friday in Sydney, I meet Emil's brother Erwin and his entire extended Binetter family. Learning all four sons' relations is as overwhelming as this description: Erwin's son Michael was named after Etelka's husband, who died in Auschwitz. A son practices law and has two sons. Michael's brother, Ronny, works as an ophthalmologist, and he has a son. A third brother, Peter, is a dentist but works as economist; he has a daughter. The youngest Binetter brother, Andrew, manufactures juices. We are thirty-two descendants of the firstborn Etelka Bäck, all sitting around a large oval Sabbath table. Erwin blesses me along with other children.

Affidavits (2002–2003)

Myjava

July 19, 2002

Dear Mr. Matustik,

I am sending you the affidavits about the persecution of the family of your grandfather, Pavel Veselý, MD. Today, with the passage of time, those who remember are hard to find. Many of those people died; it is almost half a century! By the way, today is the sixtieth-year anniversary of the day when your ancestors received Lutheran baptism. I know that both my parents and those of Ing. Borsuk did everything possible for the survival of your grandfather, grandmother, mother, and uncle. In those days many people in Myjava tried to help. We were able to find several other people to sign the testimony.

Ján Vrana

Testimony about the persecution of the family of Pavel Veselý, physician in Myjava at the time of the Slovak State:

On the basis of our personal knowledge, information, and narration from our parents, we state the following: Our families, Ján Vrana (born February 27, 1908) and wife Anna, née Varsikova—pub owners in Myjava—and Pavel Borsuk (28 June 28, 1903) and wife Elisabeth, née Bzduskova—grain and wood miller in Myjava, were friends of the family of Nathan (Pavel) Beck, physician in Myjava, who was our family physician. In the time of the Jewish persecution during the Slovak State, because of the fear of deportation, the Becks converted to Lutheranism (copy of the baptismal record is enclosed). The witnesses for the act for the parents, and the godparents for the children, Magda and Ernest, were our parents. The Becks accepted a new name—Veselý. When the Becks had to leave the family house on the main square, they rented the house of Michal Cádra, Myjava no. 189, at the downtown end of the city with the street name "Vulici." As children we used to bring them food in this house. To avoid the first transports in 1942, Dr. Veselý marked the house with the sign of the typhoid epidemic. After having to give up his medical practice, Dr. Veselý worked with others in the locksmith workshop of Samuel Bruška. After the worsening of the situation, the family was hidden by the Borsuk family— the wood miller, Myjava no. 56—in the adapted animal stall made to hide them at the mill. After their hideout was betrayed, but with a warning from the police captain Aujeský, our parents moved them to Kúty in the Zahorie region, most likely with the family of Štefan Hačunda. From one visit by our parents in this period, there survived a photo of the daughter, Magda, with her dedication to godparents Borsuk.

The journey of the Beck family after this period is not known to us. But we know that they took part in the uprising in Banská Bystrica and that they re-turned to Myjava after the war, where Dr. Veselý continued with his medical practice. His wife died in 1948, most likely as a consequence of suffering during the enforced flight.

Myjava, July 19, 2003

Ján Vrana, Myjava, Tura Lúka no. 266; and Ing. Branislav Borsuk, Myjava, Hošťáky 19/915

We confirm the above testimony:

Viera Vargová, née Cadrová; Myjava, Komenskeho 32/843; daughter of the owner of the house no. 189

Imrich Bagala; Myjava, Bodnarova 5/795; apprentice at the Borsuk wood mill during the time the Becks were hiding there

Darina Rybárová, née Boryskova; Myjava, Krmanova 10/849; daughter of Anna Boryskova, maid at the Beck home

Olga Šikundová, née Mareckova; Myjava, Krmanova 10/849; Magda's class-mate and friend

Ján Križka; Myjava, Hoštáky 25/911m; former friend and classmate of Ernest

The undersigned, Štefan Jakubec, from Myjava, Hviezdoslavova 111, testifies that I knew Dr. Pavel Veselý, formerly Nathan Beck personally. His family suffered anti-Jewish persecution: Dr. Beck was forced to work with horses at the estate of Mr. Valášek, and I was very angry when he had to give up the medical practice and become a coach driver. Therefore I visited the deputy of the Slovak senate, Šavojský, and requested that he demand restoration of Dr. Veselý's medical practice. Myjava lacked physicians at that time; it had only three physicians for more than ten thousand inhabitants. Dr. Veselý was very much liked by the Myjava people. I met Dr. Veselý in Banská Bystrica during the Slovak National Uprising, in which he took part with his entire family. That was on 2 October 1944.

Štefan Jakubec, July 19, 2002

15

"AND IF NOT NOW, WHEN?"

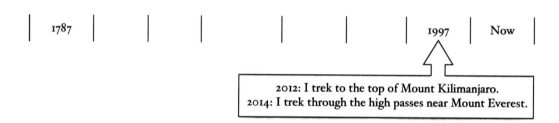

I wander in and out of several endings before passing through the bookends of my Jewish dharma: Rabbi Hillel's timeliness of *tikkun olam* and Buddha's compassion for all living beings. I ponder the impermanence of this now in its ashes and resurrections, in all that is remembered and released as suffering and joy. In one of this book's conclusions, I begin to discover another practice that gradually transforms my inherited urgency to repair: compassion across generations. With that my urgency yields to working and waiting with equanimity for a more just world in which many worlds may coexist.

Endings Are at the Beginnings (1997–Now)

"It is over there." Taking a break from mowing the front lawn, an old man points beyond his house. He is the third villager I have stopped to ask for directions. Vrbovce, nestled between the Slovak Kopanice hills twenty miles from Myjava, celebrated its sixth centenary in 2004.

"I tried to drive there on a small road behind this one, but it took me nowhere," I complain.

"There is no way you can drive there, but you can come through our backyard and reach it that way." He waits while I park my car.

"We will take you there," he says, and decides to invite his wife to join us.

"I haven't been up there for years," his wife chimes in with a heavy eastern Slovak dialect. "I'm afraid to go there!"

"Why are you afraid? It's daytime, and the ghosts won't bite you or..." I hesitate. There are no signs, no marked paths.

She offers no answer. As we approach the fenced square hidden under overgrown willows, her "there" still does not taste familiar to her. Panting for breath, she repeats, "I'm afraid to come here."

"The place has been abandoned for many years." I have been looking for the Jewish cemetery; this is where they are taking me. The man, in late sixties, gibbers on, "Somebody tried to steal the gravestones, but they caught him." Bending over the falling-down stones inscribed in barely legible Hebrew, we move into the thick growth.

"Somebody came after nineteen eighty-nine with a proposal to pay for the clean-up, but nobody followed up," the man says. "They repeatedly attempted to steal the stones—the masons who make graves. Look over here...The headstone was lifted from its place and carried toward the wall." There are voids that neither cry nor laugh; their loneliness robs us with abysses. The man takes me to the spot of the graveyard theft.

"My ancestors lived in your town in the nineteenth century." I explain the reason for my visit as we descend into a comfortable brick house.

"What was their name?" the man asks, and invites me to sit down.

The winding Kopanice road climbs the peaks and slowly descends. Grandpa rode its curves to his patients in his Tatra; the sick sought him from the opposite end. He was a legend.

"That is a well-known name. I was born here, and I have heard it many times. Wait..." He stops in midsentence, thinking. "There was a well-known and liked Dr. Beck."

"My great-great-grandfather Nathan Adam Beck, born here, is over *there*." I point toward the feared location we just visited. "Adam's youngest son, Jakub, married one of the Reisses' daughters and settled in Myjava. My grandfather, Nathan Beck, was one of Jakub's ten children from Myjava," I explain.

An old lady sitting in her local folk robe on a small stool is the man's mother. The son speaks to her loudly. She is hard of hearing; the man addresses her in a customary formal "you" and me in a formal "they."

"We came to ask you if you remember Dr. Beck from Myjava. He is his grandson."

"Yes, sure I do," she says with a big smile. "I went to his clinic in Myjava with a terrible toothache, and he pulled out my tooth. Everyone in our village went to his clinic. He was our main doctor."

"We were talking about the Jews," her son interjects, "how our people hid them, how other Jews went away to Israel." He wants his mother to confirm that all "those Jews" from the region were either saved in hiding by "our people" or managed to flee. She knows how it all happened but just cannot remember. Her one remaining tooth smiles with veiled ignorance.

The man pours me cold water from a big clay jug, and I hear the post-Communist story of Vrbovce, in which a prosperous collective farm was privatized then sold to new owners for cash. The village woke up with its prosperity gone. The new Communist-cum-capitalist owners carved out the community's old wealth and left the village empty. The Communists sold what machinery there was; fields, pastures, and animals once well tended were neglected; the townspeople were languishing, unemployed; all lived in fear for tomorrow—and of "those Jews." The old man didn't think he was being ushered into a better, brighter future. A story circulated about a factory, Armatúrka, in Myjava. The plumbing-equipment factory, with its five-thousand-strong work force under Nathan's medical care, was fragmented and sold off.

The son returns to the other topic about "those Jews" weighing on his conscience. Thanking him for their help and hospitality, I'm not going to leave him the last word.

"In 1942 most Slovak Jews were taken into ghettos then to concentration camps, and a great many were killed and never returned home," I offer, to which he repeats that most Jews were either saved by Slovak villagers or emigrated. Laughter engulfs the tears at the comic; rituals cry with joy to embarrass shame; tragic beauty lightens the sorrow. The man is visibly uncomfortable with the idea that many Jews were deported from nice Slovak villages to the camps. Tears don't destroy laughter any more than they diminish beauty or render silence empty. The old man's wife is afraid to visit the Jewish cemetery, and he is afraid to learn the truth.

I go to see my ailing father. He has a year to live.

Our Fathers: Steiner's Kosher Bauhaus
and Libeskind's Deconstruction

On September 7, 1944, after the Slovak partisan uprising began, Reb Dov was arrested in Nitra and taken to Sereď. Eichmann sent Alois Brunner to replace Wisliceny in Bratislava, which would speed up the deportation of some 18,500 Slovak Jews. Brunner refused to negotiate with the mystical Rabbi Dov Weissmandl; in fact he had him photographed in twenty-two positions so he would be recognized in case he escaped from the train to Auschwitz. Reb Dov used a small saw to get himself out of the carriage. Unable to take his family with him, he jumped off the train and ran away to a bunker near Bratislava where he stayed until the liberation in 1945. Weissmandl died in the same year as my grandfather, a year before my birth.

In 1944 Andrej Steiner fled to the partisan territory in the Tatra Mountains with his wife Hetty and little Peter. After the defeat of the partisans, the Kučarek family rescued them. After operating an orphanage for Jewish refugees in the Tatra Mountains, the Steiners relocated to Cuba in 1948 and moved to the United States two years later. Andrej testified in absentia at Eichmann's trial; he returned to Slovakia only once, because his two sons wanted to learn about the untold Slovak chapter of their father's life.[45] In Atlanta Andrej is known for designing Stone Mountain Park, as well as a mini city in downtown for 130,000 people and buildings at Emory University.[46]

In 2004, it was my third summer school for the undergraduates in Prague, and I needed to learn how Daniel Libeskind, an American-Polish architect of Jewish origin, articulated unspeakable histories. So I took an intercity train to Berlin to spend a day in Libeskind's Jewish Museum. This museum cuts space-time by three diagonal passages of architectural voids. I entered through the first passage that took me down, as if into the underground. I knew what to expect from having studied the photographs, but I didn't imagine I'd be entering an architectural epiphany of my Jewish odyssey. The first void architecturally refracted any memorial to my "self." The path leading to nowhere expressed an antimonumental and countermemorial way of narrating history. This passageway brought me to an outdoor square with a series of stone pillars that rose in different heights and thicknesses to the blue Berlin sky. The pillars stood rooted as mute witnesses on an asymmetrically leveled ground. The entire diagonally skewed stone platform made me dizzy, as if I were on a boat or suspended in space. I was allowed to walk among the pillars, moving in all directions without a guide, but I was losing my horizontal and vertical bearings. I became aware of silent stones speaking. Libeskind had planted here an architectural Garden of Exile. The stone-pillar plants recorded historical ejections from the mythical Eden.

The second void ran through all levels of Libeskind's cave, and I couldn't access it directly. The museum led visitors by blind alleys; it exhibited through small windows and slanted walls. I was unable to reconstruct any narrative history about the Berlin Jews. No easy consolation. From the underground I arrived in a tall, empty space called "The Nothingness of Memory." A pile of corroded metal, expressionless faces rose up several floors high. I touched the cold, clinking abrasiveness of Mother's traumatic amnesia. She neither remembered by telling, nor could she forget by keeping herself in a monastic cloister.

The third void rose in a dark cathedral tunnel. No Gothic roses refracted this entropic light. Wailing walls wallowed, empty, more iconoclastic than Jewish, Protestant, or Islamic niches. Tears fell, inconsolable, more alone than hermitages on Mount Athos. Nietzsche's madman failed to envision sepulchers of godless time. In Libeskind's "Tower of the Holocaust," Mother's muteness could sing in audible frequencies. Nihility grew here, large enough to touch personal voids. Peering in through this iconic barrenness, I gathered crumbs of light. I wanted to glue vowels as if this were a cosmic Scrabble that could inscribe missing names into the Book of Life. The moist European sun stroked the air for a full year before I took my last trip to see Father.

Aging and limping at seventy-seven, my father had to climb down six floors. Nina didn't want me to see him in "her" apartment, so Father and I met in a Bratislava street café next door.

"The best years of my life were in my childhood and youth," he said with faint joy in his voice. "Then everything went downhill."

I told Father that I was completing a memoir; I was eager to define his place in my life. He walked down his memory lane as if to meet mine. Since his close brush with death the previous summer, he had been reading my essays in the Czech intellectual weekly *Literární noviny*. Articles became my indirect letters to him. Father read them with interest but did not write me. Now we chatted about his failing health and about his struggle to make it on his small pension. He lamented a great deal about things that had passed him by or that he missed doing or that were simply incomplete. Nostalgia was mixed with some regrets.

One could always live better, I thought, then asked myself, *What can one do at the end of life with a sorrow that doesn't know how to feel the passing of time?*

"But you seem to have loved all your wives at the time you were with them, and you had many more women to love than the four you married." I put an upward spin on Father's brooding.

"Magda and I didn't make it past seven years." I couldn't tell if his voice betrayed his sorrow.

I had no other purpose for visiting the city of my birth than to experience Father at the end of his journey. He had recovered some strength and even worked on some writing projects. We spoke about various Slovak modern artists he knew or whose work he had documented and showcased at various times. Father devoted time to his lifework in contemporary Slovak art history. He will be remembered as one of the great scholars in the field.

"Do you still have any letters you wrote Magda or those she wrote you?" I didn't volunteer that I had inherited a shoebox full of intellectual love letters Mother had written to him in their youth.

"Some time ago I gave your brother a letter Magda wrote me when he was in jail." In the 1970s Pavel was arrested ostensibly after a skirmish with a police officer but in truth because of his participation with an antiestablishment student campaign regarding governmental elections.

"I know she loved Pavel very much, and his imprisonment was an occasion for her to show it." I remembered her concern for my brother. "You told Pavel recently that you love all your children," I said, reminding Father about his conversation with Pavel earlier that year. I didn't ask why he didn't want to receive me at the hospital and why he had his daughters carry out that rejection instead of doing it himself.

"I was born when your marriage was almost over; perhaps you were no longer faithful to it. I wonder if the lateness of my birth is why you nurtured doubts about

me. Or was it because your marriage was over or because of your mutual infidelities?"
I was direct.

"Not everything should be said," he responded. I didn't know whether he meant
to say that partners should keep quiet about infidelities, or that Mother shouldn't
have confessed her affair to him, just as he hadn't confessed his, or that my question
about paternity should neither be asked nor addressed. I wondered whether his ambivalence always had been rooted in self-doubt and insecurity about being a *good* father to anyone. What can good fathers say? He didn't find words to say more on this.

"From all the things you have done in your life, which do you consider to be the
most important?" I turned our conversation sharply away from myself.

My father thought long and hard. Looking with glazed eyes far into distance,
he said something Sisyphean yet at odds with any real effort at speaking. "I do not
know; if I knew, then I would not have made such a mess out of my life." I was astonished by the naked poverty of his truth. What would make him happy? Was there
anything he loved with all his heart?

"But you seem to have loved your writing and speaking about art more consis-
tently and faithfully than anything or anyone else. It survived even your interest in
women. Is that not something worthy and genuinely true about you?" I wanted to
find the core of his regrets and agitation. I could find peace in knowing whether or
what or whom Father loved. He didn't respond, and the full answer has eluded me
ever since. I sensed a false modesty in his capitulation. I was unsure whether I should
regard his claim to ignorance about the greatest love of his life as his Socratic insight
into human finitude. Or were those words of emptiness, the expressions of life that
has not found itself? I had no privileged access into his heart to witness whether it
beat with epiphanies granted in inwardness or with panic and confusion. His words
made him sad and tired; his weary spirit had exhausted him. The fragile space of intimacy between us cracked from his inability to name the love that had built up his
life. Sorrowing over a life with tears of anxious self-love took my father further from
me than his physical death ever could.

"I arrived in Myjava just in time to pay the rental fee for the plot of the Beck
grandparents," I told him. "*Pan* Vrana renewed the grave sites for another ten years."
Father remembered Jan's name from his first wife, my mother Magda. Father must
have honored my mother's silence; it was a way of his love.

Father perked up and sat up higher. "I'm curious to know how much renting
costs."

"One thousand five hundred and fifty four Slovak crowns." Fifty dollars was the rental sum I had paid Vrana.

"The cost of a burial plot is but a fraction of the monthly fees I pay for the Bratislava apartment." Father burst out laughing then pulled the napkin from under his cup and calculated all the years of eternity he could afford on his meager Slovak pension.

"Father, take care of yourself!" I told him.

We did not make another date before he made his with death.

Summits and Valleys

I meet a wandering Jew in my dream.

"I am not Buddha. Spare my life," he says.

"Where is my home?" I ask him with the opening words of the Czech anthem. The Slovak hymn responds, "It thunders above the High Tatra Mountains."

"Don't look at your shoes. Behold your face!" he shouts back. I wake up.

I am a wanderer with worn-out shoes who does not claim to possess the master repair books.

As in my dream, so also in this book I arrive at archetypal scenes of birth: *the burials, the unions, and the ultimates.* With each scene I sample archives and afterlives of questions. They spin like children's dreidels yet are unable to spin forever. Questions call out to generations whom I may not claim to save.

Scene One: How Do I Come Home to Myself?

"Your father transformed himself through his deeply moving spiritual testament and meditation on Ján's work," Ján Mathé's wife, Eva, tells me at my father's funeral.

Father slipped away like the wolf he always was, alone when everyone was far and near. Nina takes her long-awaited vacation in the Mediterranean; Kyra enjoys a scholarship for art work in Stockholm; Pavel returns from his Prague trip only minutes too late to hold Father's parting hand; and I am stuck in Wisconsin, out of telephone and Internet contact. Patricia joins me for a trip to Bratislava in late August 2005 for Father's funeral. Nina's sorrow entirely melts any residues of hardness in her heart and mine. The magnitude of her grief utterly overwhelms her. As if sensing that life has prepared me for this moment, sorrow surrenders her whole being into my embrace. Looking at Father's quiet shell, Nina falls to the floor like a suddenly cut birch. The loved one is there neither in space nor in a linear memory of the past. The frost of late August resembles still lives even less than canvases or photos. The burials cradle us with renewed urges to repair and give births.

Father left behind a secret gift. In the last two years of his life, he completed a manuscript of a portrait of the Slovak sculptor Ján Mathé, whose large-scale figures religiously transformed many post-Communist housing projects and their spiritless landscapes. In the arid gardens east of the lost Eden, did this engagement with this modern religious artist irrigate Father's desert?

"When your father's book is published, it will dramatically change the reception of his place as the most important art critic of twentieth-century Slovak art," Eva Mathé assures me.

She reveals that the original inspiration for Father's unpublished opus was not only his lifelong friendship with Ján but also a citation he found in volume two of *Theology of Agape* (1994) by Jozef Zvěřina. Zvěřina was one of the most important Czech Catholic thinkers of the twentieth century and influenced the period of my early Christian conversion. He also was among those who frequented the house of the MJ Catholic family who adopted me in Prague after Mother's death. Life's mystery is coming full circle to me; I am still in the eye of a snowflake.

Eva discusses a quotation from Zvěřina, marked by Father on page 217 of *Theology of Agape*:

> There are works that belong to the Marian songs of praise [the *Magnificat*], "Many nations will bless me." I can mention only one work of our abstract art; it is called "The fruit of your life" by Ján Mathé, a Slovak sculptor from Košice [the town in East Slovakia which is also the birthplace of Andy Warhol]. The scultpure is from stone in a monumental proportion. Mary is signified by a line in the image of letter "C"—a body line of medieval madonnas that are motherly, tender, protective. Here is the line truly motherly in whose womb is a fruit—a sphere, conception, the beginning of the new cosmos. It is not a painting; it is a fundamental archaic form— "the mariological principle"—expressed in the sculpted matter. No

other plastic art would truly fit among the high beton buildings [the Communist housing]. There stands something mariologically essential and fundamental—a promise and hope.

Did Shekinah speak to my father at the end of his life through a madonna face? I wonder. *Were Father's two wives, my mother and Nina's mother, beckoning him from other shores?* While all these faces could appear in my father's death, no decent theology obliges one to doctrinally reconcile such singular intuitions of birth.

Scene Two: Is Love as Strong as Death?

"What took you so long?" people ask me.

"I asked her twenty years ago," I reply.

The banquets of love punctuate death, and they sketch good endings. Life cycles hurry disrepair from earth dust to birth milk. *If not now, when? Now* is the year of my fiftieth birthday, the thirtieth anniversary of my escape, and the twentieth marker of my meeting Patricia.

"We lacked a sense of community that we could invite. We blessed each other by silent vows," Patricia says, explaining the twenty-year delay.

"We matured for this moment, and now we dare to invite everyone into the same room," I add.

Patricia and I tear pieces from an unleavened challah and drink the May wine of joy. A Loyola Jesuit officiates, and a Jewish-Renewal rabbi blesses our wedding. A few Marxists complete our cycle of blessings. Neither Jews nor Catholics nor atheists easily fit into interfaith weddings. *Is it holy to hold the vows in a chapel or under the canopy of stars? Do I cover or uncover my head? Can hybrid lovers invent kosher cooking for Jewish-Christian communions? Do we cut or tie the knot for covenanted betrothal?*

Jesuit Father Dan Hartnett, who returned to Chicago's Loyola University from years in Peru, is a humble priest in his middle years. The smiling, jovial man requires of us no final exams to prove that we are ready or worthy. Extensively educated as Catholics, we have our baptismal credentials. For all the conspiracy of circumstance to the contrary, my flesh never has been cut off from its Jewish matrilineage. The shortest path, without either the Catholic Cana or the Jewish covenant's requirements, is to have Dan officiate and Rabbi Menachem Cohen from the Mitziut Jewish

Renewal community in Rogers Park give us his priestly blessing. The Chicago bishop prohibited outdoor weddings, and we imagine our chuppah under the Adamic heavens. Dan is prepared by his work among native Indian Catholics who often live together then marry, like us, twenty years later. He offers a name for our practice, not recommended but tolerated by the Church in Peru, *servinaqui*. Rabbi Menachem works alongside Christian pastors in a night ministry for runaway youths. He's an intuitive young man with deep spiritual yearnings, long wild hair, and a thick beard. Patricia and I met him while he was drinking a beer in Heartland Café with his college buddy, a Chicago activist and secularized Jew. *Who would receive strange Jewish-Christian hybrids like us?* I wondered. We were both spiritual mutts and cooked unorthodox brews together. Menachem, however, embraced us as we were.

Patricia wears an array of light green, pink, lilac, and yellow, and I accentuate her spring palette with rose pink. There you see the couple continuing hand in hand, giving one to the other without an intermediary. Leaving the worlds of our religious-cum-atheistic families, we enter the Garden of En-Gedi, where King Solomon sings an ode to love. We eat of the liturgies choreographed by our mysterious chefs. Isaiah serves his bold promise that even should our earthly parents forget us, G-d will not abandon us. Saint John reveals G-d as love, and Matthew has Jesus sum up the Torah under two essential Commandments out of 613, to love G-d with all one's heart and to love one's neighbor as oneself. Beatitudes of justice and peace are, for Christians and Jews alike, the messianic age that is yet to come. We dramatize a dialogue, at once spiritual and intimately erotic, composed from the Song of Songs. Patricia and I sing to each other; we are a bit older now, have more wrinkles, emit more sonorous vocals.

"Love is as strong as death." We taste the words together. I tremble, and I forget where I am.

We speak our vows, leaving out the customary mention of death: "until G-d makes us part." My Maoist best man brings our necklaces; Father Dan blesses them; and we place them on each other with King Solomon's words imprinted on them.

"I am my beloved's, and she is mine. My beloved is mine, and I am his. *Ani l'dodi, v'dodi li*."

Rabbi Menachem covers us with his prayer shawl. He whispers the ancient blessing given to Adam and Eve. Seven friends and family members bless us—*Sheva b'rachot*—and many recite in Hebrew. Father Dan blesses our daily bread and wine; we share communion and believe it to be changed into kosher delights. Patricia and I stand still in a twenty-year afterglow. We listen to Khalil Gibran's words. My mother cherished that poem of independent love; Patricia chose it for our interfaith ketubah. An artist sets the wedding ketubah in the Garden of En-Gedi; it needs no human contract. I step hard on a glass to cut our covenant. "Mazel tov!" As Patricia and I walk out with Beethoven's "Ode to Joy" playing, the moment tastes imperishable.

It is May 2007, and Beck's ten-year wedding anniversary cup from 1937 claims the center among the witnesses who survived the Shoah and my exile. The phantom limbs of survivor's shame become chimeras. The brass cup melds the irreparable without hiding its secrets. Under Mary's side of the chapel stand the still lives of Mother and Father; next are Patricia's grandparents; and they are joined by the grand wedding party of the young Beck grandparents. Pavel, and my nieces—Katka, Meghan, and Sasha—draw near. Other wedding guests chip into the cacophony from all strains of our journey: believing Communists and disenchanted ex-Communists (my parents would be happy in this row), staunch Catholics and liberated lapsed Catholics, secular Jews and kosher Jews, Jewish-Christian crossbreeds, new age spiritualists, heady philosophers and headier atheists, activists of every sort, straight guys and gay lassies, white working-class folks and the black elite. The arrival of the Sabbath bride marks the Judaic "now time" of creation and redemption. The Eucharist marks the Christian "now time" of creation and redemption. The secular-cum-socialist-cum-market-dreams of a better world promise the same without their being named by religious recipes. The kiddush cup saved from the Holocaust by my grandparents, guarded by my mother's silence, and preserved for this nuptial moment now overflows with an open future.

"I want to tell you about our wedding," I start slowly.

Ten years after those uncanny letters from Sydney took my breath away in our Chicago living room, Rabbi Menachem celebrates the founding of the Mitziut (Reality) Jewish-Renewal community, which Patricia and I began to frequent after my father died. With a progressive postmodern admixture of Orthodox and Reform Judaism and Kabala, our rabbi cooks from old and new pots. I speak to this group.

"When I hit a roadblock in myself, I went to see Rabbi Menachem. 'I am scared,' I told him. 'I don't know how to wed because I don't know how to accept myself as either a Jew or a Christian or neither or both,'" I explain. "So Menachem encouraged us to cook up a Jewish-Christian ceremony."

A month before Patricia and I were married, I wasn't ready to invite friends from this community to our wedding, to risk being seen. *If not now, when?*

"I could not bear another withdrawal of blessing." *I could not bear another letter from Martha.* "Can you receive someone with our hybrid genealogy?" I ask them.

Surrounded by latter-day hippies, Kabala students, professionals, artists, activists, and mixed couples, I stand on the beach of Lake Michigan, not far from Loyola University. My Kafka once thought he had parted the Red Sea and also arrived in the promised land en route from Prague. The Great Lake Michigan breaks over the rocks, welcoming Sabbath's awakening at dusk. I don't need to wait for an answer. Writing a midlife memoir instead of having a midlife crisis yields an open-ended book. I drink up the remnants of survivor's shame. As rainbow dew shoots through the air, I glimpse Menachem's tears.

Scene Three: Are Peaks, Valleys, and Plateaus Our Ultimates?

I survive my gifts of healing and become my own antiheroic witness. Thus I find myself deeply conflicted about what the November 2011 symposium "Memory and Countermemory: Memorialization of an Open Future" is supposed to be. A major international academic event at Arizona State University in Phoenix gathers significant voices in post-Holocaust and memory studies as well as Eastern European and Native American studies. I write myself into this event's archetypal scene of transgenerational dis/repair. This banquet has been cooked for me alone. I dream to be its convener, facilitator, and recipient. Having opened my mother's shoeboxes, I can name what she hid in her version of Helen Epstein's iron box. My mother is joining the symposium with Helen Epstein, Lawrence Langer, Marianne Hirsch, Leo Spitzer, Sandor Goodhart, Lewis Gordon, Gabi Schwab, Simon Ortiz, Leslie Marmon Silko, Berel Lang, Sasha Etkind, Karl Figlio, and Rainer Schulze. Survivors are not gods— their lives can be messy; they can both heal and harm. I know this about my mother. I am the dreamer who can at once heal and harm. The symposium guests enter from my dreams and writing. *We* have lived through our gray zones. A notice about this event later appears in the *ASU News*.[47] My story of dis/repair across the generations becomes public. I'm surviving my mother's secrets; I'm forgiving the author of my life for revealing them. I can now read valleys and peaks with my readers.

In early January 2012, Patricia and I climb Mount Kilimanjaro. The six of us trekkers—assisted by porters, cooks, and mountain guides—take five days to reach the Uhuru Peak, which towers 19,341 feet (5,895 meters) above sea level. The telling of the story of our Kilimanjaro ascent belongs elsewhere. I conclude this memoir journey with the penultimate day before our nighttime assault on Uhuru. Even though I prepared for more than a year, this is one of the most difficult things I've ever done, and in midlife it's my hardest and the most magnificent journey. The Shira trek to Kilimanjaro is designed for acclimatization. We walk higher and sleep lower. With increased altitude, the air gets more rarefied. I practice deep yoga breathing and often stop to catch up with my heartbeat. On day four, a day before we'll reach the summit, I lose control over my breathing during the morning trek. I tremble at first with the anxiety of losing my grip on life. Awaiting my next breath, I know that I cannot hold up the world. In paying attention to my breathing on the way to the summit, I learn the same life lesson I have been discovering while writing my memoir. My urgency to repair traumatic silence suffers its own inability to mourn.. Summiting to the valley of fear, I descend to my peak without mastering a new plateau. I shed unspoken burdens. I no longer need to transmit the traumatic consciousness I inherited from the prior generations. This transgenerational wandering through suffering and healing leads to meditative silence out of which I may speak about trauma with compassion.

Who walks my plateau walk when I reach valleys and descend to the mountain peak? I give up the heroic versions of myself, my family, my story. I tell and remember across the generations liberated by compassion to live free of shame.

Jewish Dharma

Rabbi Hillel the Elder, born in Babylonia, lived in Jerusalem at the time of King Herod, Caesar Augustus, and Jesus of Nazareth. Hillel was a Jewish sage of Mishnah and Talmud and a founder of the dynasty of sages that lived in Israel until the fifth century BCE. He addresses the mindful silence of all generations: "If I am not for myself, who will be? If I am only for myself, what am I? And if not now, when?" ("Ethics of the Fathers," Mishnah, *Pirkei Avot* 1:14). "That which is hateful to you, do not do to your fellow. That is the whole Torah; the rest is the explanation; go and learn" (Babylonian Talmud, *Shabbat* 31a).

"We all lived in the gray zones during the entire Communist period," Fedor says in a conversation about the meaning of moral ambiguities of the oppressive regimes. *Malostranská kavárna* in Prague was a traditional coffeehouse that was overtaken by Starbucks. My dissident art and film friends will not deign to meet there, so we meet next door. Fedor Gál is a leading Jewish activist and writer from anti-Communist Slovak dissent circles. A contemporary of Havel, he was among those who formed the Public against Violence, the counterpart of the Civic Forum at the time of the Velvet Revolution in 1989. After the Czecho-Slovak political divorce, Fedor escaped from Slovakia to the Czech Republic. Slovakia has not yet come to terms with its anti-Semitic legacy, and the successor statist forces have not become free of Jozef Tiso's clerical-fascist nationalist moods.

"Some eighty percent of children and young adults suffer some form of violation of intimate boundaries," Fedor continues. Political gray zones are complicated by personal violence.

"So the two groups must overlap: eighty percent of intimate-boundary violations include other gray zones," I speculate.

"It makes no difference to your story," Fedor says.

"But the overlap makes a difference," I respond.

"It's really your decision. You're the author of the story," Martin Hanzlíček chimes in. He's a filmmaker and producer of sharp documentaries about the Communist period in Czechoslovakia. In 2010 Martin and Fedor produced a film about Fedor's father, who died on the death march from Mauthausen.

"The personal dimension of totalitarian abuse makes absolutely no difference in judging the Nazi and the Communist era atrocities. I repeat, it neither adds nor takes away an iota," Fedor insists.

"I agree—it makes no political difference to the story of the camps and extermination. But in the untold story of my mother, the personal makes all the difference," I say.

It neither adds nor takes away an iota from the political, I think. *But why is the story incomplete if I take away the personal dimension, which neither adds nor takes away an iota from the political? How does one mend the world with compassion—with closed or open eyes?*

"Neither the atrocities of the Nazi camps and gulags nor the stories of survival can be judged through moral lenses," Martin adds. I agree with him and mention Primo Levi.

"The personal dimension of my mother's public story now makes sense to me; it *all* makes sense together—only now it all just makes sense. The Becks' generations tell a story of greatness, survival, woundings, and dis/repair," I say, speaking my mind.

"Perhaps you should speak with our psychiatry friend, P. He's been working with victims of intimate-boundary violations all his life. I'll send you contacts for other archives in Slovakia and Prague. There may be documents about the Hlinka Guards, postwar affidavits, and who knows what else." Fedor gets excited. "And you definitely should do something about Beck's Myjava house, just because it is right to do so."

"Fedor and Martin, I have to tell you something else," I say, changing the tone. "Pavel and I did the scariest thing on our brother-brother trip last week. We went on a forty-minute tandem paragliding flight in Beskydy." I pull out my iPhone and show the pictures Pavel took of me in the air and the ones I took of him landing.

Martin laughs. "You had the nerve!"

"Pavel and I talked about my memoir, and he confirmed that he knew as little about our origins as I did, even though his boyhood friend was Jewish, and our mother and that boy's mother were Jewish survivors living in Bratislava. After I discovered our Sydney family and after my visit there, Emil Binetter visited with Pavel in Los Angeles. Pavel experienced in LA what I did at Bondi Beach in Sydney. 'Walking and talking with Emil was like seeing our grandfather Nathan again. He sounded and looked just like him,' he said."

"Does your brother remember Nathan?" Martin asks.

"He does; Pavel is six years older. I only imagined that Emil looked like Nathan on the basis of transmitted memory. After our paragliding flight, my courage failed me, and I didn't tell Pavel about our mother's second secret—her personal reasons for hiding where we came from. He doesn't know the end of our story. Please don't say anything to him until I do," I plead. I would meet with my brother several months later to complete this conversation.

Martin nods. "It is for you to tell."

"It's your book. You are the author," Fedor seconds.

I wanted to ask them how they would produce a script for this story, but I left that for another time.

"Do you know who the Buddha of compassion is?" a Tibetan monk from Takthok called out and invited me to sit down next to him on a meditation platform.

Takthok (means rock-roof because its roof and walls are made up of rock) is a monastery in the Nyingma tradition of Tibetan Buddhism situated in Sakti village in northern India approximately 450 miles east of Leh. The monastery was founded around the mid-sixteenth century during the reign of Tshewang Namgyal on a mountainside around a cave in which Padmasambhava is said to have meditated in the eight century. Patricia and I visited Tibetan India in the summer of 2014 before I trekked through the high Everest passes in Nepal.

Someone who works for tikkun olam, who repairs the world and heals all sentient beings, I thought in silence but answered the monk with something less articulate.

This was a teaching moment. He took me on a journey through Siddhartha Gautama's fourfold discovery that all beings suffer (Sanskrit, *duhkha*), that suffering originates from craving and aversion toward the impermanence of all beings (*samuda-ya-satya*), and that meditation and its living practice on this nature of reality are ways out of suffering (*nirvana*). Siddhartha Gautama became the enlightened one, the Buddha of compassion, who taught that there is a path to end all suffering (*magga*).[48]

"It is time to leave your preoccupations with the traumatic past and dedicate your next ... years to the work of compassion." Assigning a number to my lifespan, the monk answered his question about the compassionate Buddha by showing me another way to be.

"I have been searching for ways of shifting my life," I said. I pondered how in the Lurianic Kabala the work of *tikkun olam*, mending of the broken world, is to liberate the divine sparks deeply buried in all beings. If there were G-d in Buddhism, s/he too would depend on our work of repair.

"My parents were shot in front of me when I was a small boy." He entered the monastery in Ladakh as a refugee from Tibet occupied by Communist China. He was showing me another way of coming to terms with the traumatic past without forgetting it and without engendering new suffering from its memorialization.

The monk learned from me nothing about my life when I sat next to him in silence. After some fifteen minutes of meditation he spoke to me as if he had just finished reading my memoir. He had not heard my accent, yet he addressed me as if I had arrived from Eastern Europe with a heavy baggage (also an image of karma) of inherited and redoubled family trauma. He had no knowledge of my lifework, yet intuited that I came to Ladakh contemplating midlife changes.

The monk turned toward Patricia who entered the temple while we were in silence and sat down quietly across from us. "You have been thinking about your retirement, but it is time to leave the suffering of trauma; one could carry it forever, right?"

"Trauma can continue without end, unless you decide to begin anew," Patricia nodded in agreement. She understood his question.

Is she a Buddhist at heart? Or has the monk lived with me for over twenty years?

There is no terminus to suffering except realization of its origin and cessation. Trauma is redoubled suffering, an attachment to harms we suffer and carry as our inheritance, labor, duty, burden, responsibility, obsession, craving and aversion.

"Look at me, I am meditating!" he pointed at his own face. "Look at me, I am meditating," his eyes were wide open. "Nothing would change my awareness of impermanence, whether an attacker or a beautiful woman entered the room. And all these Buddhist images," he pointed at the Buddhas and Bodhisattvas, "are only my reminders."

I was born with an urgency to repair the irreparable; however, until the summer of 1997, I didn't sharpen my transgenerational memory to touch and taste the traumatic past of my family. Until now I haven't been aware of the radical impermanence that pervades all things. My inherited urgency all along has been embodied in the transmission of suffering and in the specific form of suffering that arises, passes, and transmigrates in the karmic memory traces of trauma. Trauma holds the present hostage to the woundings of the past, and therefore all traumatic memory reduplicates suffering and conditions the future possibility of suffering.

There is suffering of human finitude and the impermanence of all things, and this marks how we live life in the present. Nostalgia for the past and longing for the future bring more suffering in the present because archives cannot forgive the past, and the future cannot be lived as an afterlife of memory as if ahead of itself.

The past provides access to memory, but archives cannot reverse time, so remembering the wounded past, as much as forgetting it, cannot grant equanimity. Walter Benjamin was correct in his assertion that past generations have expected our coming so that we may rescue the messianic promises of a more just world. Yet an anamnestic solidarity of the present generation with victims of history does not culminate in salvational acts by a messiah or buddha. Kafka poetically predicts that the messiah will arrive only when we no longer need one,[49] and the nonviolent communities of compassion counsel us that if anyone sees a buddha, we should know that it is a mirage that may be killed.[50] Memories of woundings can guide future generations through the museums of suffering, ensuring that no age will forget the traumatic past. Yet repair work devoted to the afterlives of memory alone cannot enlighten or redeem the present. Transgenerational trauma transmits future incarnations of suffering as the karmic inheritance of woundings one passes to others.

When I gave up the creation myths of my youth and passed through the adult cosmologies of a/theism (I've thought a great deal about Max Horkheimer's concept that both theism and atheism have their martyrs and tyrants), I began to get glimpses of my present. I've unlocked the iron box with keys that repair without the terrifying costs of survivor's shame.

How can I forgive the future for this open wound of disrepair? But if not now, will there ever be an end to humanly made and transmitted misery? Can I embrace the present without keeping alive the traumas of the past or awaiting saviors who heal generations? If ending human misery isn't possible now, when will it be?

Tears tremble with the tragic beauty of love sparring with death. *Are tears as infinite as tastes of the sublime? Can tears that also laugh heal all wounds?* No theory or storytelling can make promises to heal the wounds of history without one's own practice of wakeful silence.

What if there are sorrows that to us mortals seem unredeemable? Must not tears we shed learn compassion from the infinite face of mercy?

I laugh when scholars do not cry, and when they cry too much, I learn to smile. There is a dimension of the world cooked entirely from compassionate tears. I would fail to practice compassion if, in my urgency to repair, I were unwilling to bear disrepair. This sorrow and joy belong to wanderers who have become liberated from the cycles of suffering and ignorance—from the trauma of *samsara*.[51] Spirit's untamed freedom intones the first sound of equanimity and bliss out of emptiness that is silence.

Our Female Rabbis (*Rabínky*): Gisi and Magda

Gisi Fleischmann was a major female leader and rescuer of Jews in Europe from 1938 until her deportation from Bratislava on October 17, 1944. The SS officer Brunner (he was seen in Syria after the war), who presided over these deportations, allowed Gisi to stay in her office at Edlová Street 6, the building that also housed the headquarters of the Bratislava Gestapo. Gisi was given the task of providing for the Jews imprisoned in Sereď. On October 15, alone in her office, she was answering a Jew in hiding who had asked for help.

As she wrote, "Regrettably, I am in the lion's mouth,"[52] Brunner opened the door, tore the letter to pieces, and sent her immediately to Sered'. Promised release in exchange for the names of Jews in hiding, Gisi endured interrogations. Two days later she traveled on the last transport to Auschwitz. Himmler stopped killing by gas at the end of October 1944. On Brunner's explicit order, the letters *R.U.* (*"Rückkehr unerwünscht"*—"Return undesirable") were added to Gisi's name on the transport list. When the train carrying her arrived at Auschwitz, Gisi's name was one of two called out on the loudspeaker. According to a Slovakian survivor's eyewitness account, she was taken away by two SS officers and never seen again.[53] In 1939 Gisi had sent her two daughters, Alice and Judith, to Palestine, but refused to save herself. Her daughters died in Israel within the time frame that leads up to the opening of my story in Chicago.

I imagine my mother and Gisi sitting in our Prague apartment or in Café Steiner in Brno or strolling on the banks of the Danube River in Bratislava. They're speaking dramatic lines about mending the irreparable across generations, which I invented for Samuel Beckett's drama that he did not write, *Waiting for the Messianic Age*:

Gisi: Didn't you want to be a Jew after what you and your family went through?

Magda: But I was too Jewish! That is why I could not be seen with the Jews anymore.

Gisi: I saved my children from "the lion's mouth" by sending them to Palestine.

Magda: I saved my children for a better universal future.

Gisi: Good-bye, my children. I am leaving on the last train to Auschwitz.

Magda: Good-bye, my children. I am leaving betrayed by my generation's promised land.

This is the story I imagined my mother and I would tell each other one day.

37. Martin Matuštík with his mother

38. Martin and Pavel Matuštík with their mother in Prague, the 1960s

39. Martin Matuštík with his first camera, circa 1967–69

40. Martin Matuštík at the end of the ninth grade, 1972

41. Martin Matuštík in Prague, 1970s

42. Martin Matuštík at his high-school graduation ball at Lucerna Hall in Prague, spring 1972

43. Martin Matuštík speaking at his high-school-graduation ball, Lucerna Hall in Prague, spring 1976

44. Nathan Beck (right) assisting in anatomy class, before 1939

45. The Beck family in hiding with the Granec family, Kúty 1943-44

46. Martin Matuštík with Uncle Ernest and Patricia Huntington in Karlovy Vary, 1987

47. Martin Matuštík with Patricia Huntington on Mt. Kilimanjaro, January 2012

ACKNOWLEDGMENTS

I'm grateful to many individuals who accompanied me in person or appeared at various stages during this project: my uncle Ernest, whose memoir letters became part of my own narrative; the Binetter families in Sydney, who gifted me with the oral history of my past; my father Radislav and brother Pavel, who encouraged me to complete the work; my sisters Nina and Kyra for being part of my life; Gary, Olga, Blanka, Brano, Jan, and Peter, who shared with me their transgenerational memories of my past; and my life companion, Patricia Huntington, the first witness and reader of the the book. I benefited from three close editorial readings of the book, by Hillel Black, former editor in chief of William Morrow, publisher of Macmillan, and executive editor of Sourcebooks, by Alan Adelson, director of the Jewish Heritage Project, and by Angela, a skilled editor who wishes to remain anonymous. At various stages of the project, I also received feedback from Eva Fogelman, Helen Epstein, Fedor Gál, Sandor Goodhart, Anna Grusková, Martin Hanzlíček, Maryš Hošková, Katarina Hradská, Larry Langer, Bill McBride, Sol Neely, Gabriele M. Schwab, Simon Ortiz, Arthur Sabatini, Hava Tirosh-Samuelson, Janet Rabinowitch, Ivica Ruttkayová, and others.

Book Subventions

Award for "Heritage and Memory: Sites of Transgenerational Trauma, Moral Reminders, and Repair." Institute for Humanities Research Seed Grant. Arizona State University (2012).

ACLS conference award for "Post-WALL-memory of Eastern Europe: Ghosts, Afterlife, and Conflicted Legacies in Post-1989 Eastern Europe" (2011).

Book subvention awards from the Institute for Humanities Research and the Center for Critical Inquiry and Cultural Studies at Arizona State University.

Sabbatical leave from Arizona State University and the Lincoln Center for Applied Ethics (2014-2015).

Presentations of the Book Material

The Association for Critical Theory and the Doctoral Students' Council at CUNY Graduate Center (New York; March 13, 2013).

University of Alaska-Southwest, DVD by UAS Media Services (Juneau, AK; Apr. 5, 2013).

Arizona Jewish Historical Society Book Club (Phoenix, AZ; Apr. 18, 2013).

"Helga Weiss's Holocaust Diary," www.broadstreetreview.com (Philadelphia, 2012).

"Midrash on How the Pasts Will Have Remembered Their Futures" at the symposium "Memory and Countermemory: For an Open Future" (Arizona State University; Nov. 8–9, 2011).

North American Levinas Society Conference (Anchorage, AK; May 14, 2012).

"Connecting the Links to Our Chain of Tradition" at Temple Chai (Phoenix; May 1, 2011) at The Future of God, a conference sponsored by Gonzaga University (Florence, Italy; Feb. 23–26, 2011).

"Unforgiving Memory and Counter-Redemptive Hope" at Nordic Summer University (Falsterbo, Kursgård, Sweden; July 31–Aug. 6, 2011).

"Where Do People Go? Postsecular Meditations on Václav Havel's *Leaving*" at the Wilma Theater, after-performance symposium on Havel's legacy (Philadelphia; May 30, 2010).

Interviews

"Professor Rediscovers His Past—and Gains a New Life," *ASU News* (Oct. 26, 2011).

"The Traces of Silence," http://radio-arch-pp.stv.livebox.sk/devin-20131227-697-Parnas-18-30.mp3, an interview by Ivica Ruttkayová, Radio Devin (Bratislava, Slovakia; Dec. 27, 2013).

NOTES

1 See http://www.deathcamps.org/reinhard/slovakia%20transports.html

2 Helen Epstein, *Children of the Holocaust: Conversations with Sons and Daughters of Survivors* (New York, Penguin Books: 1988). Epstein's opens her story of the Holocaust: "For years it lay in an iron box buried so deep inside me that I was never sure just what it was."

3 See any stock web images of a potato pancake and latke.

4 See http://www.yadvashem.org/yv/en/exhibitions/communities/bratislava/fishers.asp

5 Abraham Fuchs, *The Unheeded Cry* (Tel Aviv: Mesorah Publications, 1983, 1986, 1998).

6 See http://www.yadvashem.org/yv/en/exhibitions/communities/bratislava/working_group.asp

7 Anna Grusková, *Rabínka (A Woman's Rabbi)*, documentary about Gisi Fleischmann (Bratislava, Slovakia: K2 Production, 2012).

8 See http://pionyr.cz/EN/

9 See http://digitalassets.ushmm.org/photoarchives

10 Dieter Wisliceny's testimony from trial October 27, 1946 trial can be found in Yad Vaschem, Israel. Wisliceny worked as Eichmann's superior in the 1930s then helped to promote him. Himmler and Eichmann's policy of extermination replaced Wisliceny's Jewish emigration plan. Wisliceny testified against Eichmann in Nuremberg in 1946, and his testimony is cited in the transcripts of the 1961 Jerusalem trial of Eichmann. The testimony in Nuremberg did not save Wisliceny from death by hanging in Bratislava in 1948.

11 Transcripts from the Eichmann trial come from the Nizkor Project: http://www.nizkor.org/hweb/people/e/eichmann-adolf/transcripts. See also http://www.un.org/en/holocaustremembrance/2012/Eichmann_events.shtml

12 Ruth Lichtenstein, "The Road to Atlanta," http://rappaport75.weebly.com/lessons.html

13 Archive footage of the location where a fourteen-year-old boy was shot on August 21, 1968.

14 Reference to a photo by Pavel Štěcha on the cover of *Postnational Identity: Critical Theory and Existential Philosophy in Habermas, Kierkegaard, and Havel* (New York: Guilford Press, 1993; Phoenix: New Critical Theory, 2013).

15 "Yehudah Loew of Prague, also known as the Maharal, was one of the outstanding Jewish minds of the sixteenth century. He wrote numerous books on Jewish law, philosophy, and morality, and developed an entirely new approach to the aggada of the Talmud." Maharal is also assumed creator of a golem. See https://www.jewishvirtuallibrary.org/jsource/biography/Loew.html

16 Cited from Claude Lanzmann's interview with Andrej Steiner, in *Shoah,* the film transcript, pages 22ff. See http://resources.ushmm.org/intermedia/film_video/spielberg_archive/transcript/RG60_5010/90A3EE59-27DC-49A1-AEAA-CECD8626A9EB.pdf

17 See Epstein, *Children of the Holocaust.*

18 Ludwig Börne (1786–1837) was a German journalist and writer who was of Jewish origins. In *Letters from Paris,* he criticized German despotism and upheld the rights of the individual.

19 Lichtenstein, "The Road to Atlanta." See also David Kranzler, *Holocaust Hero: The Untold Story and Vignettes of Solomon Schonfeld* (London: KTAV Publishing House, 2004).

20 See Lanzmann's interview with Andrej Steiner in *Shoah,* the film transcript, page 31.

21 Sarah Kofman, *Smothered Words* (Evanston, IL: Northwestern University Press, 1998), pages 65–66. Robert Antelme, *The Human Race* (Marlboro, VT: The Marlboro Press, 1992).

22 Michel de Montaigne, *Essays* (Kindle e-book, 2012). Ernest Becker, *The Denial of Death* (New York: The Free Press, 1973), page 31.

23 Václav Havel's "The Power of the Powerless" empowered East-Central European dissidents in 1978.

24 Milan Kundera, "The Tragedy of Central Europe," *The New York Review of Books,* Vol. 31, Number 7 (Apr. 26, 1984).

25 Herbert Marcuse, *An Essay on Liberation* (Boston: Beacon Press, 1969).

26 Primo Levi, "The Drowned and the Saved" and "The Canto of Ulysses" in *Survival in Auschwitz* (New York: Simon & Schuster, 1958).

27 Eduard Nižňanský et al, eds. *Holokaust na Slovensku*, Vols. 1–7. Dokumenty (Bratislava, Slovakia: NMŠ, ŽNO, 2001–2005).

28 The facts are compiled from open sources: www.holocaustresearchproject.org

29 Karol Janas, *"Židovské obyvateľstvo v Trenčianskej župe a jeho perzekúcia v rokoch 1940–1945"* in *Dokumentačné stredisko holokaustu 2005–2010.* See http://sk.holokaust.sk/wp-content/janas2.doc

30 This story varies in its tellings by my uncle Ernest, Brano Borsuk, and my father. I was unable to confirm that this person indeed was Štefan Hačunda. See chapters 9 and 11, "Letter from Uncle Ernest to His Nephew Martin."

31 Cf. Claude Lanzmann's film *The Shoah.*

32 Primo Levi, "The Gray Zone" and "Shame" in *The Drowned and the Saved* (New York: Simon & Schuster, 1988).

33 In his letters to me, my uncle writes about "Kubala's ill mother," while both Brano Borskuk (chapters 8 and 11) and my father referred to "Štefan Hačunda's ill wife." The core of the midrash about this miraculous doctor, Nathan Beck, is the same. The Slovak Hlinka Guard leader Otomar Kubala was executed in Bratislava on August 28, 1946. It is unlikely that this Kubala would be the person who had received an affidavit from Nathan or my mother after the war.

34 Kundera, "The Tragedy of Central Europe." See Judith Butler, "Who Owns Kafka?" *London Review of Books*, Vol. 33, No. 5 (3 March 2011), pages 3-8.

35 Genealogy archives of the Church of Jesus Christ of Latter-Day Saints www.familysearch.org

36 See http://www1.yadvashem.org

37 Štefan Čúvala is listed as the Myjava head of the Hlinka Guard from 1943. See http://www.upn.gov.sk/hlinkova-garda/data/velitelia.pdf A person with the same name was reportedly also one of the regional organizers of the Slovak National Uprising in August 1944 in the Myjava hills. See http://www.krajne.sk: "29th August [1944] erupted in central Slovakia uprising. Soldiers in western Slovakia fled from his crew with their equipment and adding to the guerrilla groups, organized by Milos Uher on Javorine (partisan section Hurban), John Repta in Brezovský mountains and teacher Stefan Čuvala in Myjava mountains. In the woods Vlčia Valley was formed another guerrilla group, whose commander became captain bears" (cited from the web article on the history of World War II in Slovakia).

38 Havel's speech upon receiving an honorary doctorate from the Hebrew University in Jerusalem, "Kafka and My Presidency" in *Projevy* [*Speeches*] (Praha, Czech Republic: Vyšehrad, 1990), pages 100–103.

39 See my book, *Jürgen Habermas: A Philosophical-Political Profile* (Lanham: The Rowman & Littlefield Publishers, Inc., 2001).

40 Grusková, *Rabínka*.

41 Peter Baruch's father was born in 1921. He was twenty-one or twenty-two years old during 1942 to 1943. He joined the partisans in 1944, mostly in Nízké Tatry and Banská Bystrica.

42 I used numerous open-source documents for compiling this factual information, including http://www.holocaustresearchproject.org, http://en.doew.braintrust.at and http://www.ushmm.org

43 Sonja M. Hedgepeth and Rochelle G. Saidel, eds. *Sexual Violence against Jewish Women during the Holocaust*, edited by (Waltham, MA: Brandeis UP, 2010). "US Holocaust Museum Studies Rape of Jewish women in the Holocaust," *Jewish Journal* (June 4, 2011). Cynthia L. Cooper, "Holocaust Women's Rape Reports Break Decades of Taboo," *Jewish Journal* (June 3, 2011).
Jessica Ravitz, "Silence Lifted: The Untold Stories of Rape during the Holocaust," CNN.com (June 24, 2011).

44 Cited from Cooper (preceding note). Also see Fogelman's concluding chapter in *Sexual Violence*.

45 *Andre's Lives*, documentary film (1999). See http://icarusfilms.com/new99/andre-liv.html

46 *Andre's Lives*, see http://icarusfilms.com/guide/andreliv.pdf

47 Professor Rediscovers His Past—and Gains a New Life, *ASU News* (Oct. 26, 2011).

48 The monk taught me the essence of Buddhism: The Four Noble Truths regarding the suffering and the Noble Eightfold Path out of suffering presented in the fourth truth. The eightfold path out of suffering consists of wisdom (Right Understanding and Right Intention), ethical life (Right Speech, Right Action, Right Livelihood) and concentration (Right Effort, Right Mindfulness, and Right Concentration).

49 "The Messiah will come only when he is no longer necessary; he will come only one day after his arrival; he will not come on the last day, but on the last day of

all." See Kafka's "The Third Notebook" (December 4, 1917) in *The Blue Octavo Notebooks* (Cambridge, MA: Exact Change, 1991).

50 The ninth-century master and founder of the Rinzai school of Buddhism, Lin Chi, is the source of the following admonition to a young monk: "If you meet the Buddha on the road, kill him." One never should think that he or she has found the right doctrine or savior.

51 One meaning of the Sanskrit term *samsara* is "wandering existence." The fictional, often pejorative figure, of the Wandering Jew refers to the peculiar *samsara* of those who have no home on earth. The Buddhist liberation from wandering in the beginningless cycles of births and deaths lived in suffering does not require a Jewish sacrifice. The similes of shoes, shoeboxes, and wandering I used in this book fit the journey of a Jewish Buddhist (Jewbu, Jubu, Buju), Martin Beck Thubten Gyatso, who recovers his Jewish beginnings and practices Lamrim.

52 Joan Campion, *In the Lion's Mouth: Gisi Fleischmann & The Jewish Fight for Survival* (Lanham, MD: University Press of America, 1987).

53 Katarína Hradská, *Gizi Fleischmannová. Návrat nežiaduci* (Bratislava, Slovakia: Albert Marenčin, 2012). See http://kultura.pravda.sk/kniha/clanok/60329-katarina-hradska-gizi-fleischmannova-navrat-neziaduci

ILLUSTRATIONS

DETAILED CONTENTS

BY THE SAME AUTHOR

Postnational Identity:
Critical Theory and Existential Philosophy
in Habermas, Kierkegaard, and Havel

Specters of Liberation:
Great Refusals in the New World Order

Jürgen Habermas:
A Philosophical-Political Profile

Radical Evil and the Scarcity of Hope:
Postsecular Meditations

Neklid doby:
Eseje o radikálním zlu a jiných úzkostech dneška

ABOUT THE AUTHOR

Born in Slovakia in 1957, Martin Beck Matuštík grew up in Prague behind the communist Iron Curtain. A firsthand witness of the fall of communism in Czechoslovakia in 1989, Matuštík was raised in an atheistic home by communist parents until he was orphaned at the age of fourteen. Fleeing Prague in 1977 at the age of nineteen, he spent five years in training with California Jesuits, studied with Jürgen Habermas in Frankfurt a/M, and returned to Prague after the fall of the Iron Curtain.

Matuštík received his PhD from Fordham University in 1991 and went on to teach in Purdue University's philosophy department. In 1995, he was a Fulbright fellow at Charles University in Prague. The author of six books and the editor of other distinguished works, Matuštík is on the faculty at Arizona State University as the Lincoln professor of ethics and religion and professor of philosophy and religious studies.

For more information about the book, please visit the author's Publisher's page at www.newcriticaltheory.com

CPSIA information can be obtained
at www.ICGtesting.com
Printed in the USA
LVOW09s2300300418
575393LV00021B/185/P